Rainbow Nation
Without Borders

RAINBOW NATION WITHOUT BORDERS

Toward an Ecotopian Millennium

ALBERTO RUZ BUENFIL
Introduced by Starhawk

BEAR & COMPANY
PUBLISHING
SANTA FE, NEW MEXICO

LIBRARY OF CONGRESS CATALOGING–IN–PUBLICATION DATA

Buenfil, Alberto Ruz, 1945-
    [Arcobaleno. English]
    Rainbow nation without borders : toward an ecotopian millennium /
Alberto Ruz Buenfil.
        p.   cm.
    Translation of: Arcobaleno.
    Includes bibliographical references.
    ISBN 0-939680-75-0 (pbk.)
1. Social movements. 2. Subculture. 3. Life style. 4. Rainbow—Mythology.
5. Green movement. 6. Peace movements. 7. Twenty-first century—Forecasts.
I. Title.
HN17.5.B83 1991
303.48'4—dc20   90-49818
                                                             CIP

Bear & Company, Inc.
Santa Fe, NM 87504-2860

Cover illustration: Javier de Maria y Campos, "Ixtlaccihuatl, the Mother
    Goddess from Anahuac, giving birth to a new civilization"
Cover & interior design: Chris Kain
Author photo: Marya Legrand
Editing: Brandt Morgan
Typography: Buffalo Publications

PHOTO CREDITS. Jan Svante Vanbart © 1991: Prologue photo, 1, 2, 4, 5, 11, 12,
13, 14, 15, 16, 20, 21, 22, 23, 25, 26, 28, 29, 33, 34, 37, 39, 40, 41, 42, 43, 45, 46, 47,
48, 49, 50, 51, 52, 53, 54, 55, 56, 58, 59, 61, 62, 63. Alberto Ruz Buenfil © 1991: 10,
17, 24, 30, 35, 36, 44, 57, 64. Gunnar Hansen: 6. Ira Cohen ©: 7. Courtesy of Bauhaus
Situationist: 8. Mercedes Galvez: 18. Liora Adler: 19. Paolo Silkworm: 27. Courtesy
of Arcoiris Community Archives: 31, 32. Lourdes Ondategui: 38, 60. Unknown
photographer: 3, 9.

Printed in the United States of America by R.R. Donnelley

9   8   7   6   5   4   3   2   1

For all our relations in the universe

Contents

Acknowledgements and Dedication

I want to first thank life itself, for being the source from which all the manifestations of reality are born and exist, around and within ourselves.

I thank my great grandfather, the Sun, the masculine force of the universe, for bringing to life all the knowledge coded in the cosmic spiritual realms.

I thank my great grandmother, Tierra, Gaia, the Earth, for her nurturing wisdom that flows through all our beings and for being the loving womb in which life is manifested.

This book is the result of a more than twenty-year-old quest, during which I have looked for the meaning of my personal destiny as a carrier of changes in social reality and tried to make possible and real our individual and collective desires for a better world here on Earth, both now and for tomorrow.

In this first English-language version of the book, I want to thank those close brothers and sisters who helped with the long process of translating the original Italian and Spanish pages of my manuscript, especially Roberta Friedman, Marya Legrand, Dr. Jerilyn Rose, Alberto Buenfil, Roberto Lunardello, Pilar Elias, Susan Keyes, Micheline Penninck, Vasumati, and Giovanni Ciarlo. I also thank those even closer allies and road companions who contributed pieces to this seven-color puzzle-bridge symbolized by the rainbow. Thanks to Garrick Beck, Ria Bjerre, Emilio Fiel, Sandra Comneno, Octavi Piulats, Paolo Silkworm, the Sun Knights, Urs Fleury, Nina Schär, Andres King, Fantuzzi, Thaddeus Dr. Now, and Ara and Danais Tokatlian; to Javier de Maria y Campos for his artwork for the cover of this book, "La mujer dormida dando a luz"; and very specially to my brother Jan Svante

Vanbart, for his piece on our family and his incredible collection of photos from the last two decades.

I also wish to acknowledge, for the process of making this collection of messages, visions, and tales available in this form, the contribution of a great editor, Brandt Morgan, and the enormous help of Barbara Doern Drew, Gail Vivino, Debora Bluestone, and the two main forces behind the powerful Bear & Company clan, Barbara and Gerry Clow.

For the first steps of this book's co-creation, I want to especially thank my former companion and the mother of our daughter Ixchel, Sandra Comneno, who is also the cofounder of Huehuecoyotl and the main inspiration for this book. I also thank John Masnovo and Rosa Sbalchiero for the editing and publication of the first version of this book in Italy.

The original Spanish and Italian version of this book included some contributors whose writings will unfortunately not be found in this edited English version, due to a lack of space. Nevertheless, I wish to honor their help and to tell them that they are all true Rainbow Warriors of our times. The spirit of this book would never have been real or possible without their deeds, thoughts, feelings, and words. Thank you, Arturo Pozo, Carl Perry, Pip Wilson, Rainbow Hawk, Barry Plunker, Sunny Adams, John Masnovo, Gino Sansone, Pino de Sario, Maurizio Di Gregorio, and many others.

Finally, I want to dedicate this book to my three children, Odin Govinda, Mayura Natalia, and Ana Ixchel, and to the mother of my coming child, Lourdes Ondategui, who has helped me in every moment and has accompanied me with her laughter, her high and light spirit, and her incredible patience and strength in these last two very crucial years of my life.

I also dedicate this book to all the beings of the mineral, plant, and animal worlds, all the warriors of peace from the Rainbow Nation who are creating a healing millennium for the Earth, and all my tribal children, brothers, and sisters from Huehuecoyotl and Puente de Wirikuta. My greatest thanks and dedication goes to Blanca Buenfil, my Gaia, my mother, to whom I owe almost everything that I am.

Foreword

I first met Alberto Ruz Buenfil at the North American Bioregional Congress in British Columbia in 1988. It was a gathering of people both attracted to and wary of expressions of the sacred, drawn to the idea of ritual and a little timid at actually doing it. Alberto was a staunch ally. Although at the time he was unfamiliar with the Goddess traditions of Wicca that I practice, we found that our understandings of ritual, energy, and the honoring of the sacred meshed smoothly together. We planned a full-moon ritual for the end of the congress. Delayed until after the closing party and the final set of the scheduled rock band, it was attended by a small group of the faithful and/or sleepless, but the energy was wild and ecstatic as we danced on the green lawn under the round moon.

The following summer, I visited Huehuecoyotl, Alberto's community near Tepoztlan in Mexico. I was there only a short time, but long enough to feel the warm communal spirit, to be impressed by the beauty of the adobe houses; by the affectionate, confident children; and by the respect for the land and for each other that form the basis of community life. One evening Alberto told us the story of his political and spiritual wanderings over the last twenty-five years. As I struggled to follow the rapid flow of Spanish, I began to feel that I had encountered a brother spirit who had faced many of the same challenges, in different arenas. In particular, we have shared the challenges of linking the spiritual and political—change in consciousness to change in how we live and act and shape society.

Others from Huehuecoyotl were already close friends and sometime members of a collective household sister to my own. So began a fruitful and, I hope, long-lasting connection between similar-minded communities north and south.

I was especially happy to collaborate with Alberto because of my own growing conviction that members of the Euro-centric Goddess movement needed to become more aware of other traditions, more diverse and multicultural. Alberto told me, in Canada, about the awakening Goddess movement in Mexico and inspired my trip there. At the same time, he was fascinated to learn about the growing Neo-Pagan movement in North America, which shares so much with the rainbow spirit expressed in this book.

As we enter the nineties, with the old divisions of Eastern and Western blocs crumbling, we become more able to see the gulf between North and South, between Anglo culture and those informed by the tribal peoples of the Third World. Too seldom have we of the North listened to the voices, visions, and perceptions from south of our borders. *Rainbow Nation Without Borders* is both a vision and a contemporary social history as seen from the tail of Turtle Island. It gives us an opportunity, first, to hear how the last thirty years of our own history appear from that vantage point, and, second, to become acquainted with a vision of the future that draws on myths and dreams and symbols of peoples all over the world.

Rainbow Nation takes us on a journey through many of the alternative movements and countercultural experiments that have arisen in the United States, Mexico, and Europe. Those of us who identify with one or another of these movements too often perceive the United States as being at the cutting edge of alternative culture. It is humbling and illuminating to learn what is being explored in other parts of the world. Attempts that failed here have sometimes succeeded elsewhere, sometimes with remarkable longevity—for example, the anarchist city within a city of Christiania, which began back in 1971 and continues to thrive today.

Alberto is a magical guide on this journey that is to some extent the journey of his own life, much of which took place literally in motion, on a bus that traveled four continents, participating in Rainbow Gatherings, rituals, and political actions; networking between far-flung groups; and building and sustaining his own community. He is able to bridge differences of language, culture, and ancestry because of his own background and life experiences. He brings to his vision a rich awareness of multicultural possibilities and respect for diversity.

Alberto is himself the son of a French-Cuban archaeologist father and a Mayan mother. In Huehuecoyotl, I met community members from Spain, Sweden, and Italy, as well as Mexico. As alternative movements in this country strive to become inclusive, multiracial, to reflect the many mixtures of cultures and ethnicity that make up the population of the United States, we can learn much from the experience of those who have been steeped in multicultural environments all their lives.

Mexico itself is a synthesis of races and cultures; of ancient and powerful sacred sites, shamans, healers, *curanderas y curanderos*; of cosmopolitan mixtures of artists, writers, dancers, performers, and refugees from many revolutions; of tribal groups that still maintain their identities, overlaid by a worn veneer of Spanish Catholicism, giving way in places to movements to revive pre-Christian traditions of art, culture, dance, and religion. *Rainbow Nation* conveys some of this vitality and diversity.

The book is a catalog of countercultural experiments in the Americas and Europe all linked by the symbol of the rainbow, many of which were either unknown or only vaguely known to me. What strikes me, first, is the scope and longevity of many of the projects. The Rainbow Gatherings in the United States began in 1972; in Europe, 1977. Christiania has been functioning as an anarchist free zone for nearly twenty years. Alberto's own community is based on a group that has been together since the late sixties.

In the United States, the media would have us believe that all such endeavors failed in the early seventies. We are taught to laugh at the efforts of the hippies and scoff at naive idealists. But those seeds took root in other places and flourished. Some readers, who, perhaps like myself, remember the sixties, may find themselves perturbed by Alberto's idealization of some aspects of these movements. But if we can suspend cynicism, there is a lesson to be learned from that era. For myself, it was precisely the incredible optimism that I remember. We believed, in spite of our growing realization of the severity of social and environmental problems, that we could and would make a better world. That belief may indeed be naive, but without that naiveté, nothing will change.

Today we need a dose of optimism more than ever, as an antidote to despair. Despair has been manipulated by the media's insistence that each movement was dead as soon as its novelty value had worn off; by our lack of communication, in spite of all our modern technology, with people from other places and cultures; by our ignorance of the success of experiments in alternatives.

What these experiments have in common, besides the symbolism of the rainbow, is that they are decentralized, cooperative, and nonhierarchical, with a respect for diversity and process. They encompass spirit, culture, and art along with politics, organization, and practical skills. They challenge the constructs of power as we have known it.

My own writings have been concerned with the redefinition of power. "Power-over"—control and domination—is not the only form of power. We also have access to what I call "power-from-within," which is closer to the root meaning of the word *power*, from the Latin *potere*, linked to the idea of potency, ability. These stories of the rainbow record attempts to organize societies, large or small, rooted in power-from-within, that evoke and challenge each person's ability. In so doing, they tap a power that is close, also, to what we mean when we say "spirit."

Most exciting, to me, was the report from the Rainbow Networks of Mexico, telling of their work to raise issues of ecology, and to organize and aid people after the great earthquake of 1985. That natural disaster also sparked tremendous social upheaval in Mexico, with many positive results. People came together to provide help for each other in the vacuum left by the failure of the official government agencies and services. It left a legacy, building on Mexico's traditions of social revolution, that has encouraged many, working against enormous odds, to challenge oppressive structures of political and social control.

The story of Christiania also fascinated me. I knew something about the history of this community and had even strolled through its open squares and alleys on a trip to Copenhagen some years back. But I appreciated having its full story set out for me as clearly as Ria Bjerre does here.

I am always amazed to discover how little we know of what goes on even in the First World. The TV news and the newspapers present us with a carefully selected sampling of world affairs. For example, last year, in February of 1990, I spent a week in Italy and discovered that hundreds of college campuses were being occupied by their student bodies in a widespread rebellion against a new law that would have allowed private investment (and corporate control) of these institutions. Nothing was reported in the U.S. press; even my radical friends knew little or nothing about a movement reminiscent of the Berkeley Free Speech Movement of 1964 or the wave of occupations following the U.S. invasion of Cambodia in 1970.

In this high-tech world of instant, global communication, there is still a need for personal contact, for stories passed by word of mouth, for traveling bards and gossipers who can bypass the corporate control of the media. This book is in that tradition—tales of hope and inspiration told by the travelers themselves.

As much as we can learn from what is present here, we can learn also from what is missing. For me, of course, the most noticeable omission is the feminist movement, mentioned in passing but not really spotlighted as part of the Rainbow vision. I find this lack disturbing, for without an examination of the power dynamics between women and men, no new movement is going to be truly different from what has come before.

However, I am not surprised at this lack. Although I have spent more time in Europe than in Mexico, I have observed that the feminist movement in both areas has a different character than in the United States. It is much more a movement of and for women only. Here, I have taken part in direct actions around many issues in which women and men both use "feminist process" to make decisions by consensus. Women have challenged the de facto male leadership of many groups and organizations, and feminism has been seen as a challenge to power relationships that informs many different movements. The connections between feminism and ecology, especially, have given rise to the eco-feminist movement, which is just beginning to be widely discussed abroad.

The movement for lesbian and gay rights, which in the United States has also sparked multiple alternative cultures, is also absent here. Stories of communal support and mutual aid to those living with and dying from the AIDS virus might be our own counterpart to the activism arising from the Mexican earthquake. These omissions show us where

U.S.-based movements do, also, have important challenges to pose and insights to give to global alternative culture.

Nevertheless, the challenges to centralized, hierarchical power embodied in these stories draw on many of the same insights and understandings articulated by feminism. They are experiments in lived process from which we can learn much. I would hope that feminist insights would begin to inform the politics and culture of the rainbow, overtly and directly as well as from out of the political background. Alliances between issues, groups, and ways of viewing and challenging power could be named and strengthened. Feminists can find much in this book to stimulate thought and provide another lens for viewing our own changes.

Also missing from these stories is specific mention of the Goddess movement, or Neo-Pagan movement, which is my own spiritual home. This Earth-based spirituality has much in common with Native American religions and other tribal and shamanic traditions. Common to all are the belief in the sacredness of the Earth and the interconnected systems that sustain life; the focus on ritual, on ecstatic experience and lived ethics rather than on dogma; the heritage of persecution and resistance to oppression; the stress on spirituality as communal healing rather than on personal salvation or enlightenment; the rich symbolism rooted in the cycles of birth, growth, death, and regeneration in nature and human life.

The Neo-Pagan movement has focused on its roots in pre-Christian, native European cultures. In order to avoid becoming cultural imperialists, grabbing half-understood pieces of tradition from the very people Europeans have oppressed and slaughtered for five hundred years, we need to recover the Earth-centered knowledge of our own ancestors, as well as the history of its brutal suppression in the witch persecutions of the sixteenth and seventeenth centuries. Images of the Goddess have a special appeal to women who find themselves dissatisfied with exclusive male imagery and leadership in so many other spiritual traditions.

This, too, is an idea and a movement not yet widespread in Europe itself. Outside of England, where a Pagan movement has been growing for years, and Germany, which is desperately hungry for any new spiritual ideas, it has yet to flourish. The linking of spirituality and politics is especially problematic in Europe, because of the heritage of Nazi pseudomysticism and the Marxist ideology that sees all spirituality as suspect. In the United States, the Goddess has been a central image inspiring action both toward women's issues and toward protecting and restoring the Earth. Myth, theater, poetry, music, and ritual are often joined with direct action. People have hungered for a spirituality that can express their understanding of this Earth as sacred. And, moved by that understanding, spiritual people have hungered to act to prevent the destruction of the Earth.

Thus, in the United States, the Pagan resurgence has strong ties to feminism as well as to the ecology and peace movements, and some ties also with the broad spectrum of human growth and potential movements termed "New Age." In Mexico, the resurgence of indigenous traditions, the renewed interest in sacred sites and in ancient goddesses and gods, in techniques of healing and achieving altered states of consciousness, is linked to a renewed pride in the mixed ancestry and diverse cultural heritages of that country. It is a revaluing of the *Indio*—the poor, the dark-skinned, the oppressed—a cultural revolt of the South against the North.

Countercultural movements in the United States, whether Pagan, feminist, anarchist, beat, or hippie, are always to some extent a revolt against the lack of rich, sustaining culture in our society, the dearth of ritual, the absence of community, the repression of emotion, sexuality, life, color, and drama. Mexico, in contrast, abounds with traditions, festivals, processions, rituals, and strong family and community ties. All the color we seek is already a part of communal life.

Alberto draws on this tradition, and we can learn also from the scope and daring of many of these projects that do link the political and the cultural, the spiritual world and the material world, art and life. "All of [these groups] are trying to pave the way for a millennial change, for the dramatic and permanent shift from a world of exploitation to a world of ecological harmony and balance." In this crucial decade, as we approach the end of the twentieth century with life itself hanging in the balance, faced with the necessity to choose change and healing or continue destruction with unparalleled power, may we be guided by the spirit of the rainbow, toward harmony, cooperation, and respect for diversity.

Starhawk
San Francisco, California
January 1991

Starhawk is author of *The Spiral Dance, Dreaming the Dark*, and *Truth or Dare*.

Prologue

*A Letter to Dr. Alberto Ruz Lhuillier
from His Son, Alberto Ruz Buenfil*

Author Alberto Ruz Buenfil with his father, Dr. Alberto Ruz Lhuillier, University of Mexico City, 1976.

Editor's note: The following is an edited letter from the author to his father, the famed anthropologist who discovered the Royal Tomb of Palenque. Written shortly after the professor's death, it expresses not only the agony of the loss of a loved one, but more importantly the clash of cultures and ideologies and the search for meaning that characterized the postwar generation. In a sense, it is both a short autobiography and an introduction to this book, for all these forces conspired to shape the thoughts, yearnings, travels, and convictions of the author. For more than two decades, they led him all over the world, ultimately creating the broad perspective and the "path of the heart" that allowed him to produce this book.

My Very Dear Doctor:

We were all gathered at our temporary home at Round Mountain Ranch in California. We were sitting in a circle inside a yurt, a circular Mongolian tent, watching a videotape about the natural home birth of one of our children. Tears were rolling down my face as I wondered about the magic of life. Then, when the film was over, I received a long-distance telephone call from Mexico, from brother Jorge, telling me you had died.

One hour later, I went alone on a long walk toward the lake, at the same moment the full moon was disappearing behind Round Mountain. Then I knelt and entered the sweatlodge, where the members of our community frequently celebrate together in the tradition of the Lakota Sioux.

The moon cycle, Round Mountain, the sweatlodge, the yurt, the circle of people holding hands—all remind me of the magic of life and death, and prompt me to reflect on the life we spent together.

In my oldest memories, I go back to the Yucatán, to you and me sitting in front of a chess table, concentrated and serious. I remember, too, the baseball and croquet games in Mérida and the beach house in Chikchulub, as well as the fishing parties in our little boat *Saeta*.

Then there were my birthdays when you took me to the bookshop to choose four or five new classics for children: Verne, Cooper, Stevenson, Twain, Salgari. And the long holidays in the summer, when for two months I would share your expeditions and adventures in Chichén Itzá, Uxmal, Dzibilchaltún, or Palenque. It was then, I remember, that you gave me my first jobs: carrying stones for the reconstruction of the Pyramid of Inscriptions; cleaning and classifying clay pots and bones; putting together the pieces of Preclassic and Postclassic puzzles; mixing sand, gravel, and cement for the building of the new museum. Always you were there—my biggest hero, my best teacher, my most demanding tutor, my most loving and patient father.

I also remember that the rediscovery and reopening of the Royal Tomb of Palenque brought important changes to our lives: our first family trips out of Mexico; the lecture tours in the United States and Cuba; and the widening of our world and its marvelous possibilities.

Then, when I was thirteen, came our forced exile from the Yucatán and our tropical paradise, as a result of the corruption of the state governor. With that painful event came the end of a cycle and the beginning of a new one. It was the end of my childhood and a certain wild innocence that had only been possible on the beaches and in the jungles of the Mayan centers. It was also the beginning of my youth in the streets of Mexico City, life on the third floor of an apartment building, and a new discipline at the Franco-Mexican high school.

This, I remember, was about the time you had your first heart attack, which forced you to stay at home for almost a year and brought us closer together. During those months, I learned a great deal about your revolutionary past in Cuba and your association with legendary figures such as Juan Marinello, Tony Guiteras, Calixta, and Julio Le Riverand. It was also then that I first heard about the times you had been imprisoned in Cuba, in the jails of the Machado and Fulgencio Batista regimes.

You taught me about the struggle for freedom, and you told me amazing stories about my great-grandfather, Francisco Ruiz, the first Cuban to free his slaves. All of that began to shape my destiny, setting fire to my teenage imagination, awakening a new admiration for you.

During this time in Mexico City, you also made contact with your old bohemian and revolutionary writer friends again—people who through their art, writing, and deeds continued to give me an education far beyond the walls of the classroom. No longer were my readings limited to the classics of my youth; now you began loaning me books from your own library. One book in particular, *The Good Conscious People* by Carlos Fuentes, helped to confirm my future direction. We shared a certain ideological complicity, you and I.

Then the first ideological conflicts began to erupt with my friends and teachers in high school. For the first time in my life, I began experiencing the realities of social injustice, political activism, and the strong impact of the Cuban Revolution. I remember describing all this in one of my first political essays, written in 1962 for a modern-history course—an essay dedicated to the two figures in contemporary times who had most influenced my life. I well remember your smile and the look in your eyes when you read my work, entitled "Fidel Castro Ruz and Alberto Ruz Lhuillier."

A new cycle started in our family life when you began working with Mother at the Seminar on Mayan Culture at the University of Mexico City, about the same time I entered college at the Faculty of Chemical Sciences. While at college, I was surprised to discover that you were very worried about my helping to organize the first street marches in support of the Cuban Revolution. Perhaps I could not blame you; these demonstrations were usually repressed and often ended with hundreds of people wounded and jailed. I also noticed that you seemed worried about my waning interest in a career in petrochemical engineering. Even then, I remember, you had a very clear vision about the effect oil was going to have on Mexico and the rest of the world.

One year later, I left the Faculty and Mexico to go to Cuba, hoping to get some firsthand experience in the revolutionary process. I went with some close friends of yours: author Sol Arguedas, theater director Jorge Godoy, economist Elena Huerta, and others—I felt like a young apprentice on an initiatic journey.

I returned from that journey with full sympathy for the Cuban Revolution, and I began spreading my enthusiasm in lectures, study circles, protest songs, and the publication of one of the first books in Mexico about Fidel Castro's historical speeches.

In 1965, I entered the school of economics, then the most important center for political activities in the Mexican university world. It was a focal point not only for classes but for strikes, rallies, elections, and fascinating roundtable discussions that pushed my education in many new directions.

The trip to Cuba had given me a new critical perspective that began to conflict with the ideas of the intellectual left to which you and most of your friends belonged. I was young, filled with enthusiasm for new ideas, and I began to feel that you and most of the people in your generation were happily "sitting" on some very small achievements, and that many of your advanced ideas did not correspond to the way you were living your own lives.

This was also a time when your work at the Seminar for Mayan Culture was taking most of your time and interest, a situation that led to some distance between us—a distance that I knew was good and necessary both for your growth and mine. During those years, our family unity was broken, too, with your divorce from Mother. Yet this, too, I took as a sign of our mutual need to grow, a step that helped to free each of us to follow our own destinies.

The next time we met was in Cuba in 1967, during your sabbatical. It was your first visit to the island since the triumph of the revolution in 1959. On your return there, you lived like a prince—recognized, admired, in a suite in the Habana Libre Hotel, eating steak and lobster along with the other important guests of the Cuban government. I remember you even had a car at the door of the hotel with a private chauffeur.

In the meantime, I was living much closer to the way most Cubans lived, sharing with them not only the wonderful achievements since the revolution but also the daily frustrations, mistakes, and criticisms. These I saw not just as seeds for counterrevolution, but also as the most precious and important elements necessary to keep the revolution alive.

Our experiences in Cuba, then, were very different, and this fact created more distance between us. But even then, I considered it a healthy process for our mutual independence and freedom. By then you had also formed a new family of your own, and I had begun sharing my life with a companion named Gerda.

After six or seven months, we all went back to Mexico, and the distance between us was growing wider. I had no interest in continuing the study of economics because I knew the school was becoming a training center for administrators, a trampoline for political leaders, teachers, and school directors to get into the party's sanctioned institutions.

None of these alternatives pleased me—I only wanted to take free courses for no particular career. I wanted a nonspecialized education. I wanted to become a whole human being, not just part of a politico-economic machine. Thoroughly frustrated, I finally I decided to leave the university altogether. I decided to leave Mexico and the influence of you and your friends who had served as my primary teachers until then, and to enter into the open university of the world.

My post-graduate studies abroad lasted seven years, from 1968 to 1975, and those studies took me to no less than four continents and twenty-five different countries. During those years, I confronted many social realities: war, revolution, affluence, and hunger, as well as societies both primitive and industrial, capitalist and socialist. My journeys forced me to use my head, hands, and spirit to survive, meeting and sharing with people from almost unbelievably different backgrounds and ideologies. This was an education that no university could have offered. Also during those years, my first two children were born: Odin and Mayura, your grandchildren, one on each side of the world.

During the seven years I was gone, I remember, we communicated by letter, from one side of the planet to the other. By this time, your Seminar on Mayan Culture had become the very important Center for Mayan Studies, and your well-deserved fame took you all over the globe. Yet my journeys and yours were as different from each other as our experiences in Cuba had been. I always respected the whys and hows of your life, but in all those years I could never make you understand the whys and hows of mine.

During those seven years, we met only once, by coincidence, at the London airport between flights. You were waiting for a plane to take you to Paris, I for a flight to New Delhi. During the two hours we together, you met my son and daughter, your two new grandchildren, and I met your new son, my half-brother Claudio.

Unfortunately, during that short time, we shared only our differences. I tried to help you see some of the things that moved my life, some of my visions and needs, but we ended taking our own flights, each feeling frustrated over our mutual lack of comprehension. Neither of us had given the other what we both wanted most to share: our love.

Years later, in 1975, when we met again in Mexico City, I hardly recognized my home or my friends. I felt like a foreigner in my own country. Many people I knew had chosen to travel paths I would not even consider possible for myself, nor would these former friends have considered my road possible for them.

Each time I came to visit you at the Center of Mayan Studies, you seemed glad to see me, but I also know that my long hair, earrings, and way of dressing caused you great confusion. Your own hair had become longer, too, in those years—long and silvery, like the aura that surrounded you. Yet in spite of your brilliant light, I always felt your uneasiness and never understood it. It was an uneasiness that did not correspond to your age, wisdom, or achievements. I would have loved to see you calm and wise in your last years, your serenity unaffected by the little things in life.

After those two years in Mexico, once more I felt the need to leave the country. Yet I also felt that I might not see you again, and this caused me some anxiety because I truly wanted our relationship to be clear. I wanted us to be able to leave one another with feelings of mutual acceptance and respect.

I left in 1976, and we maintained a periodic correspondence. It lacked the intensity of previous years but fortunately it also lacked the ideological and emotional clashes. Ours was a long, slow process of mutual acceptance. I sent you copies of my poems, essays, and published articles, and you sent me copies of your more recent books. We even talked about future projects that might bring us together again. It was a careful and loving process of polishing our mutual respect, of slowly coming together.

Our last letters were all gentle ones—the first such letters in ten years of correspondence. And finally, in one of your last letters, you sent me proof of your acceptance—an acceptance that I had not known since I was a teenager. Your "yes" finally healed a wound between us that had been open for many long and painful years. And it did not require me to change my lifestyle or beliefs. It was an uncompromising yes, a yes that had no bait, no hook.

When a father says yes to his son, this is more important than any social affirmation. It may be even more important than a yes from the spiritual realms, for our father is one with us, and we cannot complete our own growth process if our earthly father continues to reject us and refuses to give us this acknowledgment.

Only two months ago, in June, you called your visiting grandchildren to your office at the museum to give them a gift. It was a book called *The Night Guardians*, which included a couple of real-life stories about the adventures of the archaeologist who discovered the Royal Tomb of Palenque. "For my dear little grandchildren, Odin and Mayura," you wrote, "as a remembrance from a great adventure lived by your own grandfather."

Your present arrived along with my two children when they came to visit me in Arizona. Since then, I have never missed an opportunity to show it to people I sense might benefit from seeing it.

When we were camping in the land of the Hopi, for example, near the ancient town of Oraibi, some of the Hopi elders came to visit our camp. I showed them the illustrations of Palenque with great pride. They were very impressed and showed great interest in what I had to tell them about the Maya. Some of them—especially one of their leaders called White Bear, who was then governor of Oraibi—told me that he thought one of their sacred cities, "the mysterious red city of the

Hopi, a city in the south called Palatkwapi," could very well have been the center of Palenque.

My last words to you were sent from the land of the Hopi, the People of Peace. Then, two days ago, came word of your death. Jorge said you had died in Montreal. He said your wish was to be cremated and have your ashes taken to some place near the Tomb of Palenque.

I know that even in this moment that I write you, many people are paying homage to your memory, and that your body will be traveling for the last time from Canada to Mexico. I also know that in Mexico your spirit will begin traveling to the clouds with the smoke, and that your ashes will return to the land of power, that sacred center that you yourself unearthed and gave back to humanity.

Thus closes a perfect cycle as the tears roll down my face and I wonder about the magic of life and death. Wise and impeccable warrior, my very dear doctor, you are a part of me, just as I am a part of my own children, just as we both will be a part of their children. I will love you forever.

Yours always,

Alberto

RAINBOW NATION WITHOUT BORDERS

Chapter 1

The Rainbow:
A Universal Archetype

In all cultures and times, nature has been the object of a great many forms of veneration. The divine forces of nature have included not only the visible planets and stars, but also such forces as lightning, thunder, rain, solar and lunar eclipses, earthquakes, oceans, and the Earth herself.

Most early human cultures considered all of these forces living entities in their own rights. They worshiped a Father Sun and Mother Moon, a Heavenly Father and a Mother Earth; they celebrated the first celestial couple created by the Supreme Being; and they worshiped the gods and goddesses of thunder and fertility, as well as those of chaos and the Creator of all living forms.

Such disparate peoples as Africans, Asians, Americans, and Northern Europeans, for example, all had ritualistic cults of the sun. The ritual similarities between such far-flung cultures, which had no apparent contact with one another, support the concept of a "collective archetype" advanced by Carl Jung. These archetypal memories are part of our genetic inheritance. We are all, and have been in other times, conscious or unconscious adorers of the sun, the moon, the rain, and the Earth. We still have within us a need to relate symbolically to the manifestations of nature.

The purpose of this book is to uncover the hidden story of a natural archetypal symbol that has been little explored in the studies of the modern world: the rainbow. Unlike the sun and the moon, the rainbow is a subtle element whose presence can neither be predicted nor fully apprehended. It appears and disappears as an enchantment, as if by magic; it has no predictable cycles; it does not produce heat, cold, or humidity; it is not particularly seasonal; and it has no material structure that can be transformed and used for "practical" purposes. In a literal sense, the rainbow is an apparition, a mirage.

In spite of the rainbow's elusiveness, however, few symbols have been more universally accepted as harbingers of good news. The rainbow has always presaged the end of trials and catastrophes, and few natural phenomena are of comparable beauty and magnificence. In different times and cultures, the rainbow has been given a plethora of names that suggest its inspiring beauty—for example, Rainbelt, Dove of God, God's Arc, the Arc of Time, and Floating Bridge of Heaven. These names alone suggest that the roots of the rainbow in the human psyche are far more than illusory, and far deeper than science can ever measure. In fact, the premise of this book is that the rainbow symbolizes a transformation in human consciousness the world has never known.

Before considering the implications of this transformation, let us first quickly examine the roots of the rainbow in various cultures and times. This will give us a better idea of what the rainbow archetype means in our own lives and in the life of modern society.

Roots of the Rainbow in Africa and Australia

For lack of written records, the African legends are among the least available. The traditional knowledge of African people has been preserved and passed on from generation to generation in the form of stories told by elders around tribal campfires.

Students of African customs and beliefs have documented the rituals and practices of various groups regarding the rainbow. Thus, we know that among some African tribes the rainbow is the bridge between celestial and earthly realities. For other tribes, the rainbow is a gigantic snake that arrives after the rains to graze on the wet soils. The Zulus believe that this "rainbow snake" can devour anyone who stands in its way. Due to this belief, they show great respect and even fear when confronting a rainbow.

In Australia, the aborigines have also represented the rainbow as a snake. This is beautifully illustrated in the cave paintings of the Namarakain tribes, some of which are many hundreds of years old. The Kaitish tribes of central Australia believe that the rainbow is the son of the rain and that he is always trying to prevent his father from falling to the surface of the Earth.

The legend of the rainbow serpent in Australia goes back to aboriginal stories of the beginning of time. In 1979 in Sydney, William Collins recovered one of these legends, which reads:

> In the beginning, the Earth was flat. As the Rainbow Serpent wound his way across the land, the movement of his body heaped up the mountains and dug troughs for the rivers. With each thrust of his huge, multicolored body, a new landform was created.
>
> At last, tired with the effort of shaping the earth, he crawled into a water hole. The cool water washed over his vast body, cooling and soothing him. Each time the animals visited the water hole, they were careful not to disturb the Rainbow Serpent, for although they could not see him, they knew he was there.
>
> Then one day, after a huge rainstorm, they saw him. His huge, colored body was arching from the water hole, over the treetops, up through the clouds, across the plain to another water hole. To this day, the aborigines are careful not to disturb the Rainbow Serpent as they see him going across the sky from one water hole to another.

Roots of the Rainbow in Asia

Among Asians, there have been many different interpretations of the rainbow. The Chinese have used it to answer questions of fidelity between husband and wife. They have also used it to make important political decisions. Among the Tartars, the rainbow has always been considered "the thunder drinking the waters of the rain." And to the Japanese, who call the rainbow *Niji*, it symbolizes a floating bridge that leads the way to heaven.

For Buddhists, the colors of the rainbow are related to the seven sacraments, and among the Tibetans the rainbow is used to illustrate the auras of spiritually advanced individuals. Here is how Lama Anagarika Govinda sees it:

> The rainbow is the symbol of the intangible nature of reality, a reality that evades us in our world of apparently solid things and hard facts. . . . It is at the same time a bridge between the real and the unreal, the tangible and the intangible, the visible and the invisible, as well as a door that leads into the world of imagination and fairy tales.[1]

Some of the best representations of the rainbow are found in Tibetan art. In many instances, these are connected to the seven chakras, or psycho-physical centers, of the human body. The seven colors of the rainbow are also used when referring to the auras of certain people, such as saints, prophets, and gurus who have achieved a high level of illumination.

Once, when Yogi Dzeng Dharma Bodhi was teaching his disciples about the principles behind the rainbow, which he symbolically called the "luminous bridge of diamonds," the sky was suddenly filled with rainbows for no logical reason. This unexpected phenomenon caused a great deal of fear and nervousness among his Tibetan students. In order to calm them, he explained that when he himself was receiving the same teachings from his own master years before, exactly the same phenomenon had taken place. His explanation was this:

> The rainbow is only a manifestation of the unspoken, an illusion without real existence, and this is the reason why the Tibetan artists use the seven colors' natural spectrum to illustrate the general principle that all phenomena has no real substance and has qualities of pure spirituality.[2]

Thus, the rainbow transcends the distinction between the physical and spiritual worlds. Often, Tibetan Buddhists use the seven colors of the rainbow to represent the sacred word "Hum" (also "Om" or "Aum"). These colors correspond to the seven levels of wisdom that can be achieved through the study of Buddhist philosophy.

The Rainbow in Native America

The rainbow also figures into a common symbology among many different native peoples of the Americas. For example, the Mayan *Chilam Balam*, one of the oldest books of humanity, records the destruction of one of the Mayan worlds due to a terrible deluge:

> A fiery rain fell, as ashes covered the heavens and trees trembled, crashing to the ground. And the Earth shook, and the trees and rocks were thrown against one another. Those who had escaped came to their places, knowing the annihilation was finished, and they were settled in their places. And a rainbow appeared as a sign that the destruction was over, and a new age was to begin.[3]

Among the Inca of Peru, the rainbow god is called Chuychu and is known as a servant to the sun. Among the Maya, the goddess of the rainbow is Ixchel, the wife of the supreme god, Itzamna. Ixchel is also the deity of inundations, the moon, sexuality, childbirth, weaving, and medicine. She is also known to be entertained by a court filled with very special beings, including dwarfs and magicians who attend to her every whim and fancy.

Similarly, among the Tarascans from the Mexican state of Michoacan, there is a fertility goddess named Mauina, who lives under the rainbow in the gardens of the lords of the rain and waters. This place is filled with beauty and pleasures, and Mauina, like Ixchel, is served by a legion of dwarfs, hunchbacks, and clowns.

For the Mojave Indians of the deserts of Arizona, the rainbow is one of the mightiest powers of the Great Spirit and part of an enchantment necessary to stop the rain. Similarly, the Yukis of California believe that the rainbow is the multicolored dress of the Great Spirit, the Creator of all existence.

The spirit of rainbow is frequently represented in the sand paintings and sacred drawings of the Zuni, Hopi, and Navajo. Among the Navajo, the rainbow is a goddess who appears in the midst of ritual chants that are intended to heal the sick. For the Shoshone Indians, the rainbow is a gigantic snake that scratches its back against the celestial world, which is considered to be an enormous ice dome.

The rainbow as a snake is a recurrent image among many ethnic groups and nations. The Pomo and Kato tribes of California consider it to be an aquatic, horned snake that provokes floods and earthquakes. The rainbow is also identified as a water snake among the people of South America. The natives of the Amazon believe it represents a bridge between the Earth and the temples of the royal kingdom of heaven.

Among the rainbow myths of North America (often called "Turtle Island" by Native Americans), there is one worth reporting in some detail. It comes from the Zuni people, neighbors of the Navajo and Hopi and inhabitants of the plains and deserts of New Mexico.

This legend, which is enacted year after year by the maidens of the Zuni villages, was first offered to the public by Helen P. Blavatsky in 1888, in her famous book *The Secret Doctrines*. Following is an abridged version of a description published by Paedric Column in his book *Myths of the World*, in 1930:

> Among the Zuni people there is a god of the dawn and the evening called Paiyatuma, who is a talented flute player. Once upon a time, Paiyatuma brought to the Earth seven maidens decorated with feathers and magic wands, and he introduced them to our grandparents singing this chant:
>
> > The corn that you see, growing, rising
> > Is the present of my seven bright maidens.
> > Never forget to feed and nourish them
> > And do never try to change their presents
> >   and offerings.
> > They represent the fertility of flesh in all
> >   human beings,
> > They carry the children of humanity.
> > Do never forget them or lose them,
> > You'll never find them again.

Paiyatuma left amongst our grandparents seven corn plants, each one of a different color, and the elders all said, "Yes, we truly appreciate the seven maidens and the essence of their flesh." Since then, when the season was favorable, our elders have built a bower with a big roof of branches and started a fire in the entrance.

In the night, the seven maidens danced to the beat of drums and rattles and to the tunes of the chants of our elders. Each one of the maidens danced with her corn plant, and they helped it to rise with their magic wands and their colored feathers. The first maiden embraced the first plant, and it fired a flame of yellow lights. The second maiden illuminated her plant with blue flames; the third with reds; the fourth with whites; the fifth with a multicolored luminosity; the sixth with a warm light; and the seventh with a brilliant light of all the colors of the rainbow.

At dawn, the seven maidens left behind their feathers, their wands, and their white robes, and they came out of the arbor to dance with the people. One day, the messengers of the village listened to an incredible music that came from the top of thunder's mountain. They immediately believed it to be much nicer than their own music. Following the notes, the messengers arrived at the rainbow cave, where they found Paiyatuma playing his flute. He was accompanied by seven maidens, who were also playing and dancing with their seven flutes.

The messengers were so insistent that Paiyatuma bring these new seven maidens to the villages that he finally answered them: "These maidens are the same as yours, in the same way that the seven stars reflected in the lake are the same seven stars that you can see in the sky. The only difference is that your seven maidens carry the seeds of corn, and these maidens carry only the water that allows your seeds to germinate."

Because of the insistence of the messengers, Paiyatuma agreed to come down again to the earth, accompanied by the seven sky maidens, playing the music of the rainbow for the seven corn maidens. Their dance was so beautiful that all the youngsters of the villages fell in love again with the seven corn maidens, who, when the dance ended, embraced the seventh plant and afterwards disappeared forever.

The people cried louder and louder: "Where are our seven maidens?" But they could not find any trace of the way the maidens had taken when they left. The elders first decided to send an eagle to look for the maidens, but the eagle could not find them. Then they decided to send a falcon, but the falcon could not find them, either, and the people cried more and more, louder and louder. Finally, they decided to send a black crow to look for the maidens, and this one returned to the village, saying, "Only Paiyatuma can find them and bring them back again."

The council of elders had to climb the mountain to ask Paiyatuma to bring the seven corn maidens back again, but Paiyatuma received them as a clown, mocking and punishing them for their weakness. Then he forced the elders to enter the sweatlodge several times to purify themselves, and he selected the four most chaste young men from the village. He departed with them toward the faraway lands of the summer, playing his flute until the seven corn maidens appeared among millions of butterflies and birds of all colors.

The seven maidens agreed to descend to the earth once again, following Paiyatuma and the four young men of the village. They were received with great happiness. A new arbor was constructed immediately, and the sacred fire was lit at the entrance. Then the dance and the chant of the elders started, and it went on all night long, just as it used to in the old times.

The seven maidens embraced the seven plants again, each of them infusing her plant with the essence of her own flesh and with a different color of the rainbow. When the last maiden had sent her beam of light, the seven maidens disappeared as if they were shadows. Since then, they have never returned to the Earth.

The only one left was Paiyatuma, who had these words for our elders: "The corn will keep on growing every year, because the seven maidens have left their essence in each one of the seven plants. In the next season, seven maidens of each village should repeat the dances and chants of the seven corn maidens to the beat of drums, flutes, and rattles. They should embrace the new plants that are growing. But the other maidens, the rainbow maidens dressed in white, will never return, because you humans have broken the contract that we had at the beginning of time."

And this is the reason why, even today, the Zuni consider sacred the corn seeds they use to plant. When they put them inside the ground, the village performs a ceremony of death, for they consider the seed to be the soul of a very beloved person they mourn at the same season each year.

Once this part of the process ends, Paiyatuma uses his breath to keep the seeds fresh until Tenatsali, the god of time and seasons, helps them reach full maturity. To finish the cycle, Kuelelel, god of warmth, heats them with a divine torch, giving them vitality. In the meantime, the seven maidens of the Zuni tribe dance and embrace the seven corn plants for the whole night, showing them the way up to the sky.

For the Zuni, there is a correspondence between the four directions and the four colors of corn: north is the yellow, south is the red, east is the white, and west is the blue. The black corn corresponds to the fifth region, the underworld, while the rainbow ears (those that have grains of all colors) are considered to belong to the upperworld. And finally, there is another variety of maize, brilliantly striped and spotted, that corresponds to the Mother Priestess and to the seeds of all races of past, present, and future. This variety is considered to be the mother of all living things.

This Zuni legend of the sacred relationship between corn, rain, and people and the symbology of the colored corn are well worth pondering. The main reason I have recounted the legend here, aside from its sheer beauty and simplicity, is that it expresses much better the essence of the newly emerging "rainbow consciousness" than any political essay, anthropological study, or religious doctrine I can think of. I will say more about the development of this consciousness in the last two sections of this chapter, as well as in chapter 2.

European Roots of the Rainbow

When we consider the early cultures of the Mediterranean and Northern Europe, we discover the rainbow myth found in the *Book of Genesis* of the Bible. In the Judeo-Christian tradition, the rainbow is a token of the covenant between God, the Creator of all things, and humanity, represented by one of God's favorite children, Noah. With the rainbow, God gave a promise that the Earth would never again be flooded as it had been during the universal deluge.

In *Genesis* (also called the *First Book of Moses*) 9:13-16, we read:

> I do set my bow in the cloud, and it shall be a token of a covenant between me and the earth.

> And it shall come to pass, when I bring a cloud over the earth, that the bow shall be seen in the cloud.

> And I will remember my covenant, which is between me and you and every living creature of all flesh; and the waters shall no more become a flood to destroy all flesh.

> And this bow shall be in the cloud; and I will look upon it, that I may remember the everlasting covenant between God and every living creature of all flesh that is upon the earth.

For the Greeks, the goddess Iris was, together with Hermes, a messenger of the god Zeus's orders and desires. Iris personified the rainbow, and she symbolized the bridge that binds together the heavens and the Earth.

Iris was the daughter of Thaumas, an intrepid and gifted sailor from ancient Greece, and of Elektra, a glittering oceanic nymph. She incarnated and reflected the colors of the sky in the waves of the seas, filling them with the lights and the seven beams of the rainbow. Iris always appeared after a storm, but she was also the goddess of the tempest, and her messages often announced the approach of war.

Iris was also known as the goddess and messenger of the flying feet. She flew as the wind, as the breath of a storm, descending from the heavens to the Earth. Like Hermes, she carried in her hands a caduceus, the symbol for peace and the healing arts. The only goddess who possessed winged sandals, she was, like the rainbow, a fleeting presence who disappeared before anyone could grasp her. Iris served similar functions for the Romans. According to the poet Ovid, she was the one who "feeds the clouds with the water from the oceans."

The Estonian tribes believed that the rainbow was the head of an ox drinking from the waters of the rivers. For the Germans, the god of light and keeper of the bridge that links the dwelling of the gods with the homes of simple humans was named Heimdall. He was also the guardian of the Bifrost, the rainbow, and from his position in the sky, he could foresee the arrival of enemies both day and night.

Among the Lapps and Finns the rainbow was a part of Thor's bow, and his arrows were lightning and thunder. For some other Germanic groups, the rainbow was the gigantic bowl in which God began the creation of all living beings.

In the mythology of the Celts, the rainbow was the chair of the goddess Ceridwen. This corresponds to Judeo-Christian tradition, in which the rainbow is compared to the luminosity of God's throne—a symbol of hope that shines to reassure all God's children.

The Rainbow in Science and Philosophy

While the rainbow has been an integral part of mythology and religion for thousands of years, only in the last few centuries has it become a subject of study for the natural sciences. Today, however, the rainbow is an important topic of research in physics, chemistry, astronomy, and optics, as well as in alchemy, metaphysics, and philosophy.

One of the first "scientific" explanations of the origins of the rainbow was offered by the Greek philosopher Aristotle in the year 350 B.C. According to Aristotle, "In some mirrors we can see the reflections of things, and in some others we can only see colors. The rainbow is a reflection of the light over the drops of water that react as if they were mirrors."[4]

For many alchemists, a "philosophic rainbow" indicated the seven stages one had to pass through in order to attain inner peace. According to the alchemical tradition, an initiate had to ascend, color by color, level after level of consciousness, until the moment when he or she obtained the "alchemical gold."

Today it is common knowledge that rainbows are formed in drops of water, whether in mist, waterfalls, waves, spray, fountains, or water spouts. We know that rainbows can also form at night, as when a circular rainbow forms around a very bright moon; and that sometimes a double or even a triple rainbow can coalesce under the right conditions.

These and other rainbow phenomena have been studied by a number of scientists and philosophers. Among the most noted of these early researchers was the British philosopher Sir Francis Bacon, who rightly concluded that rainbows are formed in storm clouds when the last drops of rain are hit by the light of the sun. Then, in 1637, in order to erase the "superstitious and mythological thinking of the past," the French mathematician and philosopher René Descartes rebaptized the rainbow "Arc en Ciel," or "Arch in the Sky," a name that has lasted up to the present.

A few decades later, Sir Isaac Newton discovered that light travels in the form of waves, and that different colors are produced by different wavelengths of light. He also discovered that when a light beam hits a crystal prism at an angle of forty-two degrees, the beam is divided into seven smaller beams, each one appearing at a slightly different angle and each one of a different color. From this discovery comes our present-day understanding of the physical properties of rainbows.

After Newton, a new theory suggested that color was formed by tiny particles and that different colors were produced by different densities of such particles. With this discovery, spectral analysis was born, and the mystery and wonder of rainbows began to take a back seat. From that time on, color was analyzed primarily from a rational, scientific point of view.

Nevertheless, colors evoke sensations that are deeply rooted in our unconscious memories, sensations that have no rational explanations. The fact that we know exactly how our eyes and brains distinguish color does not lessen our pleasure each time this marvelous natural phenomenon manifests before our eyes.

Ironically, in recent years, even science has contributed to this sense of wonder. In 1814, a German optician named Joseph von Fraunhofer invented the spectroscope, an instrument used to study the composition of matter through its constituent colors. In 1900, with the help of this instrument, physicist Max Planck discovered that the range of light is much wider than had previously been realized. He detected more than sixty new luminous beams of color, among which the visible spectrum represented only a very small portion.

Today, spectroscopy is used to determine the components of the sun and stars, to diagnose certain diseases, to analyze pigmentations in the paintings of old masters, and even to determine the components of objects found in the ruins of ancient cultures.

Even more wonderful, Johann Jakob Balmer has recently proven that the other planets in our solar system are composed of the same elements found here on Earth and that all the elements in the human body are also parts of major bodies found in the heavens. Thus, we are all tiny parts of an immense body that includes everything from microbes and whales to stars and galaxies.

When the ancient philosophers intuited, "As above, so below," they were neither ignorant nor naive. These recent discoveries confirm that the rainbow is, in effect, the bridge between heaven and Earth, between the conscious and the unconscious, and between the material world and the illusive world of energy and light.

The rainbow helps us to see that the microcosm is indeed an accurate reflection of the macrocosm, and that whatever happens on one level happens on all levels. We can also see that the very road we have traveled as a historical and intellectual species is a part of our evolutionary development. We are now able to integrate the intuitive emotions of our past with the clear reason of the seventeenth-century philosophers and scientists. And we are about to do exactly that—not just individually, but as a species—through the creation of a new mythology, a new paradigm for a new age.

Energy, the Rainbow, and the Aura

Another marvelous scientific discovery made in recent years is that everything that exists moves and pulsates, transmitting signals in the form of waves, or "vibrations," of colored light that carry messages about its makeup and essential being. Through the centuries, this emanation of "rainbow" energy from rocks, plants, animals, and humans has been called by many names: odic force, halo, nimbus, aureole, prana, orgone, human atmosphere, energy field, bioplasma, St. Elmo's fire, and aura, to name a few. Mention of this luminosity is found in the alchemical doctrines of Hermes Trismegistus, in ancient Egyptian texts, in the teachings of Indian yogis, and in illustrations depicting Oriental philosophers and sages of all eras.

In 1915, in his book *The Human Atmosphere*, Dr. W.J. Kilner described several methods for observing the human aura. He also invented a machine through which auras could be perceived through a special screen. For several decades, Wilhelm Reich tried to isolate the vital energy the Hindus call "prana." In the 1940s, he invented a sort of generator called the "orgonic box," which he used to revitalize the bioenergetic fields of human beings.

Then, in 1939, a Russian scientist named Semyon Kirlian discovered that the flow of energy floating between an electrotherapeutic mechanism and a patient's skin could be photographed by placing a simple photo plate between them. Thus was born Kirlian photography, a technique that captures the coloration, intensity, and frequency of the flow of life energy. In a healthy, living organism, Kirlian discovered that the colors are shiny and very bright, but in organisms that are sick or dead, the flow of energy and its color diminish or disappear.

With these twentieth-century discoveries, we can affirm today that the luminous spectrum and the colors of the rainbow are capable of indicating changes in the emotional and vital tones of almost anything—people, animals, plants, and even "inanimate" objects. Following is a table showing some of the most accepted correlations between colors and the specific qualities they indicate among human beings:

Violet: A tendency toward spirituality, love for ceremonial forms.
Indigo: A capacity for perception and intuition.
Blue: Inspiration, love, religious sentiments.
Green: Vital energy, sympathy, compassion.
Yellow: Knowledge, wisdom, intelligence.
Orange: Health, pride, ambition.

Red: Desire, life, anger, passion, rage.
Black: Hate, ignorance, fear.
Gray: Depression, lack of energy, lack of character.
White: Illumination, madness, innocence.

Many different physical and emotional factors are reflected by the coloration of the human aura and its luminosity. The study of these relationships is not just a matter of interest for mystics, but for healers and holistic physicians as well. Some healers use their chromatic skills to determine which colors produce psychosomatic changes in their patients. They also use colors, sounds, and visual impressions to help harmonize their patients' energetic fields and flows.

Chromotherapy is a new branch of the medical arts directed to revitalizing the life centers of the patient using specific colors for various symptoms or diseases. For example, violet and lavender are used to increase concentration and to achieve mental harmony. Green restores vigor and strength. Yellow and orange increase inspiration. Blue lowers fevers. Red stops shivering and stimulates the sick person. Orange relaxes and produces heat in the organism.

Color, Sound, and Perception

Investigations have also proven that the visual spectrum has exactly the same wave frequency as the auditory spectrum; therefore, there are seven notes that correspond to the seven colors of the rainbow. Associations between sounds and colors are as old as time itself. Many musicians, such as Beethoven, Rimsky-Korsakov, and Handel have identified notes with colors, moods, and meanings. In the sixties, music and color became an integral part of the so-called "psychedelic culture," popularizing the use of new electronic appliances that translated each note into a color. Such music created a concert of images and sounds.

Now, some thirty years later, a combination of sound and color is used in psychology, psychotherapy, medicine, anthropology, chemistry, and the arts. Associations between colors and musical notes are part of a new way of perceiving the universe.

These new perceptions are also among the first indications of a change in human awareness—a paradigm shift that will ultimately allow us to recover a holistic, ecological vision of reality. This change of perception we will refer to in this book as the "rainbow conscious-ness," or simply "the rainbow."

The Rainbow and the Psyche

In the last few decades, the use of psychedelic and psychotropic substances has given millions of people their first look at energy fields and their colorations, as well as a new look at the world around them. Experimentation with LSD began in Basel, Switzerland in 1943, when Dr. Albert Hofmann accidentally took a dose of the new synthetic substance. Forty-four years after his first experience, in a 1987 interview published in the Spanish magazine *Integral*, Dr. Hofmann declared:

> Under very favorable circumstances, and in many cases thanks to LSD, the borders between the "I" and the external world can dis-appear. A human being who for the first time in his life has the op-portunity to blend with all that surrounds him—from his feet all the way to his head, and to feel each one of his cells—that person will never again consciously destroy his environment. He will feel that as a part of it, he is protected by and living inside of a larger ecological system.
>
> Thus, one of the main uses that LSD could have in the medical arts is as an auxiliary agent for increasing awareness and for practic-ing meditation. It could also be used in psychotherapy, in brain re-search, and in the treatment of terminal diseases. Many people who have been conditioned only by a materialistic conception of reality and existence could find out, with the help of LSD, that it is possi-ble to explore another hidden face of reality.

People who were in their twenties during the late sixties found that LSD, as well as natural substances such as hallucinogenic mush-rooms, marijuana, and peyote, provoked many different changes in perception. Those who dared to experiment with these drugs in the internal laboratories of their own psyches acquired an altogether new awareness. Admittedly, there were dangers; the absence of any guides or "maps of consciousness" made these internal "trips" risky affairs. But through such inner journeys, many experimenters came to under-stand themselves and their surroundings in a deeper way, and many of them learned things that modern humanity had forgotten during centuries of "rational" and "scientific" conditioning.

One of the areas open to exploration through drugs was the hidden symbology of color. For the first psychonauts of this generation, these trips were truly immersions into the deepest mysteries of the luminous spectrum—a process of gradual initiation on the path to rainbow consciousness.

During these psychedelic journeys, the tonalities of objects, places, and people took on more meaning. Initiates began to perceive unspoken, unintended communications; people and things were felt or "vibed," as if they were surrounded by colored tints. Little by little, after several such trips, many initiates began to see auras. Eventually, they noticed how energies tended to attract similar energies and how people surrounded themselves with objects, forces, and beings that reinforced their own dominant qualities. As a consequence, trips came to be defined more and more according to their predominant colorations.

Yet one does not need drugs to perceive the effect of color on the psyche. For example, inside a discotheque, the red lights and general darkness generate both the hidden, black energies of the unconscious and the red, sexual energies of the customers. On the other hand, inside a temple, church, synagogue, mosque, pyramid, pagoda, or ashram, the prevailing colors are white and blue—an atmosphere that inspires a flow of energy to the higher chakras and results in feelings of peace, brotherhood, unity, compassion, and spiritual love.

In a green, natural setting, the physical body is invigorated. With this awakening comes the need to use the body again—to breathe deeply, to run, move, climb, jump, sit on the Earth, and be covered by mud or sand. Similarly, brown is the color of the soil, the bark of trees, the roots to the primal mother. In the brown, loving arms of the Earth, we learn once again to go back to the land, to come into close contact with the primal reality, to become one with roots and trees, sand and mud, and with the essential matter of our own bodies.

To today's Western mind, orange and ochre imply journeys into Eastern spiritual realms, evoking images of the Buddha, the smell of incense, the sounds of mantras and cymbals, and the whispering of "Aum," the original breath of the universe. Yellow is associated not only with cowardice, jealousy, jaundice, and loss of health, but also with sunshine, intelligence, and illumination.

Violet and indigo are related to the development of the intellect beyond dualism and dialectics, the path of the heart. White can mean innocence and holiness, but it can also denote madness. And black, the absence of light, evokes ignorance, apprehension, and the unknown, as well as sadness, loneliness, and grief. All the external truths can be seen and known through colors.

After traveling through the deeper meanings of red, orange, yellow, green, blue, indigo, and brown, and after experiencing roads both black and white, some of the pilgrims of the sixties arrived finally in the midst of the rainbow, a fresh, new consciousness. The rainbow was the alchemical gold that so many seekers had been trying to find by physical means during the Middle Ages. This luminous spectrum is the bridge between the seen and the unseen, between the inner and the outer, between this world and the heavens.

Not only those who experimented with psychedelic substances and mind expanders were able to reach rainbow consciousness. It is also true that not all who used such substances were able to achieve it. Tragically, many people of the psychedelic generation remained permanently stuck on one particular trip. On the other hand, many returned to devote themselves only to the colors of their beloved national flags, churches, football teams, and political parties. Some even tried to forget their "multicolored" experiences and ultimately embraced only the roles and colors assigned to them by others.

The New Rainbow Movement

However, since the early seventies, large numbers of people have begun showing signs of a new awareness. A part of the psychedelic generation *did* graduate after the journey, and this graduation implied not only seeing more deeply but living life in a different way.

In the end, all who achieved rainbow consciousness began living according to the urgings of their hearts, and the movement of their collective thoughts, visions, words, and actions eventually generated a number of organizations dedicated to social change. In the last twenty years, all over the planet, dozens of different groups have formed under the symbol of the rainbow. All of these, in different ways, have the shared intent of working for the healing of the Earth.

Among these multicolored "seeds" of change are families, tribes, communities, cooperatives, networks, councils, villages, banks, political groups, and parliamentary factions. Today, the rainbow has become a planetary symbol for a new social myth and a radical transformation of the world's consciousness. It evokes a spirit that is helping to uproot the forces of ignorance all over the Earth.

Traditionally, organized religions and established ideologies have tried to unify people based on creeds and dogmas—on "monochromatic" principles and symbols. Unlike the cross, the swastika, the hammer and sickle, or even the white dove of peace, the rainbow does not belong to any nation, party, sect, or organization; nor do tyrants, dictators, priests, and presidents use it to subjugate others. As a universal archetype, it is known and appreciated by people all over the globe. With its own natural subtlety and transparency, the rainbow cannot be categorized. It is a symbol of unlimited freedom, and within it are the seeds of all nations, creeds, and colors.

The rainbow is for people who are able to see the universe, the Earth, themselves, and others as a net of subtle interrelations that can never be broken. It resonates for people who understand that each thought, movement, word, and action has repercussions throughout the universe. The rainbow is for people who know that we are all part of a gigantic web that includes everything, from the smallest microorganisms to the remote stars and galactic systems. The rainbow is the spirit of love that embraces and contains all things, and that spirit is returning to transform the world.

Chapter 2

Return of the Rainbow Warriors

Today, we are nearing the end of the Piscean, or Christian, Age. We are now on the threshold of a new millennium, which makes these times propitious for a radical paradigm shift. This shift was announced in brilliant form by Marilyn Ferguson in her book *The Aquarian Conspiracy: Personal and Social Transformation in the 1980s.*

According to Ferguson, the Aquarian revolution implies a radical change of consciousness, the releasing of old concepts of nation, class, race, and politics. Some of these limiting concepts began with the myth that launched the Christian Age nearly two thousand years ago.

According to the Bible, when Jesus was born in Bethlehem, three wise men came to pay homage to him. These three, guided by the eastern star, represented the three known races or families of the world. They were Balthazar of the black race, Gaspar of the yellow, and Melchior of the white.

However, it is a mistake to conceive of the world community as being formed only by these three families. This is one of the distorted historical and cultural patterns of the Christian Age. We tend to forget the fourth member of the human family, one of the oldest and yet the last to have been incorporated into the great council of world nations: the red family, the American Indian. One of the prerequisites of the new paradigm is to include in our thought processes the wisdom and experience of the Native American.

Interestingly enough, many Native American tribes have held such a unified vision of humanity for hundreds, if not thousands, of years. According to ancient wisdom of the Hopi, for example, the world is divided into four regions or directions, each with its own predominant color: yellow in the east; red in the south; black in the west; and white in the north. In his book *American Indian Myths and Mysteries*, Vincent H. Gaddis writes, "Hopi prophecies are not to be taken lightly. Prophecy is an important part of their religion, and their sages seem to be able to tap a psychic source of information. They knew there were races of white, yellow and black-skinned peoples long before they had any contact with other races."[1]

Furthermore, he says, for many centuries the Hopi knew that the arrival of the white man would be accompanied by a long period of persecution and difficulty for the red people.

The Hopi were not the only ones who realized this and whose world was divided into the colors of the four races. Similar prophecies and divisions were recognized by the Maya, the Aztecs, the Tarascos, and numerous other tribes throughout the Americas.

Even more remarkable, however, many of these tribes shared a vision of the return of a spirit that would bring all the races of the world together in harmony and peace. These tribes saw the Earth as the mother of humanity in all its diverse colors. They foresaw not so much a blending of bloods as a cultural blending of traditions in the creation of a new society and a new world view. And this vision, which has only become possible in recent years, was to be brought about by the return of a group of people called the "Rainbow Warriors."

What is a Rainbow Warrior? That question was first answered for the modern world in 1962, in a book called *Warriors of the Rainbow* by William Willoya and Vinson Brown. In it, the authors compiled the interlocking visions and prophetic dreams of numerous individuals and nations, including those of the Iroquois, Crow, Sioux, Paiute, Blackfeet, Hopi, and Eskimo, as well as the Aztecs, Javanese, and even the Hindus.

One of the most useful of these is a simple Native American tale called "The Return of the Spirit," the essence of which I would like to recount here. The story that follows is an abridged version of the original that was translated into Spanish by Alfonso Gonzales Martinez and which appeared in the Mexican national paper *El Dia* on July 8, 1984.

❖

"Grandmother," asked little Jim, a twelve-year-old boy from the tribe, "Why did the Great Spirit in the sky allow the white men to take away our lands?"

The old woman, Eyes of the Fire, was sitting by the creek. When she heard the little boy, she turned her face to look at him with her deep opal eyes. She realized that Jim, just returned from the city to the village of his ancestors, had a real interest in knowing the answer to his question. Something vibrated within her spirit.

"Listen to me, my grandson who speaks his mind and feelings," she said. "This is a big question you are asking me. In ancient times, when a boy your age asked such a question, the elders would look at him and say, 'This is a big question for someone so small. We must send this boy through the hardest tests to try his spirit. Only a big person can answer such a big question. Let us see if he can prove that he will grow to become a real warrior.'"

"What do you want me to do, Grandmother?" asked the boy.

The old woman asked Jim to call his parents. She spoke to them, saying that the boy had the right to try to purify himself in order to look for an answer to his question. According to the traditions of the village, there was a special way to do that.

From that night on, when the grandmother was telling stories by the fire, Jim was always sitting close to her, drinking in all of her words. And in those nights, it seemed that something new was floating in the wind—a new feeling, as if the spirit of old had returned from the high mountains and was trying to come back to the village.

For the next ten days, Jim bathed every morning in the cold stream and prayed at dawn on top of the hills. On the last night, the old woman asked him to bring from the highest of the hills a rock that would strike fire. She also asked him to make himself a bow and arrows, and to go hunt a deer so that his people could eat of his hunt.

These things were not easy jobs for little Jim. He had never made a bow. In order to have a successful hunt, he had to learn to track deer and know their habits very well. On the night that he was lucky enough to return with the meat and skin of a deer, the old woman, Eyes of the Fire, smiled and said: "Very well, my grandson, you are becoming a man."

She then tossed some seeds on the fire, and one became red as a cherry fruit. Jim was so silent that his grandmother watched him until her gaze reached the bottom of his eyes. When she understood what was happening with the boy, she caressed him gently and said: "This little one has seen pain in others. Look at him, all of you, my people. This boy has been close to the Silent One, and his spirit will be great in the years to come."

In the warm silence, the rest of the people seemed to understand. In the middle of the night, someone began to play a drum, and the thumping of the drum was followed by chanting. The song was an old one, a beautiful chant that lifted the spirit of the people back to the days when the prairies had no barbed wire fences and the voices of the villages could be heard, clear and wonderful, for miles and miles.

The training of the child continued. He had to learn to climb rocks and mountains, to hunt for food, to learn about edible and medicinal plants, to listen in silence, and to eat properly. Then one day, Jim stood in front of his grandmother with fiery eyes and asked her again: "Now, Grandmother, tell me why the Old Man Who Brings the Light, the Great Spirit, allowed the white men to take away our lands."

Eyes of the Fire laughed with her full heart, with a deep, warm laugh that can only be heard among people who love and care for each other. Then she took a stick and drew a mountain in the dust, and on its peak she drew the figure of a man with his arms raised to the sky.

"You have climbed the hills and you have hunted the deer. You have searched and you have found. You have strengthened your muscles as a mountain lion and trained your eyes to be like the eagle's. You have done all of these things, and now there is only one more thing you must do in order to become a man. You must climb to the top of the highest mountain over there and fast and pray until you have a vision from the Great Spirit. But before you do that, I will tell you why the Grandfather of Everything allowed the white man to take the land of our people. Sit and be quiet. All I will tell you will be helpful when you seek your vision."

Jim sat down and kept still, as a young wolf does when he listens to his mother howl in moments of danger. Eyes of the Fire drew a circle on the floor with her stick, and inside this circle she drew many other smaller circles.

"Those small circles represent all the nations and religions of the world," she said, "but the big circle represents the great nation and the great religion that encloses and gives meaning to all the rest. The big circle is like a mother quail who covers all her chicks with her wings to protect and love them equally.

"A long time ago, our people lived more united than they do now," the old woman continued. "They were united by the wisdom and love they held for each other. The elders, both men and women, were wise, and they taught their children how to love and care for each other. The land belonged to all the people, and the children knew they had a father and mother in each person in the tribe. There were no babies left alone or unloved, and there were no old people who had no one to care for them. When the young hunters went to hunt buffalo, deer, or elk, they brought the best pieces of meat for the elders, the widows and the sick people. This way, there was love, goodness, and unity among our people, and we almost never had thieves, murderers or other harmful people like we do today."

"But were there wars among our own people?" asked little Jim.

"Yes, it is true that there were wars, but these were very few before the arrival of the white men. The white men came from the east, crossed the Great Ocean, and when they came to our lands they started to move quickly toward the west. As they moved, they shoved the Indians up against each other. This created more and more wars and resentment among nations. The more the white men pushed, the worse it became for our people. There was fighting everywhere. And to make things even worse, the white men brought their whisky, which made the Indians drunk and crazy, and they did things to themselves and to each other that they had never done before."

"Now tell me, Grandmother, why did the Spirit of the Earth let the white men take the land of the red people?"

Eyes of the Fire laughed again, a laugh as loud as thunder resonating inside a canyon, and she said: "All these things I just said will help you to understand. Our wise elders of long ago told me once why the white men had been sent to our lands. They said the Heart of All Being sent them here because they lived in a land where there were only white people, and they needed to learn how to live with other races; and that one day, when the Indians got the old spirit back again, they would teach the white men how to love one another and the rest of humanity. But now the Indians have been humiliated and impoverished, and through this process they have also been cleansed of all egotism and selfish pride. That is why they are ready for a great awakening and to help others awaken as well.

"In their dreams, our elders saw that the Indians would have to go through the worst of times, that they would lose their spirit and be split into many parts by many different religions of the white men, and that they would also try to achieve what the white men call success. But the elders also saw that one day the indigenous people would start to wake up. They would see that the white people who chased only after personal pleasure were leaving behind all the things that are truly important in life. And in this moment the Indian people would understand that their ancestors lived in harmony with something that is much more important and wonderful: the Spirit of Life itself.

"And these were not the only things our wise elders saw in their dreams. They also saw that just when the Indian people began acting as crazy as the white men, and just when everyone thought that the old ways were forgotten, in that moment a great light would come again from the east. This light would enter the hearts of some Indian people, and they would become like the prairie fire, spreading love and understanding, not only among different nations, but among the different religions.

"This is the clarity you should seek, oh son of my son, my beloved one. And I think that when you go out to seek your vision on the mountain, you will receive the answer to all of your questions. And that answer will be so wonderful, so deep and wide, that all kinds of people will be able to find shelter under your vision. That day, all the small circles will enter again inside the great circle of unity and comprehension."

When Eyes of the Fire stopped talking, she and her grandson turned their faces to the east, and they saw a great rainbow spanning the vastness of the sky. "The rainbow is a sign from Him who is in all things," said the old woman. "The rainbow is a sign of the unity among all people into one big family. Go to the mountaintop, son of my flesh and blood, and learn to become a Warrior of the Rainbow, for it is only by spreading love and joy among the people that we will be able to transform all the hate that exists in this world. Only through great understanding and goodness will we be able to stop all these wars and destruction."

❖

The second section we would like to quote, this time directly from Willoya and Brown, contains more specific advice that Grandmother Eyes of the Fire might have had for Jim—advice that is valid for all present and future warriors in their quest for vision and purpose in their lives. This section serves as a kind of blueprint that outlines just how the Indians (and others) are going to make their dreams and prophecies come true.

The Task of the Warriors of the Rainbow

We have seen how the golden threads of the prophecies foretell the day of the awakening of the Indian peoples and the formation of a New World of justice and peace, of freedom and God. We have seen how the Warriors of the Rainbow (the new teachers) are prophesied to come and spread this great Message all over the earth. But how are the Indians going to help these prophecies come true?

For long years the Indian peoples have been sleeping, physically conquered by the white people. For all this time they have been taught to believe that the white men were superior to them, that they must learn to live in and become a part of this white civilization, as it exists, even if a lowly part. It will not be easy to awaken them from their sleep. It can be done if we realize that the Indians are sleeping giants, that within each of them are marvelous powers of the spirit that need only be started into action to create miracles of work done for the good of all and deeds of shining heroism.

The world is sick today because it has turned away from the Great Spirit. When men turn once more to the Ancient Being with love and world understanding, the earth will become beautiful again. Indians can help mankind to return to the Wise One Above by obeying the following principles.

Like the great Indians of old, they will teach unity, love, and understanding among all people. They will listen no more to the little people who say they alone have the truth, but shall see that He who listens to all is too big for little things, too full of justice to accept but one self-chosen people, too free to be caged by any mind. They will listen instead to those who teach harmony between all men, even as the wind blows without favoritism into all the corners of the world.

Like the pure Indians of old, they will pray to the spirit with a love that flows through every word, even as the breeze sings its song to the Silent One among the needles of the pines. In solitude and in council their hearts will lift with joy, free of the quarrels and petty jealousies brought by men, free to love all mankind as brothers. As the Great Spirit loves a smile and happiness, they shall sing of the coming glorious union of men.

Like the glorious Indians of the past, by their joy, by their laughter, their love and their understanding, they shall change all men whom they meet. Like the rushing torrent of a river that wears away the hardest rocks, they shall wear away the hardest hearts with love, until the whole world begins to bloom with the new growth of man.

Like the radiant Indians of old who strengthened their muscles by hard exercise and then nourished their souls by fasting and prayer, so shall they make themselves heroes of the new age, conquering every difficulty with the strength of their bodies, the fire of their love and the purity of their hearts. Filling their mouths with only pure foods and liquids, and seeking the beauty of the Master of Life in every thought, they shall scorn harmful drinking and unclean habits that destroy and weaken men. They shall run to the hilltops to pray and fast and into the solitudes of the forest and desert to find strength.

Like the Indians of old who let their children run free in the prairies, the woods and the mountains to help them grow into men and women worthy of their Creator, so the Warriors of the Rainbow today shall work to bring to all children the magic blessing of the wild, the delight of bare feet running through green grass over the hills, and the cool touch of the wind in their hair. The spiritual civilization that is coming will create beauty by its very breath, turning the waters of rivers clear, building forests and parks where there are now deserts and slums, and bringing back the flowers to the hillsides. What a glorious fight to change the world to beauty!

Like the Indians of old who loved, understood and knew the powers of animals and plants, who killed or took no more than they needed for food or clothing, so the Indians of today will brighten the understanding of the ignorant destroyers. They will soften the hearts of would-be killers so the animals will once more replenish the earth, and the trees shall once more rise to hold the precious soil. In that day all people shall be able to walk in wildernesses flowing with life, and the children will see about them the young fawns, the antelope and the wildlife as of old. Conservation of all that is beautiful and good is a cry woven into the very heart of the new age.

Like the kind Indians of old who gave work to all and kept care of the poor, the sick and the weak, so the Warriors of the Rainbow shall work to build a new world in which everyone who can work shall work, and work with joy and with praise of the Great Spirit. None shall starve or be hurt due to the coldness and forgetfulness of men. No child shall be without love and protection and no old person without help and good companionship in his declining years.

Like the joyful Indians of old, the new Indians shall bring back to their own people and spread to other races the joy of good-fellowship and kindness and courtesy that made the life of the old Indian villages such a happy time for all. How they danced together! How they ate together in loving harmony! How they prayed together and sang together in joy! It shall come again and better in the new world.

Wise Indians do not speak without reason, and they shame a boaster by their silence; so today the Indians shall teach all people to make their deeds count bigger than their words. Deeds of love and kindness and understanding shall change the world.

Even as the wise chiefs are chosen, not by political parties, not by loud talks and boasting, not by calling other men names, but by demonstrating always their quiet love and wisdom in council and their courage in making decisions and working for the good of all, so shall the Warriors of the Rainbow teach that in the governments of the future men will be chosen out of the ranks by quality alone and then will counsel together in freedom of thought and conscience. In counsel they shall seek truth and harmony with hearts full of wisdom and prefer their brothers to themselves.

Among the Indians of old, children and youth were respected by the elders and were taught love and unity, strength of character, love of the Great Chief in the Sky and good deeds from babyhood. Today young people, who should be the hope of mankind, have wandered far from this strength of soul in their pursuit of pleasure and "success." The Warriors of the Rainbow will bring back this lost spirit before it is too late and the youth shall once more do great deeds of selflessness and heroism. The glory and the purity of their lives shall light the world.

The thoughtful and devoted chiefs of old understood their people with love; the parents of old educated their children with love; all new Indians will associate with other religions and people with love. One minute of such love and understanding brings wealth from the Great Spirit and creates miracles of accomplishment. It is love then with understanding that the Warriors of the Rainbow will mix in their medicine to heal the world of its ills, leavened with pure hearts and humble minds.

Those who do not understand think that when their Messiah comes He will do their work for them. But always, when a great Prophet comes to the world to change the hearts of men, he calls for heroes and those who work with happiness and dedication. Great are the tasks ahead, terrifying are the mountains of ignorance and hate and prejudice, but the Warriors of the Rainbow shall rise as on the wings of the eagle to surmount all difficulties. They will be happy to find that there are now millions of people all over the earth ready and eager to rise and join them in conquering all barriers that bar the way to a new and glorious world! We have had enough now of talk. Let there be deeds.

From north and south, east and west have come a great number of a similarly prophetic words and visions. Even Vinson Brown himself has been the recipient of such visions. After being introduced by his physician father to the wisdom and spirit of the Indians, Brown once had the opportunity to gaze upon a medicine bag that was used to keep a ceremonial pipe of the Oglala Sioux. His father had received this bag from the hands of an Oglala chief and pipe carrier in 1890, in thanks for the doctor's having saved his son from pneumonia. Following is Brown's account of his dream.

> In my dream I seemed to be floating in the sky looking down at a land of many round hills. On the top of each hill was a group of Indians. Some of them were lying on the dry grass, with their fingers digging into the ground despairingly. Others lifted their arms hopelessly to the sky. Women were huddled together, weeping. All were wearing old, cast-off white men's clothing, just rags. Their faces were filled with a deep sadness, and their skin seemed drawn over the bones, so that I felt both bodies and souls were hungry.
>
> There seemed to be growing a strange light up in the sky. Looking up, I saw the sunlight flashing on the wings of a beautiful white bird,

a dove. The dove circled down from the sky, its body and wings pure as new-fallen snow. Fluttering and circling it came slowly, but there was a feeling about it of immense power, as if all that was in the sky centered upon it.

As the dove came near the top of one of the hills, a strange and remarkable thing happened. The Indians there suddenly sprang to their feet, gazing up at the dove. The white men's rags fell from their bodies and disappeared. Instead they now lifted their heads proudly under handsome headdresses and their bodies were covered with clean buckskin that glittered with beads and with buckles of shell. Their faces glowed with happiness and joy. Their bodies arched like bows drawn back to send forth humming arrows. Then, to my amazement, they began to march up into the sky after the dove, marching with the springing steps of conquerors like lords of the world.

As the dove dipped low again and again, other dark-skinned peoples rose joyously from hill after hill and marched up into the sky, following the beautiful white bird. I saw many costumes in my dream, but did not know what they meant or what tribes they represented, only that feathers were waving, beads of many colors glittered, and brown arms gleamed with bronze and gold. Drums began to mutter, lifting and rolling into thunder, and pipes shrilled with triumph. Voices chanted ancient songs and shouted age-long cries of the peoples.

Slowly a bow formed in the sky, a rainbow of people marching to glory, a rainbow of unity and a vision so marvelous in its sense of beauty and joy that I can never forget it nor hope to see anything its equal. Slowly, at the end of each dream, this vision of glory would fade away, but the promise of it always remained, the promise of a wonderful change coming.

Finally, I want to include some more specific prophecies relating to the return of the Rainbow Warriors. These prophecies, originally presented in 1984, have been circulating among alternative networks in the United States. They indicate not only some of the changes occurring as a result of the return of the ancient spirit, but also the continuity of prophetic thought among Native Americans.

The Rainbow People
An Indian Prophecy by Grace Walking Stick
and Ruby Morning Star

These prophecies cannot be traced to any specific tribe, for they come from intertribal medicine societies. The medicine societies involved in channeling these prophecies are the women's societies of the Crystal Skull and the Black Widow.

1980 was the year of the creation of the teachings of the Eight Great Powers and the giving back to humanity of the Twenty Count, the Starmaiden Circle and the Flowering Tree Teachings, which began the evolution of the distribution of the "wheels and keys" (the esoteric teachings of the North American Indians) of Turtle Island. It was in that year that the major beginning "wheels and keys" were given away.

1981 was the year of the planting of the light seeds of the Hokseda (the higher self). Many teachers of the Eight Great Powers began to plant their seeds of light concerning the development of the higher self and began to open the teachings to the Rainbow People, also known as the Meti (mixed-blood) people.

1982 was the year of fertilization, the year of planting, the year of going within these seeds of light in order to see the potential, the road map, that a person can use. In Turtle Island lore, we say it is the year of finding one's path with heart, and many have done this.

1983 was the year of fruition, the year of seeking perfection, growth, and development. Most importantly, this was the year of trust and innocence, when people are listening and teachers are talking; when the mythologies of the world and all Eight Great Powers are finally revealing secrets and the teachings within the mythologies are brought out into the open. Because of this, there was a great deal of joy among teachers.

1984. This year is critical. This is the year of the animal, the year of Tuwalananie, the dark force. And the reason for this is that for three years, seeds of light have been planted and are starting to grow, and the teachings are starting to come out. All the ones inside each of the Eight Great Powers who have taught partial truths, who have taught deliberate lies in myth, who have used the power of the wheels to gain control of people or to gain followers, are going to be very threatened by the awakening of the consciousness of the Rainbow People, because the Rainbow People exist in every country, every nation, every land. In other words, the Sun Dancers are going to be strong enough to counteract the dark forces.

The dark forces will be extremely threatened, and they will use their power, which is the power of technology. We are going to see some of the strongest technological advances known to humanity occurring this year, and these advances are going to be a tremendous threat as well as a blessing to the survival of humanity. 1984 is also the year that we must establish balance and harmony between the light and the dark forces. It is going to be interesting, and that is why we have this sense of urgency, because time is getting short.

1985 will be the year of human-to-human communication, the year when humanity finally becomes human—if we can get through 1984. Then there will be more teachers and more teachings brought out into the open than ever before. Then we will reestablish contact in a very knowledgeable way with our ancestors from the stars. So mark that down, because it will happen. The first wave will come from the Pleiades and will be totally acknowledged by all the world powers. The second wave will come from Sirius.

1986 will be the year when Tagashala and the enlightened teachers will begin to open the veil of the crack between the worlds. We will see our memory circles. All kivas and sacred power spots will be totally awakened. The inner room of the Great Pyramid will be opened. The order of the Golden Dawn will have ceremonies there again for the first time in 20,000 years. The Temple of the Sun in Palenque will be refurbished, reawakened, and ceremonies will begin again.

The old traditional ceremonies that are still applicable for today's world will be renewed. Many of the so-called traditional ceremonies that are trying to keep us locked in the past and which do not function today will fall. It will be hard for some of the people of the Medicine Societies, because they don't know any other way. They are going to have to change or die. Many teachers who have been seen as great teachers but who have literally kept us in the dark as worshipers of the sacramental orders, will physically die and go over because it is the only way they can find the light in 1986, and many teachers will be seen for what they were. These will be the farmers, the laborers, and the gas station attendants; they will be seen as the real teachers because the Tagashala will be fully awakened.

1987 will be the year when the 144,000 Sun Dance enlightened teachers will totally awaken in their dream-mind bodies. They will begin to meet in their own feathered-serpent or winged wheels and become a major force of the light to help the rest of humanity to dance their dreams awake. A Sun Dance teacher is any human being who has awakened, who has balanced his or her shield, who has gained the dream-mind body, and who honors all paths, all teachers, and all ways.

I look for the day when I can sit down with my pipe and the Buddhists with theirs. You will see me sit down with my dagger and my Sufi drum, with my sword, my Shinto way, and my pipe, my Indian way. We are going to put our souls out on the table and say, "I love you all." This is a sacred dance. That is what 1987 is about. That is a Sun Dancer. You cannot say you have the only true way, for all ways are true.

In 1987, 144,000 enlightened souls will sit down in gathering circles, saying, "Here it is, Brothers and Sisters. Come and receive it." A lot of these are going to be so-called common people and not the teachers you see up there now. On August 17, 1987, the various winged serpent wheels will begin to turn, to dance once again. And when they do, the Rainbow Lights will be seen in dreams all over the world, and those Rainbow Light dreams will help awaken the rest of humanity.

1988 will be the year we will sit in a new circle of law. Civil and social law will tumble. All civil and social laws, by whatever governments, will have to be in conformity with natural law, or the people will not accept them, and the people will have the enlightenment necessary to reject the laws. Science will once again become metaphysics, will once again become magic. Four laws will be discovered that will help us jump from natural to magical law and transcend the time/space continuum, which is the limitation of the age, and once again we will begin to take our power and to work with rules and laws that are magical and cosmic.

1989. In this year we will once again see the way to continue a new dream. We will be given the road map back to the stars and will see the star people come out of the illusion of their two-legged form and into their actual Great Sleeper-Dreamer form. And so you will see some very powerful, totally enlightened masters in 1989, and that is the year of the second coming of the Christ spoken of in the *Book of Revelation*. It will be the awakening of a new circle, a new design of energy movement for humanity. Christ means circle. So the second coming of the sacred circle is all enlightened humans dancing as one consciousness.

1990 will be a powerful year, and it is very hard for me to talk about it. I am a great dreamer, but I don't know if I dream that large. We will see a real shift in planetary consciousness. Many of the enemies of humans will begin to drop away. In 1990 you will see the Twelve Sacred Driver Wheels of each of the Eight Great Powers scored and put together to create the figure "8" of the infinity sign. 1990 will begin through the Feathered Serpent Medicine Wheels those groups of seventeen Great Sleeper-Dreamers. The first migration to the next world will begin, leaving behind on this planet another world of enlightened humanity to join the many already on other planets throughout our universe.

When we speak of this migration to other planets, are we speaking of the creation of a new race? Another dream, another dance, another series of dances in another dress, in another world. What is the difference between this world and the new creation? It is those that go on ahead who are the pathfinders. There are always the pioneers, and they are always the people who choose to do it the hard way, in a sense. In other words, they are totally willing to sacrifice and to step out on the path of the unknown, simply because it is a pleasure to make it known.

1991. For those who stay here on Grandmother Earth, they will totally gain the light of the Great Light Wheel. There will be one humanity, one planet composed of all the different ways of dancing in complete harmony in the great gathering together circle. In 1991 the seeds will be planted.

1992. The Earth will have the true reality formed. It will join the sisterhood of planets, the Daughters of Copperwoman, and it will create within itself all forms of all things in harmony with the Everything.

1993. In this year we will see a whole new way of perfection. There will be plants on this Grandmother Earth that will give life and sustenance as never before seen. Starvation on the earth—all these things will be gone.

1994. In this year there will be a total balance and harmony. All human beings will be balanced fives and enlightened fives—a six. And they will still be in their physical bodies.

1995. The new race of humans will begin to design their new reality of life on this planet as they intended it to be when they came from the stars.

1996 will be the year in which the second migration to the new world will occur, leaving behind on Grandmother Earth those who are choosing to continue to hold the power on this planet within the space of all the Sacred Twelve [planets]. All of these people who choose to remain after the second migration will begin to establish this planet and use the collective unconscious to hold the power of this space in harmony with the Great Circle of Twelve, all the planets, and there is a whole lot I don't even know. There is more that I am not supposed to talk about yet.

1997 will be the year the dream will be actualized, and this planet will hold its space in the great council of planets and become part of the Universal Enlightened Brotherhood and Sisterhood of Humanity. There is an intergalactic organization that is known as the Great International Brotherhood and Sisterhood of Humanity and Keepers of the Light Circles. This has happened on many planets, and it is expected to happen on many others.

1998. There will be a moment in 1998 when the population will be ready for a major jump. The Circle of Law will hold the image of fast thought necessary to allow this planet to become a starship.

1999 will be the year in which the third migration will leave this planet for the other new world and this planet will now be a starship, a spaceship, and have its design of energy movement guided by all of humanity that is living here—because, you see, it has been a starship all along, floating around a central sun but not in harmony with its sister planets.

2000. The Great Spirit will have left its seed and the egg of everything here on this planet, and this seed will create itself twenty times over at the speed of light. Thus, the prophecy ends as I have been given it by the Grandmothers that I share with you now.

The foregoing myths and prophecies, varied as they are, all blend in the common conviction that at a certain point in human history, a new "rainbow nation" would be born among the families of the Earth, and that this moment would be preceded by the emergence of the first tribes of Rainbow Warriors in different places on the planet.

In coming chapters, we will illustrate how the seeds of social change leading to such a new "nation" have begun to germinate and multiply in the four directions and how the present rainbow movement is synchronizing yesterday's prophecies with the reality of present times.

The legend of the Warriors of the Rainbow can no longer be considered a myth or simply a belief belonging to "prescientific" cultures; on the contrary, it is becoming part of our everyday reality. The diverse manifestations of this emerging rainbow nation are very different from one another, just as are the colors of the spectrum. For some people, the richness manifested by the rainbow consciousness makes the "rainbow movement" seem chaotic, anarchistic, confusing, and disordered. Part of our task in this transitional period is to learn the respective places of each of the different tonalities, to be able to see behind the apparent chaos to the true natural order of the rainbow. Only then will we be able to find the "golden pot" that is there, always, at the end of the luminous bridge.

Chapter 3

Toward a New Tribalism: 1930–1970

Though the growing rainbow consciousness first became widely visible during the seventies, the roots of that consciousness can be found in much earlier events and social trends. Beginning with the thirties, then, this chapter quickly traces the history of worldwide violence and consumerism that led to disillusionment, social fringe groups, and the powerful youth movement of the sixties. In outlining this movement, I will focus on some of the leaders, visionaries, street performers, and offbeat, experimental groups of the fifties and sixties that were precursors to a new and enduring tribalism.

During the thirties, the United States emerged as a new world power, and a generation of men and women left behind their rural, conservative, traditional pasts in search of new ways of living. The country became industrialized, and for the first time, large numbers of women were incorporated into the production system and began demanding equal rights in labor, politics, and education.

Meanwhile, in Europe, young people were being asked to give their obedience and strength in exchange for "a place in history." Most young European men had only one option: to wear military uniforms and to become pawns in the growing struggle for world control. The result of this collective madness was World War II, in which the blood of an entire generation was transformed into cannon fodder in the most brutal and destructive power game humanity has ever witnessed.

Very few people raised their voices against the war. Even most artists and so-called "revolutionaries" sooner or later allowed the wave of nationalistic pride to drag them into the "fields of glory." At the end of the holocaust, some twenty-six million people had been killed, and hopes for real change were buried in the rubble.

In Europe, the hopes for social transformation were completely forgotten for more than a decade. In order to rebuild as quickly as possible, politicians, engineers, urbanists, and capitalists turned to cement, asbestos, steel, and glass. Within a few years, whole cities were painted gray, and life was reduced to a "rat race." As a result, poetry became desperate, literature nihilistic, philosophy existentialist, theater absurd.

In North America, the war had been fuel for the growing military-industrial complex, fuel to keep the factories working nonstop, twenty-four hours a day, 365 days a year. Now it was time to start producing, developing, and expanding; time to make and sell anything; time to get rich; time to get high on the pyramid of social status. Quickly the Big Machine grew into an uncontrollable monster, a colossal empire of monolithic office buildings housing the new masters of an entire continent.

Growth became a cancer. As author and philosopher Paul Goodman pointed out, "the Organized System had turned against human nature and converted it into merchandise; people into waste and expendable spare pieces; and Nature herself into an infinite source of profitable 'natural resources.'"[1]

Millions of Native Americans, mestizos, and black, yellow, mulatto, and poor white people formed the armies of laborers, the brute force for the new empire. And for its own well-to-do white children, the system devised sophisticated means of homogenization and programming. Beginning in earliest childhood, a generation of strong, white, efficient automatons were prepared to enter the Big Rat Race.

The Postwar Beat Generation

The program progressed well for a few years. But gradually the postwar generation became disillusioned with the values of competition and consumption that they found hostile to life. As time went by, increasing numbers of young, privileged people had trouble adjusting to the norm. As they grew older, many of these misfits became rebellious, irreverent, and irascible. In the United States, their antisocial behavior gained them the name "rebels without a cause," and in

Britain, "angry young men." They were also called existentialists, hipsters, beatniks, and, finally, just "beats."

At first, the beats could hardly be found in places other than Greenwich Village in New York and North Beach in San Francisco, but soon they began to multiply and scatter, mostly to university campuses and villages. These maladjusted young people refused the advantages of the system. They rejected the bargains, gifts, and opportunities they were magnanimously offered by parents, teachers, and bosses. They stood aloof from the values of their culture. They grew long hair and beards, dressed in recycled rags and colored clothes, and wore heavy boots or sandals, or went barefoot.

Then, much to the dismay of the Establishment, some of them began to frequent the ghettos, where they hung out with jazz players, prostitutes, thieves, homosexuals, Puerto Ricans, dope dealers, and "niggers." Hipster author Norman Mailer baptized them the "White Negroes," and soon they became recognized as the tribe of "white-black beatniks."

These first cultural mulattos also started to write, to howl their poems to the skies, and to paint graffiti on the walls of cities. They lived in the street and on the road—first in the United States and then, slowly, in the rest of the world. During the fifties, they left behind a wake of ludicrous and contagious madness. And their poems and novels—*On the Road, Desolation Angels, The Dharma Bums,* and *Naked Lunch,* among others—opened the way to the new mythology of the sixties.

When some members of the beat tribe tired of endlessly walking the dirty ghetto streets and driving the long, straight highways from coast to coast, they crossed the tequila border into northern Mexico and hitchhiked to the beat of "Mexico City Blues." Starved for new highs, they experimented with "devil's herbs" and "virgin's seeds" and discovered the ancient knowledge in peyote and magic mushrooms. The "dharma bums" began walking the paths of the Hopi, Navajo, and Lakota. They smoked peace pipes with shamans, sang in sweatlodges, and were initiated in the tipis of the American Indian Church.

On their initiatic journeys, the new white Indians learned the way of peyote from Huichol healers in the high Sierras, and Mexican *curanderas* showed them the way of the *manto de los cielos,* the morning glory seeds. Eventually, their pilgrimages took them as far as the jungles of the Amazon, where Tukano Indian elders showed them the sacred uses of *yopo* and *ayahuasca*.

The apprentices returned to their native lands much changed after their journeys to the south. Now, their culture was not only white and Occidental; it was fast becoming mestiza, a hybrid of black, white, and red. Old chants and poems began sounding new tones. The pilgrims had learned to respect ways other than their own. They had overcome their forefathers' attitudes of new colonialism, unconscious tourism, and macho conquering. They had starved with people who could not afford to eat. Now they understood the value of cooperation, friendship, ancestral community bonds, and voluntary poverty and simplicity.

Then, from the cold streets of North American cities, from the stinking apartments of the ghettos, from the needles of a truly "naked lunch," the beatnik pioneers took another important step in their individual and collective growth. Some of them crossed the Great Waters and began a pilgrimage through the deserts of North Africa and Asia to spend time in the temples and mosques of Morocco, Turkey, and India, and in the schools of traditional wisdom in Japan and Nepal. With these journeys, they collectively completed their cycle of initiatic knowledge and apprenticeship. From white to black to red to yellow: thus was the sacred circle of the four directions closed at last, blending the cultural characteristics of the four original races. And from this fusion and crossbreeding, the first plants of a new tribalism were born: the tribalism of the rainbow.

The Tribal Vision of Gary Snyder

In 1957, Gary Snyder, one of the most coherent and lucid members of the beat generation, synthesized the foregoing history in a chapter called "Buddhism and the Coming Revolution" from his book *Earth House Hold*. In this text, Snyder concluded that the teachings offered by East and West were both necessary in these times and that the main goal of his generation was to integrate social and personal transformation with the void that encompasses all things:

> It means using such means as civil disobedience, outspoken criticism, protest, pacifism, voluntary poverty and even gentle vio-

lence if it comes to a matter of restraining some impetuous redneck. It means affirming the widest possible spectrum of non-harmful individual behaviour—defending the right of individuals to smoke hemp, eat peyote, be polygynous, polyandrous or homosexual. . . . It means respecting intelligence and learning, but not as greed or means of personal power. Working on one's own responsibility, but willing to work with a group. "Forming the new society within the shell of the old"—the IWW slogan of fifty years ago.

The traditional cultures are in any case doomed, and rather than cling to their good aspects hopelessly, it should be remembered that whatever is or ever was in any other culture can be reconstructed from the unconscious, through meditation. In fact, it is my own view that the coming revolution will close the circle and link us in many ways with the most creative aspects of our archaic past. If we are lucky, we may eventually arrive at a totally integrated world culture with matrilineal descent, free-form marriage, natural-credit communist economy, less industry, far less population and lots more national parks.[2]

All his life, Gary Snyder has walked, and continues to walk, the "paths with a heart." He was one of the first white Indians; he was very close to the anarchist, libertarian movements in the forties; and he was a pacifist and poet in the fifties when he began a profound study of Eastern civilizations. For four years, Snyder explored the ways of Zen Buddhism and yoga. Later, more than any of the other beats, he studied shamanism, especially the ceremonial ways of the red people of Turtle Island. Then, following all the "trips" of the psychedelic initiation, in the sixties Snyder became one of the most influential guides of a world cultural revolution.

Initially, this social movement was very much influenced by a few outspoken voices of the beat generation—voices such as those of Allen Ginsberg, Neal Cassady, Jack Kerouac, Alan Watts, William Burroughs, and Michael McClure. But what was seen in the fifties and early sixties as a weird aberration among a small group of rebellious poets, musicians, and vagabonds gradually became an extended cultural underground movement and finally a full-scale international youth revolution.

This unprecedented awakening of an entire whole generation set the whole world on fire. It caught flame first on many campuses of North America, quickly spread to almost all the nations of the Western industrialized world, and in the end even engulfed parts of Latin America and Asia.

In one of his better-known texts, Snyder prophesied the sixties awakening of the postwar generation with almost incredible precision and lucidity. His text, published in 1957 as part of his book *Earth House Hold*, is called "Why Tribe?" Following are fragments thereof:

> We use the term Tribe because it suggests the type of new society now emerging within the industrial nations. In America, of course, the word has associations with the American Indians, which we like.
> The Tribe proposes personal responsibilities rather than abstract centralized government, taxes and advertising-agency-plus-Mafia type international brainwashing corporations—a totally different style of society: based on community houses, villages and ashrams; tribe-run farms or workshops or companies; large open families; pilgrimages and wanderings from center to center. A synthesis of Gandhian "village anarchism" and IWW syndicalism, in which people take personal responsibilities rather than leaving it to an abstract centralized government. . . .
> The Revolution has ceased to be an ideological concern. Instead, people are trying it right now—communism in small communities, new family organization. A million people in America and another million in England and Europe. A vast underground in Russia, which will come out in the open four or five years hence, is now biding. How do they recognize each other? Not always by beards, long hair, bare feet or beads. The signal is a bright and tender look; calmness and gentleness, freshness and ease of manner.
> Men, women and children—all of whom together hope to follow the timeless path of love and wisdom, in affectionate company with the sky, winds, clouds, trees, waters, animals and grasses—this is the Tribe.[3]

On January 14, 1967, Gary Snyder participated in the Summer of Love and the Gathering of the Tribes for the "Human Be-In" that was held in San Francisco's Golden Gate Park. The hosts of this unusual event were the varied tribes of Haight-Ashbury, a San Francisco neighborhood that during the sixties became the most important center of the countercultural movement in the United States. One of the press releases for that event read:

> Now in the evolving generation of American young, the humanization of the American man and woman can begin in joy, and

embrace without fear, dogma, suspicion or dialectical righteousness. A new concert of human relations being developed within the youthful underground must emerge, become conscious, and be shared so that a revolution of form can be filled with a Renaissance of compassion, awareness, and love in the Revelation of the unity of all mankind. The Human Be-In is the joyful, face-to-face beginning of the new epoch.[4]

On the day of the be-in, all the leading Bay Area rock bands were at Golden Gate Park: The Grateful Dead, Big Brother and the Holding Company, Jefferson Airplane, Quicksilver Messenger Service, and many others. There were also groups such as the Diggers, one of the new radical California tribes; the San Francisco Mime Troupe; and even a few branches of the California Hell's Angels; various gurus, heroes, and leaders of the beat generation, such as Allen Ginsberg, Lawrence Ferlinghetti, Michael McClure, and Gary Snyder; and newly emerging figures on the psychedelic and political scene: Jerry Rubin, Dick Alpert, Timothy Leary, Suzuki Roshi, Dick Gregory, and Leonore Kandel, among others. Thousands of young people arrived from all over California; on hand were also representatives of new tribes and their extended families from New Mexico, New York, London, and Amsterdam.

Snyder's description of the event was brief: "At the Polo Fields, on a wonderful day, the new aboriginals gathered in bunches, with their elders and children, and some of them with their own flags and banners. Those were the real tribes and clans."[5]

After the be-in, gradually the words of Gary Snyder, as well as those of Neal Cassady, Gregory Corso, Charles Bukowsky, William Burroughs, Hugh Romney, and Jack Kerouac, became guidelines for millions, causing an awakening that soon transcended North American borders.

The Living Theatre Tribe

Equally important for understanding the roots of today's paradigm shift is the tale of a tribe of peaceful warriors of the sixties called the Living Theatre. Its founders were Julian Beck and Judith Malina, two bohemian New York artists from the forties. Beck was a painter and a poet, Malina a theater actress. Both were very much influenced by the teachings of Gandhi and the theories of the libertarian philosopher and author Paul Goodman.

Between 1942 and 1946, these two attended the New York School of Action Painting and an experimental school called Black Mountain College in North Carolina. There, they met the most advanced libertarian and experimental artists from the East Coast, including John Cage, Merce Cunningham, and Allan Kaprow. They also studied the European dadaists and surrealists, who had pioneered a new form of theatrical expression known as the "happening," based on free-form improvisation. In the fifties, happenings began to include the participation of spectators, an innovation that later became an integral part of the Living Theatre.

Beck and Malina's growing process was also very much shaped by the trial of Sacco and Vanzetti, two anarchist workers who were unjustly condemned to death in the United States, and by the Spanish Civil War, in which thousands of idealistic libertarian soldiers, intellectuals, artists, and workers were annihilated.

In 1972, a book by Julian Beck was published. Entitled *The Life of the Theatre*, it contained many of his thoughts and visions in the form of a diary that spanned some thirty years. Following is one of Beck's meditations illustrating the vision of this co-creator of the Living Theatre:

> We went to the theatre all the time, Judith and I. Everything was so interesting and infuriating. Two three four times a week. So that by 1946 Judith knew that she didn't want to work in that theatre. . . . We said we'd make a theatre that would do something else. . . .
>
> Judith studied under Piscator who knew that social action and radical politics were the only Way. We talked about Anarchism, Marxism, Greek myths and metres, dreams and Freud, youthful talks, and walked in the woods along the Palisades, and went to the sea a lot, beach beauty. Perhaps our most profound understanding: that the 1940's were not the pinnacle of human achievement, and yet that in the 1940's was, dispersed, all the glory the world would ever contain. The problem of finding, assorting, reassembling matter, feeling, and being. A theatre for that.[6]

One year later, in 1947, with the help of Paul and Vera Williams, Beck and Malina founded the Living Theatre. From the beginning, they sought to integrate acting and *mise en scene* drama with radical changes in the lifestyles of the actors themselves. They also sought theatrical action that would force the public to participate in the happening. They refused the idea of a troupe performing for a passive public, and thus emerged the name Living Theatre.

Both Beck and Malina knew that the theater they were trying to create had its roots in the mythical, initiatic journey; therefore, they began studying the ceremonial practices of the American Indians. In his "Meditation 27," Beck reflected on the struggle and suffering of the Native Americans and his hope of somehow helping to vindicate them through his new theater:

> The North American Indians saw the end of their civilization, their people. And they danced out their Vision of Death and Resurrection. They did the Ghost Dance on the Great Plains, in the snow, blanket-wrapped, cold and despairing. They danced out a vision of annihilation of the White Man and of the reappearance of the Noble Savage, and of their herds of buffalo, their red and black and yellow maize. And we see also the gleaming of something else, like our truncated souls rising up and running free, with the plenty and the beauty of the place and all the spiritual splendor that like amputated limbs clutters the landscape now. Is the leg of the chair you are sitting on the leg of the woodcutter who chopped it down? . . . End separation. End the pain.[7]

The first years of the "Living," as the theater came to be known, were extremely difficult. In the streets of New York, the air of encouragement that Beck and Malina needed in order to keep going was in rather scarce supply. They needed something different to be able to create something new. And as Beck indicates in his "Meditation 54," written in 1970, that something was a new form of tribalism:

> The tribe has its own charisma. The tribe is a group of people bound together by love. Therefore they find ways to survive, and therefore the tribe has a special fascination in a more or less loveless society. . . . The word tribe is being used nowadays to describe those groups which are close to those ethnic groups which never lost their relationship to the earth the sun the moon to wind water fire flesh. The primal things. Whose being is testament to some kind of natural, that is, non-artificial, tenderness for unspoiled life, life in harmony with the nature of things, and yet beyond the conflicts common to nature. The tribe is a way of grooving together. Each member is look-

ing out for the benefit and well-being of all the members. They constitute a community in which the individuals are not alienated from each other. Moving thru a society dying of loneliness and its terrible effects . . . the tribe, like the animals described by Kropotkin who have survived the opposing forces of the ages thru mutual aid, touches all it contacts with mysterious force and melody; it is the living symbol of useful behavior, of key, eternal rhythm. The tribe passes by; and the cold and frightened spectator, perishing in his aloneness, sees the gypsies, sees the Jews, sees the caravan of actresses and actors, scorns them for their inbred secretions, envies their ability to make it, hates, and hopes that they will transcend his hate, and knows they will.[8]

Only in 1964 did the Living Theatre begin to realize the tribal nature it had been seeking for more than a decade. From that time onward, the example it brought to the world was momentous. The tribe of the Living, with its visionary messages, plays, stages, and dramatic actions, became in a few years the spearhead of one of the most radical movements for social change in the twentieth century.

Beck believed that the theater's success was due, in large part, to its tribal nature. In another meditation, also written in 1970, he reflects on the difficulty of maintaining the tribe against the forces of society:

It was only in 1964 that finally my life, The Living Theatre, began the realization of its tribal nature; and when in January 1970, we divided, it was not to perish, but to go thru a self-imposed ordeal, in order to rebuild our tribal reality with a more intense conscious effort, in order to outwit the forces which seek to smash all tribes forever. Because the modern state cannot tolerate any group which has any feeling stronger than the dependence on its own alienated/alienating, dangerous, doom-laden self. The tribe fights for its life in such an environment. We are fighting. When the people (from behind their windows) see us as we amble down the street they know who we are, they recognize the archetypal stride, they know we are the enemy of their state, they know we are the secret lovers of their bodies who visit them at night, we are the incubi of their unconscious, we are the meat of their dreams, we are the lickers of their spirit, we wrestle with the immaterial form, they know their state is Strong and Big and Brittle, and they know the tribe is weak and small and unbreakable. . . . The weak are supple and alive.[9]

The plays of the Living Theatre, such as *Connection, The Brig, Frankenstein, Antigone,* and *The Mysteries,* became the initiatic steps leading to the creation of the troupe's most important collective master-piece, *Paradise Now*. This play, created in Cefalu, Italy, in 1967, crystallized and focused the messianic cry of an entire generation. It sparked a fire of rebellion, inspiring and animating all the disparate strands of the youth movement in the apocalyptic year of 1968.

Paradise Now offered a powerful collective vision for millions of young people who were born after 1945. It summarized the important changes of the two decades following the war: the radical criticism of the Establishment; the search for alternative ways of thinking, feeling, and acting; and the questioning of institutionalized ideologies and religions. The better part of an entire generation identified with the play, which mirrored the exuberant overflow of that generation's own energies: the psychedelic revolution, free sex, rock 'n' roll, and the transgression of all limitations and borders.

Beck recalls the spellbinding effect of *Paradise Now*, and the power of "free theater" in his "Meditation 45," written in 1968:

> The next time we did Free Theatre was in *Paradise Now*. . . . To bring this about: in *Paradise Now* we called into action mysterious forces: the influence of color, the wisdom of the *Book of Changes*, the physical-spiritual journey of Kundalini, the arousal of the energy which rests in the chakras, the holy world vision of the Chassidim, the high vision of the *Kabbala*, we energized the body segment by segment, and we devised rituals, movements, sounds, visions, and cadences that carried the actors (the guides) and the public into trance. In trance, in a spaced-out condition, maybe we could enter Free Theatre. . . . Free Theatre: a situation in which performers and public get the taste of freedom. Free theatre, free action: There is no Free Theatre until we are no longer prisoners in the world.[10]

These were Julian Beck's words just a few months before the performances of *Paradise Now* in Paris, Avignon, Berlin, and many other cities—performances that sometimes stretched on for weeks that began to unleash an unrestrainable youth revolution. One of the play's first consequences was the beginning of the generalized "Movement of Occupations" in France in May 1968. Beck reflects on that movement in one of his meditations written in Rio de Janeiro, Brazil, two years later:

> Avignon, 1968, the year the culture died, we created *Paradise Now*. As we worked on it in the late winter and early spring of that year

in the Sicilian town of Cefalu, as we composed the dialectic for a nonviolent anarchist revolution, we were already part of the movement which flowered all over the world that year, and in France in May. *Zeitgeist.* . . .

What took place the night of May 15, 1968 inside the Odeon was the most beautiful thing I have ever seen in a theatre. The occupation of the Odeon had all the elements of great theatre: a cast of vivid characters; great poetic tirades; conflict of ideas; the clash of potent ideologies; a reality surpassing the contrivances of dramatists; the emergence of the people as the hero; and the end which came a month later as awkward tragedy with the invasion of the police, tragic like the whole story of France in May, like Spain, like Kronstadt, like all the great anarchist dramas. . . .

The theatre of that spring in France was the most elevating and intoxicating thing the French people of this century had experienced: they were acting, acting great roles. . . . These dramas were written in the Book of Life. Amen.[11]

In 1971, the tribe of the Living Theatre was arrested and imprisoned for seventy-two days by the Department of Political and Social Order in Belo Horizonte, Brazil, while performing their last play, *The Legacy of Cain.* They were accused of instigating subversive activities, the same accusation that eventually led them to prison a total of twelve times in the United States, Europe, and South America. From his Brazilian detention cell, Julian Beck continued sending messages to all who would listen:

> The situation here is critical, as it is everywhere. apocalyptical vision as the year 2000 approaches. the life expectancy here is not too high. birth rate is. in the sky emergency. in the ragged huts, in the military belt, the strangle hold. in the rainbow swim, the rainbow effort, the rainbow movement, approach of many colors. white light. dark countries, dark time, also time of beauty. beauty which enhances life but does not halt the emergency, the rapid loss of blood. Bursting wounds, bursting stars.[12]

In this particular instance, the Living Theatre tribe was released from jail after an outcry from the international arts community, including people such as Salvador Dali, John Lennon, and Yoko Ono. However, life for the members of the Living Theatre, and especially for Beck and Malina, continued to be erratic, a permanent search for the roads with a heart.

After their Brazilian tour, the company created an extraordinary piece called *Seven Meditations on Political Sadomasochism*, a play that allied the theater with the movement of Amnesty International to free political prisoners. Next, they created an epic cycle of 150 plays called *The Legacy of Cain*, dealing with the six great chains that shackle humanity: war, property, the state, enslaved love, money, and death.

In the early seventies, the company took up residence in Pittsburg and later in Brooklyn, in order to become more a part of the communities in which they worked. In the mid-seventies, they returned to Europe, where they toured the entire continent almost continually from their base in Rome. Their self-exile from the United States lasted until 1983, when the Living Theatre finally returned to New York.

Three years later, in September 1985, Julian Beck died of cancer. No doubt his untamable spirit continues its struggle for the creation of an earthly paradise, now and forever. One of his meditations, written from a detention cell in Belo Horizonte, Brazil, encapsules both that struggle and that vision:

> To establish our identity as people we have to destroy the hate-filled world of nationalism in which we are divided from each other. Unification. We go from land to land, not from "country to country," to re-create our identity as a people: for holiness is in the midst of people and not ever in the midst of a nation.[13]

In 1986, Judith Malina, with the help of her son Garrick and other members of the company, produced *The Living Theatre's Retrospective*, a series of twenty-three scenes from twenty-three different productions of the company. Most recently, the company opened new quarters in a storefront on Third Street in New York's East Village. In 1989, it produced four new plays, and in the summer of 1990 the company toured Europe once again, with Judith Malina and Hanon Reznikov as directors. All told, the Living Theatre has produced more than seventy works in its forty-plus year history and performed in eight languages in twenty-four different countries.

The Merry Pranksters

In 1959, author Ken Kesey volunteered to be used as a guinea pig in a series of experiments with psychedelic substances. From his ensuing period of hospitalization, his famous novel *One Flew Over the Cuck-*

oo's Nest was born. The book, portraying life inside the prisonlike mental hospitals of the United States, gained international acclaim in relatively few years. As a result, Kesey became a notorious figure and soon began showing another side of his personality.

In 1964, Kesey bought an old school bus, a 1939 International Harvester, which he baptized "Further." He soon gathered a band of people and took off on a cross-country trip to the World's Fair in New York City. Driving Further was Neal Cassady, an almost unknown but fascinating hero featured in several bestselling novels of Jack Kerouac and Gary Snyder. When Kesey returned from this trip, he bought a three-acre ranch in California near San Francisco, which he named La Honda. One year later, the place became headquarters for a whole new group, a psychedelic gypsy tribe that came to be known as the Merry Pranksters.

During the sixties, the Merry Pranksters became the psychedelic bridge that linked the beat generation to the LSD-taking, acid-rock-listening "love generation" and its main characters and events. These included Timothy Leary, Richard Alpert, Alan Watts, Stephen Gaskin, The Grateful Dead, Jefferson Airplane, and the great rock concerts at Monterey, Big Sur, and Woodstock.

At La Honda, all kinds of legendary parties, festivals, and mythical encounters took place during 1965 and 1966. These featured not only the Pranksters but other famous tribes, including the Diggers, the Warlocks, Family Dog, the Hell's Angels, the Hog Farmers, and assorted beatniks, hipsters, and hippies.

The Pranksters developed their own style. Forming a company called Intrepid Trips, they became a tribe on the move, taking all kinds of journeys, passing around colored tabs of acid (LSD), playing and dancing to heavy rock 'n' roll, sharing a new sexual morality, and experimenting with subsistence living.

But they were not just frivolous. In their revolutionary theatrical doings, the Pranksters used collective psychodrama and Zen koans—systems that had been used two decades earlier by French philosopher Antonin Artaud, and German genius psychologist Wilhelm Reich, in an attempt to integrate left- and right-brain faculties. Beyond all else, the Pranksters' purpose was to bring surprise, aliveness, and joy to a hardened society that seemed to have lost its heart.

The Pranksters were also the first to promote and popularize a new kind of festival called the "Acid Test." These events, which took place in such settings as the Fillmore Auditorium and the Avalon Ballroom in San Francisco, were truly initiatic celebrations. "Captain" Ken Kesey became the conductor of this new "psychedelic symphony," and usually the whole scene focused on whatever was happening around him.

At each Acid Test, the watchword was *participation*: a "grooving" into everybody's trip. The Test became a collective celebration, including the most sophisticated acid-rock light shows ever seen. New stroboscopic and electronic marvels appeared at each show, with new audiovisual effects and the best Orange Sunshine, Blue Barrels, White Lightning, Owsley Purples, and Rainbow Tabs made by the now-famous Augustus Owsley Stanley III, the acid king of the sixties. Thousands of kids came to Haight-Ashbury ("The Haight") from all over the United States to be part of the scene. Gradually, the Acid Test began to move from place to place—out of the halls, onto the beaches, and into the public parks—and they were always free events, where rock music, LSD, and love were lavishly shared by all.

In October 1966, LSD was outlawed in California, and Captain Kesey was arrested. To peacefully oppose the new law, Kesey and his band, together with the Diggers and many of the Haight-Ashbury bands, decided to plan a "Love Pageant Rally." A new "Declaration of Independence" was drawn up by the Psychedelic Rangers, which stated, in part:

> ... that the freedom of body, the pursuit of joy, and the expansion of consciousness are all inalienable rights, and that to secure these rights, we the citizens of the earth declare our love and compassion for all conflicting hate-carrying men and women of the world. We declare the identity of flesh and consciousness. All reason and law must respect and protect holy identity.[14]

One month later, Kesey launched what he called the "Graduation," the last Acid Test. In this event, all the veterans of the initiatic journey received a diploma, verifying that they were truly experienced trippers, psychonauts, and "acid-heads." The awards were given out by Neal Cassady.

In 1967, there took place the first "Gathering of the Tribes for a Human Be-In" at the polo fields in San Francisco's Golden Gate Park.

One of the spiritual advisers and gurus of the sixties, John Cooke, had conceived the plan in Cuernavaca, Mexico, and passed it on to Michael Bowen, a painter from Haight-Ashbury who was also a friend of Timothy Leary. The event, the biggest ever held in the Haight, was planned as a party to celebrate the "rebirth of the Haight and the death of money." The most active tribes behind the action were the Diggers and the San Francisco Mime Troupe, a guerrilla theater group.

The idea was to bring together the two main currents of the North American youth movement of the sixties. On one side were the groups that formed the "New Left," those that opposed the war in Vietnam and that supported Third World revolutions. On the other side were all the people who identified more with the hippies, communal extended families, psychedelic heads, new tribes, flower children, and the love generation.

One of the press releases for this event read: "The night of bruited fear of the American eagle-breast-body is over. Hang your fear at the door and join the future. If you do not believe, please wipe your eyes and see." It was signed by Gary Snyder, Michael Bowen, Lawrence Ferlinghetti, Leonore Kandel, Jerry Rubin, Richard Alpert, Timothy Leary, Allen Ginsberg, and representatives of the Diggers, the Pranksters, and the Family Dog.

This event was the first attempt to bring together the disparate parts in a collective body that had been growing since the beginning of the post-Hiroshima era. Many thousands of people came to the Gathering of the Tribes—people who identified themselves as members of a generation united for a radical cultural transformation.

In 1967, Captain Kesey was arrested once again, and when he was finally freed, he decided to go into exile for awhile and let things cool. He crossed into Mexico and stayed for a few months on the Pacific Coast near Puerto Vallarta. One year later, tired of living underground and running from the law, he left the California scene, took his old bus Further for its last "intrepid trip," and bought a milk farm in the Willamette Valley of Oregon. With him went his wife, children, and some of the other Merry Pranksters.

Those of Kesey's followers who didn't want to adopt a sedentary lifestyle joined the Grateful Dead or met with Prankster Hugh Romney to create the Hog Farm tribe. Neal Cassady returned to Mexico, where he was found dead a year later near the train tracks in San Miguel Allende, a small village in the state of Guanajuato. Kesey's company, Intrepid Trips, ended its days at the farm in Oregon, where Kesey himself can still be found, together with his beloved bus Further and miles and miles of film footage from all his journeys. Also remaining there are the monologues of Neal Cassady, a rich part of the colorful history of the sixties.

One of the best known histories of that era was written by Tom Wolfe, who lived for a while with the Merry Pranksters. During that time, he taped hours and hours of interviews with Kesey and some of the members of his tribe, then collected materials from other sources to write a book that became an immediate bestseller in the sixties: *The Electric Kool Aid Acid Test*. Another part of this history is revealed in *Garage Sale*, a book that Kesey wrote in 1973. And most recently we have *The Further Inquiry*, by Kesey himself, and *On the Bus*, by Paul Perry and Ken Babb, both published in 1990.

The Hog Farmers and Their Friends

The Hog Farm was, and still is today, one of the best known of the extended families, the new tribes, the experimental clown armies of the last thirty years. It was originally formed by a group of about fifty people, including Hugh Romney, Paul Foster, David La Breun, and Bonnie Jean. These people lived on an unending trip in six different school buses converted into mobile homes. They also carried with them a four-hundred-pound pig they called "Pigasus." Originally, the Hog Farm was located at a pig farm in the San Fernando Valley, California, but it moved frequently—to New York, New Mexico, Nepal, Vermont, and then back again to San Francisco.

After adopting the pig as their collective totem, the Hog Farmers bought their first school bus and started doing road shows, just as the Living Theatre and the Pranksters had done before them. But the Hog Farm was even better organized and had a clearer intent than the other two groups, partly owing to the fact that they had absorbed their previous experiences and learned from their mistakes.

The Hog Farmers participated in all the main festivals that took place in the sixties. They created music and light shows, took acid trips, and cleaned up the mess afterward. In fact, cleaning up became a ritual

that both the Pranksters and Hog Farmers enacted at the end of all
their parties. They picked up everything, to the last cigarette butt, and
even replanted seeds whenever possible.

At many of the festivals, the Hog Farmers also acted as psychedelic
guards, and in a strange way they represented an emerging ecological
consciousness that continued to grow as time passed. In their travels,
they were connected to the best-known rock bands and radical tribes
of the times: the Grateful Dead, the MC-5s, the Living Theatre, the
Translove Energy band, and the Up Against the Wall Motherfuckers
of New York's Lower East Side.

The Hog Farm participated jointly with the Motherfuckers at
several actions in Buffalo, New York, at the National Convention for
the Legalization of Marijuana, and in Central Park, Manhattan. In
his memoirs, Romney writes about his first impressions of the
Motherfuckers:

> Now about these Motherfuckers, I think they are pretty nifty,
> although it took me a while. We're country folks, you see, and there
> ain't much country on the Lower East Side, but they are busting their
> ass to make it better for everybody, which is what our trip is about.
> They work with winos and scabby A. heads, while our scene is more
> up-town or out in the sticks.[15]

During 1968, the Hog Farmers and the Motherfuckers joined in
many confrontations with the Establishment. They could be seen
together at antiwar rallies, at the main centers of the psychedelic revolution, and as part of the new coevolutionist, ecological movement that
was gathering around Stewart Brand, an old-time Prankster and friend
of Ken Kesey. Brand's *Coevolution Quarterly* and *The Whole Earth
Catalog* were becoming spearheads for the alternative ecological movement in the early seventies, and many beats, ex-Pranksters, and Hog
Farmers were collaborating with it by putting many of its ideas into
practice in their daily lives.

In 1969, the Hog Farmers met in Santa Fe, New Mexico, for a
solstice gathering with the Merry Pranksters and the Motherfuckers.
They decided to celebrate their meeting with an "electrical bus race."

"In Aspen Meadow above Santa Fe," Kesey remembers, "the Great
Bus Further lost her silver bell to the Great Bus Road Hog in the First
Annual Summer Solstice Great Bus Race."[16] From New Mexico, the

Hog Farmers took off for the East Coast and the biggest rock festival in history: Woodstock.

Also in 1969, Romney traveled to Chicago with some of the leaders of the Black Panthers, the most radical black organization of the sixties, to start a dialogue between the Panthers and the Yippies, a political wing of the hippie movement more formally called the Youth International Party, or YIP for short.

While in Chicago, Romney also collaborated in the Conspiracy Stomp, a festival supporting the eight leaders accused of conspiracy to incite a riot at the 1968 Democratic Convention in Chicago. The leaders were due to be convicted at any moment; the idea of the festival was to raise funds for their defense and to alert the public about their plight.

In Chicago, Romney met with the two principal leaders of the Yippies, Abbie Hoffman and Jerry Rubin. From that encounter, the idea of a "People's Park" was born. The big idea was to start "liberating" city parks, national parks, and lands that were unused, and turn them over to the people to be converted into ecological, sustainable, free centers for all. The initiative was taken up by the Pranksters, the Hog Farmers, the Ant Family, Stewart Brand and his people, and Peter and Judith Berg of the Diggers, with the first People's Park to be held in Berkeley, California.

Afterward, the idea was taken by the Hog Farmers and Peter Berg to Europe and to the First United Nations Conference on the Environment, held in 1972. When the Hog Farmers first arrived in London, they bought a big city bus. Then they started traveling all over Europe with their tents, tipis, and children, organizing mini-festivals to begin planting the seeds of ecological People's Parks in all the lands they visited.

During the course of their journeys, the tribe grew to more than forty people, so in Germany they were forced to buy a second bus. The first one was named "Sterling Hog," the second, "Rainbow Repairshop." Eventually, the Hog Farmers traveled to India and Nepal, and they hoped to travel all the way to Bangladesh, intending to help its population after the catastrophic floods. Declared Romney when he arrived in Nepal in 1971: "Our best show has always been dinner, and doctors were needed indeed, but first on the menu, and what we could leave, was our love. . . . Our journey to the East is a book by itself, and someday I'll write it for somebody's bail."[17]

After their trip to India and Nepal, the Hog Farmers went to Stockholm to attend the United Nations Conference on the Environment. With them, they carried many messages, including the ways of alternative communities and the use of soft technologies, organic agriculture, and nutritious food.

Also at the conference was Peter Berg of the Diggers tribe, showing videos on some of the new eco-communities that were being founded in North America. His and the Hog Farmers' presence caused a real impact on the consciousness of European youth. They didn't accomplish much institutionally, but they built a solid, multicolored bridge between the alternative movements of both continents.

On Romney's return to the United States, he and his friends bought a piece of land in Vermont at a place called Norton. The tribe wanted it to become the site of an Earth People's Park, and they began doing workshops there to teach the principles of ecology to the public. Their intention was to start a global healing operation to help Mother Earth.

According to Romney, the idea for an "ecommunity" at Norton was to create an ecological center as a model in order to begin "freeing" pieces of land here and there and turning them into unspoiled natural areas. "The vision keeps asking for a few hundred acres in each ecological region," he wrote. "An attempt to evolve without bloodshed."[18]

Not long afterward, having already adopted the rainbow as their collective symbol, the Hog Farmers changed their name to "Earth People." As this statement from Romney's book illustrates, their mission was nothing less than to save an entire planet:

> Ecologists say we have just thirty years to get it together. The matter is pressing and requires all platforms be hopped on and tested. The system's army is rapidly dying, while ours is just being born. When I speak of our army, I don't speak of arms, but a loosely knit people who march for survival, not of the fittest but all forms of life. Sounds kinda hokey, but if you wanna enlist, all you could lose is your planet.[19]

Finally, I would like to include a colorful reflection by Ken Kesey that captures the zany, rebellious spirit of the Hog Farmers as well as its infamous reputation among the authorities. This reflection shows up in the foreword to a book of memories by Hugh Romney (also widely known as "Wavy Gravy") entitled *The Hog Farm and Friends*:

On a sweet, clear spring day, in response to an ominous sug-
gestion by Mr. Romney—who calls himself Wavy Gravy at present,
even if he used to be known as Dimensional Creemo—the Merry
Pranksters rendezvoused with the Hog Farm somewhere on what
the Hog Farm General assures us is a super secret and snugly secure
mountain far back in the high desert country of Joshua Tree National Forest—just the spot for these two revolutionary bands to get together for some uninterrupted high level plotting. Very high level.
The always-famished Hog Farmers are into the Prankster acid stash
like it was a bowl of Spanish peanuts at a cocktail party, reassuring
us as they munch down hundreds of thousands of micrograms: "Go
ahead, get ripped and cut loose all you want up here—there ain't
nobody for a hundred miles to bother us!" You might imagine our
surprise, then, when we come floating out of the sage and sandstone
back to where the Hog Farm's scruffy vehicles are parked about our
painted bus Further—come sailing out of the sage, still rushing and
preparing to peak—and see four patrol cars come skidding to a stop
surrounding us with lights whirling and radios squawking and
helicopters coming. Well, this kind of thing used to happen when you
hung around the Hog Farmers or you were one of their friends.[20]

The Diggers and Motherfuckers

The Diggers were the most radical and open organization on the
American West Coast. They brought a libertarian mystique and ideology to the street movement of San Francisco. They took their name
from an English anarchistic community of the seventeenth century,
a group who lived as farmers on wastelands and who claimed that the
Earth was for those who needed it rather than for those who owned
it. The Haight-Ashbury Diggers brought live theater, free stores, clinics,
food, art, weird looks, festivals, music, dope, fun, and culture to their
neighborhood between 1966 and 1969.

The Diggers first came into being during a violent confrontation
between black people and the police at San Francisco's Fillmore
Auditorium. The founding fathers of this nonviolent tribe were Emmett Grogan and Peter Berg, who, having witnessed the confrontation,
decided to use street theater to denounce injustice, racism, and social
violence. Later, Judy Goldhaft, Slim Minnaux, Butcher Brooks, and
the sculptor La Mortadella joined in to create the nucleus of the tribe.

Visionary Emmett Grogan, who had grown up in New York before moving to San Francisco, was convinced that theater was the best way to project his visions and involve people in radical change. He had close connections with the Grateful Dead and with the San Francisco Mime Troupe, some of whose actors also turned into guerrilla Digger performers.

At the same time, in the streets of New York's Lower East Side, another band was growing—a tribe of "dadaist situationistic guerrilla warriors" that came to be known as the "Up Against the Wall Motherfuckers." The Motherfuckers took their name from the epithets hurled at them by New York City cops every time they were stopped in the streets. Each time the police bolted out of their patrol cars with their guns in their hands, before asking anything they forced the kids against the wall for a search and "verification of identity." Invariably, they called them "motherfuckers."

Contrary to most of the other tribes of the sixties, the Motherfuckers had, from the beginning, a much more aggressive attitude when confronting the established order. The main reason for this was that they were led by several very radical, charismatic people. One was Allen Hoffman, a revolutionary poet who had been influenced by libertarian philosopher Murray Bookchin. The others were Ben and Janice Morea, two brilliant, determined revolutionary artists from the streets of Manhattan, who had been influenced by the European dadaists of the twenties.

The Motherfuckers, like the Diggers, identified with the anarchistic movements of the Middle Ages and their messianic communities. They also opened free stores (consisting of giveaway food, clothing, and other items for anyone who needed them), clinics, and crash pads, and fed hundreds of street people at public parks and abandoned buildings.

In 1966, Allen Hoffman and the Moreas created a magazine called *Black Mask*, which soon became an incendiary vehicle for many young people who were starting to turn their backs on "the system." The ideas of Murray Bookchin also conveyed a profound and radical criticism of society in the same anarchistic vein as that of Paul Goodman, Norman Brown, Noam Chomsky, and Herbert Marcuse, all of whom became important ideological figures of the sixties. An example of the extremist position held by the Motherfuckers at this time is exemplified in one of the *Black Mask*'s manifestos of November 1966:

A new spirit is rising. Like the streets of Watts, we burn with revolution. We assault your Gods. We sing of your death. *Destroy the museums . . .* our struggle cannot be hung on walls. Let the past fall under the blows of revolt. The guerrilla, the blacks, the men of the future, we are all at your heels. Goddamn your culture, your science, your art. What purpose do they serve? Your mass murder cannot be concealed. The industrialist, the banker, the bourgeoisie, with their unlimited pretense and vulgarity, continue to stockpile art while they slaughter humanity. Your lie has failed. The world is rising against your oppression. There are men at the gates seeking a new world. The machine, the rocket, the conquering of space and time, these are the seeds of the future which, freed from your barbarism, will carry us forward. We are ready. *Let the struggle begin!*[21]

In less than four years, the Motherfuckers, like the Diggers, became a legend in their own time, accomplishing dozens of actions filled with radical, subversive theatrics. Deeply rooted in the streets of the Lower East Side, Chinatown, and the Bowery in Manhattan, they expanded their range of activities to Washington, D.C., where they participated in the Poor People's Campaign in 1968. They later took part in the occupation of Columbia University and in the demonstration at the National Convention for Legalization of Marijuana in Buffalo, and finally they moved to New Mexico and California.

The Motherfuckers supported their ideas with deeds, writing, and a radical way of living. They worked alongside Puerto Ricans, blacks, Chinese, Chicanos, winos, whores, bums, freaks, and kids. They were also part of Students for a Democratic Society (SDS) and helped launch the first alternative underground papers on the East Coast. Probably even more than the Diggers, they were the first tribe of psychedelic "Indians" to integrate people of the four races. Together with the other radical tribes of the late sixties, such as the Weathermen, the Hog Farmers and the Diggers, these multicolored Warriors of the Rainbow bucked the system on all fronts.

In 1968, the Motherfuckers met with representatives of the most radical organizations in the United States—Black, Red, Yellow, White, and Brown Panthers—to define strategies of interdependence and self-defense among the different ethnic and cultural revolutionary groups. Their position was that instead of fighting each other, they should concentrate their revolutionary efforts on opposing their common enemy: the military-industrial complex.

At the same time, the Diggers were responsible for the "Summer of Love" in San Francisco. Acting as modern Robin Hoods, they fed hundreds of people at Panhandle Park. The women raided slaughterhouses, bakeries, and markets in search of "seconds," while the men picked up boxes of fruit, vegetables, rice, and fish, sometimes "liberating" these items from farms and stores. (A couple of times, Grogan and his partners wound up in jail after these escapades.) They also set up parades, free shops, and street "happenings," always protesting injustice and hassles by the police and city governments. On October 6, 1967, the Diggers celebrated the "Death of Hippie," a ceremony to mark the end of an era and to protest the outlawing of LSD in California.

In 1969, the Motherfuckers also entered into a new cycle of growth. They abandoned the cities and divided into three bands. The first band got some land in the state of Vermont with the intention of creating an "anarcho-ecologist" farm. Murray Bookchin and his companion, Bea, moved into this project, but it lasted only two years. The second band, led by Ben Morea, moved to the hills of New Mexico. In his memoirs, Hugh Romney remembers an encounter with this band in 1970:

> Stopped off at a farm to scratch the pig and hug the people. Bumped into Ben and the Motherfuckers. They had been living wild and free in the middle of a national forest maybe five miles from the nearest road. Got a small tepee town set up in a clearing, milkin' goats, shootin' deer, bearin' babies, livin' and learnin' right close to the quick. Post-graduate studies at Survival U. They shaped their black clothes for leather and feathers. Looked like they stepped out of Courier and Ives' sepia mountain-men calendar.[22]

The third group of Motherfuckers went to northern California. Among these was Allen Hoffman, who helped to create an eco-community called Black Bear Ranch. There, Hoffman and his group tried to put into practice many of the libertarian communal principles developed by Murray Bookchin in his book *Post-Scarcity Anarchism* in 1971. Peter Berg writes about this experience:

> A lot of us Diggers went and lived at Black Bear Ranch for a while, which was a heavy-duty [place in the] Siskiyou Mountains. It

was a radical commune, maybe the most radical commune in the '60s. Black Bear is the only place I've heard of where 50 adults decided to live in one room for the winter and have multiple sexual relationships. But it was also a tremendous emotional wreckage. Eventually Judy and I left there because we thought they were too insular. They were so busy having revolutions every 24 hours. But it was also at Black Bear that we started to develop a sense of place. We started to become conscious about the water of the creek, about our feces, the local vegetation, the trees. So we got into managing the resources. It was a deeply rural educative process.[23]

At the beginning of the seventies, Allen Hoffman was proposing the creation of a confederation of communities and alternative groups in northern California. He was deeply involved in this process when a car accident cut short his promising life.

At about the same time, a general exodus began from Haight-Ashbury. Emmett Grogan moved back to New York, where he wrote a novel and died from an overdose of heroin. Stewart Brand continued publishing the *Coevolutionary Quarterly*; the Grateful Dead became a big band with a large following of groupies and "dead-heads"; and Gary Snyder moved to northern California to continue writing and lecturing. Peter Berg and Judy Goldhaft remained at the Haight and created Planet Drum, an organization for bioregional and ecological projects. As for the Motherfuckers, they disappeared as a group, but some of the original members are still contributing to the growth and evolution of the alternative movement.

Woodstock Nation

At the 1968 ceremony of the Death of Hippie in Haight-Ashbury, the store sign of the Psychedelic Shop was also buried. It was only a symbol; nonetheless, it was a sign that something had started to change drastically in the capital of the love generation. The ceremony meant that a change of consciousness was necessary in order to move on to the next step. Organized groups felt that either it was time to start confronting the system in a more aggressive way or time to move out and begin doing something else.

There were suggestions for a change of name of the movement. "Hippie" was dead, and the flower children couldn't stand up to the soldiers who were pointing guns at their chests. Some urged the adoption of names such as "Freemen" and "Earth People," but none of these stuck.

Then Jerry Rubin and Abbie Hoffman came out with the Youth International Party, the Yippies. In 1967, YIP invited all the flower children to participate in a March on the Pentagon. According to the Yippies, the purpose of this ceremonial happening was to help "cleanse the karma of the building." They planned to join hands, completely encircling the building, and use the combined energies of all the people to levitate it off the ground. Thousands of young people came from all over, and many warriors of the alternative tribes were also there to help keep things running smoothly.

At that time, books such as Jerry Rubin's *Do It!* and Abbie Hoffman's *Revolution for the Hell of It* and *Fuck the System* had become cultural Molotov cocktails. These books, which were read by a generation of increasingly angry ex-hippies, most clearly synthesized the feelings, thoughts, visions, and actions that marked the end of the sixties. It was then that the protest movement became a global phenomenon; 1968 turned into the most tumultuous year of the entire century—everywhere and at the same time. Suddenly, the children of the postwar generation, the children of the atomic bomb, were marching and protesting in the streets of all the main cities of the world.

During the 1968 Democratic Convention, Chicago's Mayor Richard Daley gave orders to the police to end the popular festival convened by the Yippies. Blood began running in the streets. National television covered the news, and the terrified parents of the flower children saw their kids being gassed, brutalized, wounded, and arrested right on their TV screens.

The principal organizers of the Yippie convention were accused of conspiracy and inciting to riot. The "Trial of the Eight" began in Chicago, and among the defendants, of course, were Jerry Rubin and Abbie Hoffman. The legal process was to start in August 1969, but that same month everyone planned to go to a rock festival in Woodstock, near Bethel, New York, so the trial was postponed until September.

Woodstock was the greatest rock concert of that era. It was also a good opportunity for Abbie Hoffman to use the stage—a chance for him to attract the attention of more than four hundred thousand people, as well as the media. Hoffman loved the media, and he was in dire need of it before his trial. He also wanted to ask for the liberation of John Sinclair, head of the White Panthers, who in 1969 had been condemned to twenty years in jail for possession of two joints of marijuana.

At Woodstock there were two stages for the performers. One belonged to the superstars, who had arrived in private helicopters and were surrounded by bodyguards, and it was expressly forbidden for anyone else to climb on their stage. When Hoffman began to speak from the "superstar" stage without authorization, he was turned out, and Pete Townshend of The Who clonked him over the head with his electric guitar. Hoffman never lost his enthusiasm, however, and in the five days immediately following the festival, he wrote a classic book called *Woodstock Nation*. For Abbie, this was the first nation without presidents, just warriors and poets:

> Woodstock was an Aquarian explosion, a happening, a trip to the future, an example of functional anarchy, of primitive tribalism and a true Gathering of the Tribes. Woodstock was the welcoming into the Aquarian Age.
>
> I would like to let you know that young people here in Woodstock Nation are learning to fly in space. . . . Someday we too will fly off in some communal capsule, Blacks, Puerto Ricans, Hippies, liberated women, young workers on the line, and GIs sitting in stockades because they don't want to go to Vietnam. There will be a whole mess of us laughing and getting stoned on our way to OUTERSPACE, and the first thing, the very first thing we're gonna do out there is to rip down that fucking flag on the moon. Power to the people.[24]

Other veterans of Woodstock saw the rock festival in a very different light. When it began, the organizers asked the Hog Farmers to take care of the people, because nobody else had as much experience in dealing with large numbers of kids. Nobody had expected the arrival of nearly half a million people, nor the heavy rains, the tons of mud and garbage, and the lack of facilities to keep everyone safe and happy. According to Hugh Romney,

> It was just about time to plug in all that big-time music, when the Movement started showing up. Started setting up Movement City, but

it's hard to move a movement when it's free. Movement City in all that mud. Lots of leaflets. They're all very intense. Paul Krassner and Abbie Hoffman looking startled without sidewalks in their long-fringed leather jackets. . . .

The leaflets didn't work, because the only propaganda was survival. The Hog Farm is good at staying alive. Yet the revolution was into evolution. I mean, they could dig it, and they dropped down their leaflets and started pickin' up the wounded. Abbie Hoffman organized the hospital tent almost single handed. Then we pitched the freakouts, you know, for people on bummers, like eatin' bad dope, so here I'm telling the doctors what to do about crazy people."[25]

The Hog Farmers organized a gigantic kitchen to serve "breakfast in bed for five hundred thousand." Finally, when the festival was over, Romney remembers that they stayed there for more than a month cleaning everything up:

Well, Woodstock was over except for pickin' up the garbage, which is one of the shows the Hog Farm is best at. There's a lot of other people that wanna stay and clean up that land. Pick up the junk, plant some grass. It took them a month, and I know if you would go there, it was like it never was, 'cept these cows gave cheese for a year. But get out of your car and walk into the pasture. Just kinda sit there and feel what went down. It will be there for hundreds of years.[26]

After Woodstock, events seemed to take a completely different turn. At the Altamont Raceway Rock Festival, when the Rolling Stones were playing "Sympathy for the Devil," a young black man was stabbed to death on stage, in front of the public, by one of the Stones' bodyguards, a Hell's Angel who had contracted to keep the stage "clean." That same week, investigations began into one of the Los Angeles tribes called The Family, led by Charles Manson, regarding a series of ritual sexual crimes in southern California. Jimi Hendrix and Janice Joplin died three weeks apart from overdoses of heroin and barbiturates. And finally, John Lennon made a statement to *Rolling Stone* magazine that has become the epitaph for the sixties: "The dream is over."

These were all clear signs of a radical turn in the direction of the journey. Those who tried to live in the past or who stayed on a monochromatic trip were left behind; those who adapted to change took the next evolutionary step. It was time to start getting clear about all the things that had happened; time to mature and process certain experiences; time to get involved and committed on a deeper level.

As in all social movements, after the exuberant, exciting decade of the sixties, there came a period of decreased activity. After the gigantic wave at the end of the decade came a powerful ebb tide that cleared out the beaches, drowned a lot of hopes, and killed many newborn experiences. It was a process of purification, an autoregulation of the social organism in its own growth process.

However, the world had been changed in a subtle way by the idealism of the sixties. No longer was the counterculture composed of a few weak tribes of beatific white Indians. It had become an international movement—a movement that had directories with thousands of addresses. Alternative communities, rural and urban collectives, healing centers, barter and simple living fairs, natural food and consumer co-ops, workshops, schools, women's centers, and legal services were listed in the *People's Yellow Pages* from many different bioregions—not only in the United States, but in international directories. For the first time, alternative networks began to create a new global community.

These were times to start living in close contact with the elements, times to start doing the "real work," as Gary Snyder called it. Yes, the party was over. Now it was time to assimilate all the trips, experiences, and colors in order to integrate them into a spectrum—to create a new body of thoughts with new visions and deeds. These were good times to start building reality out of the dreams from the sixties, times to move up to the next phase of the rainbow apprenticeship.

The youth of the sixties shared a lot of things, not the least of which was a collective rebelliousness. Now it was time to graduate into adulthood and take on a deeper sense of responsibility. The people who went through this difficult graduation met again in the seventies. Now it was time to stop complaining about the things they didn't like and to stop dreaming about all the beautiful things they wanted to do. The seventies were a time to shut up and start *doing* all those beautiful things.

Chapter 4

The Birth of the Rainbow Tribes: 1970–1980

Today, it is generally accepted that the sixties gave birth to an unprecedented international movement of protest and rebellion. The seventies, by contrast, were characterized by the spread of numerous alternative social structures and communities that resulted from the maturation of that protest.

Without trying to be exhaustive, this chapter reviews—mostly through firsthand accounts—the origins, philosophies, and histories of five of the more enduring of these organizations. Though they emerged in very different parts of the world, all of these groups adopted the rainbow as their identifying symbol, and all in their own ways became models of alternative growth and transformation. Together, they express the blossoming of the rainbow consciousness, a state of mind and heart that continues to push humanity toward a planetary eco-consciousness.

The seventies, then, were a decade of inner and outer searching for new paths. Those early, sometimes faltering steps have given us the strength to walk with greater assurance. So let us give full recognition to the pioneers of this era, for without them, we would still be swimming in an ocean of unconscious dreams.

The Rainbow Gatherings
Garrick Beck

Over the centuries, the spirit of cooperation has enabled humanity to create wonders of social harmony and technical achievement. Annually for nearly the past two decades, a group of grown-up children has created a unique event dedicated to making visible the power of this cooperative spirit. This event is called the Rainbow Gathering.

Each year since 1972, during the first week of July, Rainbow Gatherings have occurred on public lands. Hosting up to twenty thousand people, they are free and open to everyone. Most importantly, they have demonstrated the potential for humans to live, work, and celebrate together without exploiting one another and without government domination or financial motivation.

The idea of the Rainbow Gathering took root in the spring of 1970. By that time, the peace movement had been badly torn by violence, divisions between neo-Maoists and neo-Marxists, CIA infiltration, and power-hungry peace-movement bureaucrats. In fact, the peace movement as we knew it had disassembled: The back-to-the-landers, food co-ops, Eastern mystics, and worker collectives had all gone their ways; rock 'n' rollers were now putting on their festivals in the face of mounting opposition from the nation's anti-Woodstock laws; Marxist-Maoists were theorizing in progressively smaller circles; and the Kent State massacre had indicated the government's eagerness to stem the tide of collegiate rebellion.

When an arts festival in the Pacific Northwest brought together a number of tribally oriented groups, it was only natural that we should share our visions of what was happening and what we could do. The idea of a gathering for all people engaged our imaginations; in the dismal and fragmented climate of the times, it was an uplifting thought.

We envisioned and planned all at once. The gathering was to be—and still is—publicized largely by word of mouth. As we talked with others, every so often someone would light up in response to the idea, as though they themselves had independently seen or desired the event to be. These people spread the word. We saw ourselves not so much as innovators as we did messengers called upon to revive an old form of human congregation and communion.

At first, we referred to the new event as the World Family Gathering. We viewed it as an event in which people of all races, nations, and clans could come together as one family. (Sometimes we thought the whole world would stop for a moment to join us.) Our own little part of this world family we called the Rainbow Family, because we felt we were part of the spectrum of all races and peoples.

In September 1970, when we regrouped at the Vortex I festival, a "biodegradable festival of life" held outside Portland, Oregon, we were named the Rainbow Family of Living Light. Mostly, I think, we saw that title as a passing fancy. But the name stuck, and by the time of the first gathering in Colorado, people were calling it the Rainbow Gathering, and we were all the Rainbow People.

For more than two years, we worked and talked our way toward the gathering. Our politics consisted of faith and elbow grease. We traveled across the country. We visited co-op food stores, yoga ashrams, street scenes, and peace action groups. We posted notices in cafes, printed "Howdy Folks" newsletters, and made announcements at rock festivals and on listener-sponsored radio and TV. We sang in parks, leafleted in shopping malls and slums, and printed and reprinted invitations and maps.

We met with a lot of doubt—doubt that such a thing could be done without financial backing or famous-name stars to attract attention and doubt that humans could gather peaceably without crime and chaos.

We also met with a lot of fear and opposition. Initially, we had agreed on the time and place to gather as being July 1–4, 1972, somewhere in Colorado. Little did we expect the roadblocks that were set before us. All along, we maintained an attitude of willingness to work with local administrators. We went to the Colorado state capitol and laid out our entire plan, but the officials there must have thought we were either joking or crazy. Months later, when they realized it was really happening, rumors began to howl through the capitol corridors, local right-wingers were up in arms, and local officials began to panic.

We had decided on an area near the headwaters of the Colorado River. There, just before we arrived, the U.S. Forest Service ordered every campground within fifty miles "closed for repairs" to prevent our gathering. Anticipating violence, the governor called up four thousand National Guard troops for maneuvers. A friendly farmer gave us his wheat field to park on, so we temporarily camped there, seven miles from our destination. Then, after much counseling, we began to move up to Strawberry Lake.

Zam! The Colorado State Police barricaded the roads. For a week, we played "cops 'n' hippies," complete with diversionary movements and secret trails and supply lines through the woods to isolated Strawberry Lake. In spite of the highway blockade, our camp grew and grew.

Meanwhile, down below, the police arrested all hitchhikers and stopped every longhair-carrying vehicle for a complete inspection. If your rig didn't pass, it was towed away. "Routine inspection for highway safety," we were told. You had to walk, or they busted you for loitering. If you didn't have enough money, they busted you for vagrancy. The records will show that more than seven hundred people were arrested—for nothing more than peacefully trying to get to the gathering.

Ultimately, the parking area down below was filled to overflowing. After more counseling, we decided to walk through the barricades. Three to four thousand strong, we shouldered our packs and began the seven-mile walk through town and out to the roadblocks beyond.

In the meantime, the encampment at Strawberry Lake had grown considerably. Close to two thousand people were already inside, setting up the village community in the woods. On the outside, we had been negotiating continuously, showing pictures of the in-camp developments, explaining how we were peaceful, gentle people and how we planned to proceed, sustain, and clean up the operation when we were done.

In response to this, the county hauled us to court. There, we maintained that our activities were all clearly permitted under the First Amendment guarantees of peaceable assembly and religious freedom. The judge ruled in favor of the county's ban on mass gatherings, which had been passed just the week before.

But in spite of the judge's ruling, our column of backpackers rounded the bend at the barricade. Faced with no realistic alternative, the sheriff's department let the swarms of singing, praying, peaceful marchers pass on by. The column continued for the next three days as people from around the world walked past the barricade and on up the next six miles to the gathering at Strawberry Lake.

In the years since, we have worked out many of our difficulties with the authorities, but each gathering, in its own way, touches on the realities of the people's rights and the forces that would restrict those rights. One year, officials in the public health department may be extremely helpful and friendly; the next year, they may lead the opposition. One set of county agents may try to scare us away, while the next may welcome us. But each year, as we express the boundaries of freedom, we still encounter the forces that would compress those boundaries around us.

Twenty to twenty-five thousand people came to the first Rainbow Gathering in Colorado, and we suddenly became experimenters in the art of community design. What we lacked in experience we made up in faith—faith that we humans could figure it out. And from that faith came a tide of creativity and cooperation. We developed community kitchens; we devised numerous prototypes for waste disposal and sanitation; we engineered water and supply storage systems. And in doing these things, we discovered nonhierarchical methods of working together, as well as the best methods to use.

Communion and Silence

From the beginning moments of the plan for the first gathering, we envisioned a silence—a qualitative "space"—at the center of the gathering where we could all come together silently to send out our thoughts, feelings, hopes, meditations, and prayers. In that silence, each one of us is left to listen to the wind, feel the Earth turn, and watch the clouds and sky with our brothers and sisters in the peaceful Cathedral of Nature.

How can I tell of the insights, emotions, visions, and experiences that occur within this silent communion? Not everyone comes to the silence in these gatherings. There is no pressure to participate. But most people come. Sometimes we have this communion right in the middle of the gathering inside the tipi circle. Other years, we choose a meadow or ridge just outside the camp. Some years, we leave the gathering site to go to a particular place. In 1972, for example, we went to Table Mountain, Colorado, and in 1976 to the U.S.-Canadian boundary between Montana and Alberta as a gesture of international goodwill. There, we did a hands-across-the-border ceremony.

Even though the latter ceremony was held in the Waterton-Glacier International Peace Park, we met with a lot of opposition. Officials threatened us, and the immigration department called in SWAT teams. As usual, we negotiated and then did what we'd planned on doing in the first place. In the end, even the officials admitted they hadn't seen what all the fuss was about.

After that, we began gathering for a week instead of just the first four days of July—four days was too short a time to enjoy the camp, the people, and all the activities. By extending the event to seven days, we had time to develop further the workshop, arts, council, and pageant aspects.

Essential Information

The design of the gathering incorporates most of the fundamental and important aspects of human society. Just because we are utopian naturalists doesn't mean we don't get all of the problems of the human experience—we do. We have the same problems as any other community, including disease, theft, aggression, and various forms of craziness. But the uniqueness of our community is that we get to apply our own techniques of healing, teaching, and cooperation to solve these problems.

The essential teachings in the context of each gathering are very simple. Human hygiene demands clean food and water, proper disposal of wastes, and the prevention of disease. These are all simple, basic lessons with which most of us in protected, high-tech nations have lost touch. Innumerable lessons in ecology are also learned in the construction of kitchens, washing facilities, water lines, and latrines.

Providing for all of these things takes a tremendous cooperative effort, and for many of us it is our most creative time of working together. There are also sprout farms to be planted and watered; water sources to be protected and conducted by pipe to easy-access taps; compost pits and trench privies to be dug and monitored in each neighborhood; and vital information to be transmitted to every person who enters the scene.

For the information dispersal, we begin with a "Rap 107 Crew," whose job it is to welcome people, help them park, and deliver "Rap 107," the traditional encampment and health-sanitation information. All this is very essential. Without it, and without a careful adherence to its guidelines, the absence of hot water and porcelain sanitation can lead very quickly to water contamination and hygienic breakdown.

Also, the information that is passed on mirrors the needs of every human community, large or small. So in the setup and maintenance of these villages, we get to see and understand the parameters of human need. We get to discover what is really necessary and what is extra. And we gradually learn how to take care of our needs independently, cooperatively, without having to depend on giant corporations and big government. This experience of community responsibility has powerful repercussions for each of us in our own personal growth. We encounter people with ideas different from our own and we have to work out solutions.

Also before the gathering, maps of the camp are given out, and booths are constructed for information and rumor control. A newspaper called *All Ways Free* is published, and workshop bulletin boards are erected showing workshop and class descriptions, locations, and times.

The workshops encompass a broad spectrum of educational opportunities and allow for the cross-pollinization of ideas. They usually include several hundred different educational experiences, including always-popular workshops on midwifery, health and diet, yoga, massage, herb walks, nature studies, handicrafts, woodcarving, and weaving.

Alliance meetings also take place at the gatherings, with people from such organizations as Amnesty International, Oxfam America, Greenpeace, and Citizens Against Toxic Sprays. "No nukes" groups, peace-action coalitions, and anarchist and justice groups also meet to share information, recruit volunteers, and inspire each other. This networking is one of the Rainbow Gathering's most important aspects. It not only strengthens the ties among often isolated organizations; it also introduces many of the younger people to the multifaceted problems of the world and to some of the people who are busy creating solutions to those problems.

Health and Healing

Our Center for Alternative Living Medicine (CALM) at each gathering is staffed by doctors, nurses, and healers. The idea of the center is to provide free health care both for immediate problems and for long-range health planning. The CALM center includes a "Mash"-type emergency and evacuation unit, an herbal apothecary, a women's center, and a massage area. Therapies include acupuncture, acupressure, and chiropractic, as well as herbal, nutritional, allopathic, and meditative techniques. The aim is to make a variety of treatments available and advise the patient on what methods are most appropriate in each instance.

Many people have never encountered an opportunity to make use of natural or alternative healing arts, so we present these alongside and in harmony with the standard medical approach. Classes and workshops also teach these and other methods.

The Rainbow Family Tribal Council

Our public forum and decision making body is called the Rainbow Family Tribal Council. Everyone who attends the gathering automatically belongs to it. One person speaks at a time, and everyone gets a chance to be heard. The council meets almost every day of the gathering as well as during setup and cleanup. But its function is not merely for decision making; it is also a forum for ideas, a stage for poets, a platform for political proposals, and a megaphone for announcements. Some people have a particular message of importance, while others just want to blow kisses.

The council can decide to focus on one issue and select a person to help keep that focus. Often a feather is used for this purpose, being passed from hand to hand, speaker to speaker. Some agenda items are decided by consensus—for example, when a resolution is clearly stated and in the ensuing silence no one raises an objecting voice. Other times it is not so easy. We sometimes use a show of hands to get an idea of how the group feels generally, but we avoid the voting process because it leads to endless campaigning and a tyranny of the majority rule.

Often the council will be of two minds about an issue. That's OK, too—we have to learn to live with our differences. And often it's better if two solutions are approached rather than one idea followed and the other abandoned entirely.

The council process is rich with alternatives. Sometimes we break into small groups to talk things out before regrouping into one large council. In other cases, consensus may be the only acceptable route. Sometimes, a straw poll may make the matter clear; other times, we all decide individually what course of action to take.

The council has entered into agreements with local, county, and federal agencies, as well as with private parties. Tribal groups from every part of the world have used council methods similar to ours. We feel this is an advanced and subtle process that has everyone's benefit at heart. It keeps poetry, music, and lightness in the midst of our debate, and it awakens us to the experience of direct personal participation.

Even when the council process is bogged down, it is full of compassion and commitment. The council is not only an effective means of self-organization but also an effective means of preventing political decay.

Tribal Roots

Some people see the Rainbow Gatherings as being associated with the American Indians. Clearly, in some ways, they are. The indigenous people are the originators of human culture on this continent, and we have learned a great deal from them. We have learned a lot, too, from the many Native American people as well as elders and spiritual teachers who have come to speak at our councils and share their insights and wisdom with us. For practical reasons, we also use many tipis as living quarters, and we use sweatlodges for bodily cleansing.

But while tipi life and traditional ways are evidenced everywhere at the gatherings, so are the high-tech wonders of the future. Windmills charge twelve-volt communications systems, solar hot-water units hang from trees, and silicon-generated electricity has illuminated the CALM centers at night. There is a balance between ancient and modern techniques. The idea, of course, is to be open and discerning enough to choose the best of each.

Indeed, the gatherings present many practical examples of communal, back-to-the-land living: homemade clothes, redesigned vehicles, horses, goats, sprout farms, composting, geodesic structures, and recycling of materials and wastes. All of these things indicate a harmonious relationship between the individual and the natural patterns around us.

Gathering Festivities

Each "neighborhood" at the gathering has its own kitchen, which often doubles as a center for music, song, and dance. In the evenings and usually long into the night, poets, storytellers, and puppeteers perform along with guitars, banjos, dulcimers, flutes, gongs, and drums. Sometimes the sweet notes of a jazz saxophone slide through the forest; other times the ground shakes with the sounds of tribal chants and dancing.

Because of all this, plus the many pageants, ceremonies, and celebrations that occur at the gatherings, we have gotten a reputation as a bunch of "partyers." While it is true that many people attend the gatherings for the "party," we make a clear distinction between the party and the process. The party is like the icing on the cake, while the cake is the process of human cooperation that keeps the whole thing together. And the process of coming from the party into responsible participation in the event is something the gathering inspires in almost everyone who attends. This discovery is one of the roots of the future growth of our species. The taste of freedom only gives the human palate an appetite for more.

Rainbow Politics

We have also been accused of being "nonpolitical"; however, we have actively supported an extensive variety of political actions. For example, we served as a medical team at the first and second Seabrook demonstrations to protest the construction of a nuclear power plant; we set up tipis on the tracks at the Rocky Flats nuclear arsenal in Colorado to blockade the infamous "White Train" that carries parts for hydrogen bomb triggers; we raised and donated food for the 1973 Wounded Knee occupation; and we have used our skills at innumerable "no nukes" demonstrations, providing coordinated child care, kitchens, and parking crews at such places as Big Mountain, Satsop, Devil's Canyon, Shoreham, and Bangor.

And these are only a few of our social-action contributions. We have also raised funds for refugee camps in Central America, and we sent a relief caravan with food, medical supplies, and tools to Guatemala after the 1973 earthquake. Within the gatherings, there have also been workshops, camps, and petitions dealing with the draft, environmental campaigns, farm labor organizing, nuclear protest education, American Indian rights, Third World communications, and prisoners' rights.

But mostly we have focused our political attention on the question of public use of public lands—the right of the people to peaceably assemble and to express their religious beliefs.

In 1986, for example, after the U.S. Forest Service rewrote its regulations to obstruct our gatherings, a district court ruled in our favor, calling the regulations "impermissibly unconstitutional." In 1988, the Forest Service rewrote its regulations again, applying the new rules against us the first day they went into effect. Once more, the federal courts ruled in our favor, citing numerous rights of expression, association, religious assembly, petition, and the long-upheld view of the public lands as a protected forum for the expression of ideas.

In his ruling, District Judge W. W. Justice declared the Forest Service's new regulations both "illegally adopted" and constitutionally "repugnant," and struck them from the books. His judgment was upheld in the Fifth Circuit Court of Appeals and has several times been used as a reference in other cases involving the rights of public assembly.

A freedom is of little value if it is only written on paper. It is when we exercise our natural rights that we truly gain the benefits that those freedoms proclaim.

Each year at the gathering, the council decides on the region for the next year's gathering. The whole process of scouting for sites, meeting the local people and officials, and setting up, maintaining, and cleaning up the encampment—right down to the last recycled can and the last car leaving the parking lot—we call "The Ride." Going for the whole ride is an immensely enlightening and rewarding experience. I recommend it highly for anyone who wants to know how the world really works.

Solving People Problems

The gatherings are like a little piece of the world. They're open and public enough so we get a little bit of everything—good and bad. The only difference is that, unrestricted by many of the world's dogmas, the gatherings give us a chance to try out new solutions and new ways of thinking.

Shanti Sena means "peace center." This is the name we give to the brother and sisterhood that attends to the security of the camp. Preparation for the Shanti Sena includes training in nonviolent techniques of persuasion, peer-group pressure, and the art of drawing an alienated person into the reality of human kindness. Ideally, when an incident arises, it is taken care of by the people who are immediately present, but the Shanti Sena maintains camps and roving teams whose mission is to help out with whatever difficulties folks may encounter. Often, these teams double up with the fire-watch crews on regular tours of the camps.

Nonviolence is a strong and powerful force when practiced as a creative tactic. Shanti Sena holds meetings to orient people to the nature of these practices. The key is communication. We are not beyond restraining someone who is violently aggressive; however, peer-group attention with understanding and love is enough to settle most disputes. This is not too different from honey bees, who, when one member of the hive flips out, have been known to form a cluster ball around that one and hum until the crazed bee cools out.

"Co-operations" is an area of the encampment set up for people or groups who need help with something or a little more cooperation. Often, disputes between camps or neighborhoods are worked out there. "Co-op" also serves as a volunteer center for newcomers and as a planning center for complex supply runs, pageants, and networking.

Another cornerstone of the operation is Kid Village. Kitchens with extra healthy snacks, activities for kids of all ages, teaching adventures, arts and crafts, hiking, swimming, rafting, and tree houses are all part of the plan. Child care also happens here on a cooperative basis. Certain areas are set aside for nursing moms and infants, and clowns, mimes, and magicians entertain the kids regularly. But the essence of Kid Village has to do with teaching the values and virtues of the sharing and caring life.

Where do all the shelters, water lines, meals, and tools come from? Much is packed in by the participants to contribute to the whole. We also have a "magic hat" that we pass at dinnertime and during councils. Sometimes we place it at strategic locations or carry it through the camp to musical accompaniment. Our banking council counts the donations and keeps open books of expenditures. The money is apportioned to our needs. As if by magic, nobody goes hungry.

But the main reason all of these things happen is because people like ourselves bring it together—not just the willpower and labor but the tents and tipis, the stainless-steel kitchen gear, the clown makeup, the puppets, and the tools. Each person who understands the process brings all he or she can, both practical and pleasurable, to make things happen in the way they do. The volunteer and participatory nature of a Rainbow Gathering cannot be overemphasized.

Drugs vs. Herbs

The Rainbow People, stemming as we do from the flower of the sixties, are sometimes repudiated as longhair types or "potheads." Actually, we make a great distinction between hard drugs, medicinal drugs, and herbs. Each of these categories is specifically different. Hard drugs are narcotics or addictive substances; medicinal drugs are compounds administered for medicinal purposes; and herbs are plants used for healing or seasoning.

In 1972, we published a document entitled *On Marijuana as Sacrament*. For many of us (though by no means all of us), marijuana is used as a sacramental medicine to bring us closer to the natural Living Spirit and to help us heal our bodies, hearts, and minds. Similarly, at a gathering one may find peyote meetings or sacred mushroom ceremonies that carry on the traditions of the tribal peoples who have been using these substances for centuries.

The More the Merrier

Another beauty of the gatherings is that they bring together so many different kinds of people. Each neighborhood and kitchen has its different character. The Krishnas come and set up Krishna's Prasadam feasts, complete with chanting, well-fed smiles, and Vedic lectures and plays. Madam Frog caters to pilgrims of all faiths with exotic teas and entertainment. The sprout gardens provide raw foods, salads, and juices. We have learned that respect for each other's diet is essential to our peace. Mostly, we are oriented toward whole, healthy foods, but you can find a little of everything.

At the traders' circle, arts and crafts are displayed alongside shells, stones, feathers, and other natural items. "Jibber-jabber"—uniquely fashioned or unusual goods—take their places alongside woven blankets, ceramics, and jewelry. This lively exchange is going on every day of the gathering except on the Fourth of July, when it shuts down during the silent meditation.

Regional Rainbow Gatherings are an important outgrowth of these annual celebrations. Although many of them are smaller, they keep folks in touch over the winter season, bring new people in on a local level, and teach the arts of community and logistics to a widening circle of brothers and sisters.

Recently, there have been much larger regional gatherings involving thousands of people. Also, the European Rainbow Gathering has truly become a world-scale event, involving people of many languages and cultures. And on an urban scale, we have seen the development of Rainbow Picnics, one-day events that give our family a chance to celebrate, council, and come together joyfully in the public parks of our big cities. The more the merrier: from the first moment, we have wanted to gather with *everyone*—and we still do!

Lots of amazing things happen at the gatherings—the stories would fill books in themselves. For example, one year, we saw a great white buffalo appear in the snow on the side of a mountain. We have seen rainbows on the Fourth of July. In New Mexico, we floated fifteen thousand organic grapefruits two miles down the Gila River to get them into camp. In Oregon, we had our first Kid's Parade—a razzle-dazzle we still use to culminate the silence on the Fourth of July. When it rained forever in Idaho, we finally took off our boots and danced in our "mudsocks" until the sun came out. And in Arizona, a giant, rainbow-colored hot-air balloon floated over the tipi circle, giving a bird's-eye view of the camp to kids and adults alike.

One of the most memorable of our gathering events was in Arkansas, when the sheriff rode in and arrested five people for swimming in the nude. Thereafter, about half the gathering moved to the steps of the county courthouse. The judge sent everyone out of town (including the original five who had been arrested), and subsequently the sheriff was so ridiculed by the press that he lost his first election in twenty-four years.

Dismantling the Encampment

At the end of the gathering on July 8, we move right away into cleanup so we can utilize the massive energies present to "disappear" our effects and revitalize the area. We call our cleanup process "Naturalization." To begin with, we recycle all our garbage based on a color-coded, seven-part separation. Red is for metal, orange for glass, yellow for burnables, green for compost, blue for plastic, indigo for lost and found, and violet for free items and giveaways. (We believe color-coded source separation can be a key to future urban recycling.)

The camp is then drawn in. The outer reaches are dismantled first. Later comes the welcome center, and finally the parking lot. The idea is to make our impact as invisible as possible. Campfires are dismantled, their rocks widely scattered, and their ashes scattered or buried. Latrines and compost pits are filled in. The tiniest bit of paper, cellophane, or litter is picked up and put in its proper receptacle. Shelters, posts, and booths are all taken apart and laid down, as are all the signs.

Then, when everything has been taken down and cleaned up, we begin to revitalize the high-use areas. Hardened ground is spaded over or aerated with shovels, picks, and hoes. The many trails that weave through the village are raked over, blocked with branches and boulders, and strewn with pine needles, leaves, and duff. Water barriers are built along all the steep places to prevent gully erosion. Often, we pack decades' worth of old scrap out of the forest—stuff that has been discarded and left there for generations.

When there is need, perhaps along a stream bank, we reinforce with matted brush to prevent erosion. Flat or open spaces are raked to obliterate every possible trace of our presence. Then we naturalize each area by scattering leaves and loose brush for ground cover. Rocks, twigs, and logs are randomly strewn about to provide habitat for small forest creatures. Lastly, when we humans have all but left the site, we broadcast specially selected seed that is appropriate to the area's climate and altitude. This process is vital; by returning the site to nature's own processes, we leave no residual problems for ourselves or the other inhabitants of the forest. And such operations have been very successful. After repeated observation of these sites a year later, we have found that it is virtually impossible to tell that anyone was ever there. Only memories and the lushness of nature remain.

The gatherings belong to everyone, not to any one person or group of people. But as in life itself, it is each individual's contribution that gives them value and meaning. This is a lesson humanity still has to learn. The end of war, the cooperation of our species, the benefits of good health and a sound environment, the nourishment of the hungry, and the cessation of economic exploitation are the real goals of the gatherings, the pot of gold at the end of the rainbow.

Editor's note: Garrick Beck is the son of Julian Beck and Judith Malina, founders of the Living Theatre performing troupe of the sixties. Having grown up under the influence of the Living Theatre, Beck started his own experimental community, "Rainbow Farm," in the state of Oregon during the early seventies. Concurrently, he became one of the organizers of the first Rainbow Gathering in 1972. Since then, he has participated in Rainbow Gatherings throughout the United States and is one of the most respected speakers in the Rainbow Family Tribal Council.

Greenpeace International
Alberto Ruz Buenfil

Greenpeace International was founded in 1971 in Vancouver, British Columbia, by a small group of American military deserters who had left their country to protest the war in Vietnam. The name "Greenpeace" comes from its founders' two main objectives: the desire for a healthy environment, symbolized by the color green, and the urgent desire for peace on Earth. In the two decades since its founding, Greenpeace has become a tremendously effective, multinational organization for the protection of the environment. Today, it has more than forty branches, several hundred full-time members, and more than three million contributors all over the world.

The members of Greenpeace International are often called "Rainbow Warriors." In his book *Warriors of the Rainbow*, published in 1986, journalist Robert Hunter explains how this name came to be. In 1971, he relates, the American government had decided to detonate a series of nuclear bombs on the Alaskan island of Amchitka. Alarmed and outraged by this decision, a small group of Greenpeace activists sailed to the site, intending to protest and interfere with the military tests. The confrontation and its widespread press coverage created a new world awareness of what was happening in the Aleutian Islands of Alaska. As a result of the public outcry, a year later the American government was forced to stop its nuclear testing at the Amchitka site, and the island is now a wildlife sanctuary. This was one of Greenpeace's first victories.

After the demonstration, a group of Alaskan natives approached the members of the fledgling Greenpeace organization to thank them for their solidarity and to offer them the name "Rainbow Warriors." Since then, the rainbow symbol has been part of the official logo that identifies the organization.

Greenpeace sees the rainbow as a very simple but very powerful image, evoking associations immediately recognizable by people from all nations and all cultures, regardless of their origins and colors. To them, it is a symbol reminiscent of the beauty of nature, the sign of a planet that has been purified.[1]

Over the past twenty years, the Greenpeace warriors have continued participating in spectacular and effective protests all over the planet. In relatively few years, they have been responsible for hundreds of direct actions in favor of ecology and life, among which I will mention only a few.

Almost from its beginning, Greenpeace has actively opposed the industrial hunting of whales. For years, its members have confronted whaleboats from the Soviet Union, Australia, Spain, Norway, and Japan. Because of their confrontational approach and the effectiveness of their actions, Greenpeace activists have been arrested frequently, and their boats have been temporarily held by the governments of various nations. But their actions have resulted in a growing state of awareness, including new regulations and laws to protect the endangered whale species.

Greenpeace has also protested the dumping of radioactive wastes, acids, heavy metals, pesticides, and oil residues in the world's oceans and rivers. Its members have never tired of telling international agencies and the public about the dangers these materials pose to the global ecosystem. In so doing, they have confronted most of the industrial countries of the planet.

For years, Greenpeace members have fought to put an end to the extermination of seals, penguins, and dolphins in the oceans and islands off Japan, England, Norway, Canada, Holland, Australia, Antarctica, the Arctic Circle, and the Soviet Union. Their efforts have met with varying degrees of success.

Greenpeace also continues attacking the producers of toxic fumes that produce acid rain and protesting nuclear bomb tests in Nevada, the Soviet Union, and the Pacific Islands. They have also opposed nuclear missile testing in Canada and other countries of both East and West.

Greenpeace activists have been arrested many times by the authorities in Belgium, Spain, the Soviet Union, Germany, France, and the United States. Many have also endured acts of anger and violence directed against themselves. In 1973, for example, when the Greenpeace III sailed into a French nuclear test site in the Pacific, the group was assaulted by French commandos, and skipper David McTaggert was badly beaten.

Nothing, however, can compare with the violence Greenpeace endured at the hands of French president François Mitterrand in August 1985. That month, when Greenpeace activists were planning a massive protest against French nuclear testing in the Pacific, Mitterrand gave secret orders to stop them at any cost. This time, their flagship, the *Rainbow Warrior*, was sabotaged and sunk in a massive explosion, and one Greenpeace member, Fernando Pereira, was killed.

When the truth came to light, Admiral Pierre Lacoste, chief of the French secret service, and Minister of Defense Charles Hernu were dismissed from office, and nearly the entire government of François Mitterrand fell as a consequence.

Afterward, one Greenpeace campaigner declared, "The French may be able to sink the *Rainbow Warrior*, but what they and the other nuclear powers need to realize is that they cannot sink the rainbow."[2] To which McTaggert added, "We Rainbow Warriors will always be there, everywhere, ready to denounce your violence and your mistakes, over and over."[3]

Recalling the rainbow itself and the Native American prophecy surrounding it, Greenpeace member Steve Sawyer recently restated the organization's commitment: "We believe that the times predicted in the legend are upon us," he said, "and appeal to the spirit of all people of all races and nationalities everywhere to come together in the spirit of the legend. Then we will peacefully take up the fight to overcome the forces that would destroy Mother Earth, also known as Gaia, and the Great Turtle of indigenous North Americans."[4]

Since the sinking of the *Rainbow Warrior*, Greenpeace has grown beyond all expectations. Its branches in more than twenty countries are not only fighting ecological insanity and destruction worldwide, but they are also producing a large quantity of educational material to awaken the consciousness of people everywhere. This propaganda includes posters, books, photos, crafts, jewelry, stickers, T-shirts, buttons, solar calculators, newspapers, magazines, and films. Activists have even produced records, such as *Greenpeace Rainbow Warriors*, an album with songs donated by U-2, Belinda Carlisle, the Grateful Dead, the Talking Heads, and many other well-known rock groups and composers.

In 1989, a book called *The Greenpeace Story* was published in London by Michael Bowen and John May. It includes a detailed description of the group's philosophy and activities. Greenpeace is not only active in the Western industrialized nations but has also opened branch offices in New Zealand, Japan, Russia, Costa Rica, Sarawak, and numerous other countries. In sum, it promises to be a powerful force for planetary healing well into the twenty-first century.

For Christiania with Love
Ria Bjerre

Christiania's history is different from the many other social experiments of the sixties. It is the fascinating story of the founding and growth of an alternative, anarchistic "free city"—a city bound neither by laws nor governments—within the larger city of Copenhagen. It is also the story of the political power games that became an integral part of its development, and of the ingenious way its people successfully fought city hall to prolong their own existence. The "rainbow action" described in this chapter is only one of many tactics used by the inhabitants of the free city to maintain their continuing exemption from all laws and restrictions, but it is also the one that has had the farthest-reaching consequences, both for Christiania and for the rest of Denmark.

The Beginning

The modern story of Christiania, an area of Copenhagen originally named after a Danish king, starts back in 1971. At this time, a thirty-acre area within Christiania filled with old military barracks had been lying unused for half a year. Moved by the urgent need for housing, a group of squatters tore down the fence and occupied the area.

As squatters, these people were part of the youth movement all over Europe whose activities included the occupation of empty houses. They were partly manifesting their desire for a communal lifestyle and partly protesting the lack of decent housing.

In Copenhagen, the squatters were very colorful and anarchistic people. They did not belong to any particular political party but floated around the city from one condemned building to another in an eternal cat-and-mouse game with the police. They occupied one building and were thrown out; they occupied another building and were thrown out again. And all the time, the struggle was followed by the media, thus educating the public to the fact that expensive individual or family-oriented housing does not fulfill everyone's needs.

But never had the squatters had such a ripe opportunity for individually and collectively trying out a new lifestyle as they had in Christiania. The thirty-acre military area included 156 large, medium, and small buildings, including dormitories, administration buildings, laboratories, riding halls, houses for officers and their families, factories, kitchens, dining rooms, toilets, watch sheds, and depositories. Some of these were located across the channel on Dyssen Lake, and at the time they had no electricity, water, or sanitary installations. This was to become the "countryside," the farm area of Christiania.

Occupation was not an easy affair. Street kids and vandals had begun to pick the buildings apart. The heating system was old and worn beyond repair. Most of the sanitary installations had gone, together with most of the door handles and electrical installations. Most of the windows were also smashed. But the squatters worked hard, and by New Year's Eve of 1973, Christiania's four hundred new inhabitants had set in for their first cold winter.

The Danish government did not know how to react. No one could determine who was legally responsible for the area. The Ministry of Defense did not want to use it anymore. The Ministry of Culture was not yet ready with its plans to build a new ballet and opera school, nor was the Magistrate of Copenhagen ready to unveil its plans for new offices there. Lacking any better solution, the squatters were temporarily allowed to stay, and an astonishing treaty was drawn up between Christiania and the two ministries, the Magistrate of Copenhagen, the social democratic government, and the police.

The treaty secured for the squatters the right to live in Christiania until plans for the area could be readied. For their part, all Christianians were required to register and pay a small amount for electricity, water, and sanitation. This unusual renting contract was most favorable for the inhabitants of the free city—and it was made, amazingly enough, between established government entities and the anarchistic Communal Council of Christiania, the only ruling body the free city has ever had.

However, as with most treaties between ruling states and minority or countercultural groups, the state did not keep its agreement. Very soon afterward came the first threats and calls for evacuation.

Growing Pains

The Christianians were up against tough odds. Amazingly, though, the free city continued to grow in spite of—and strangely, to some extent, even *because* of—the barriers and limitations that were imposed on it. As Per Lovetand wrote in the Christianian newspaper *Ugespejlet* ("The Weekly Mirror") in 1974,

> Without means or structure, against the city authorities and with a negative opinion from the Danish people ("They are parasites on society") . . . with police raids all the time, with all the social problems of Copenhagen, with 120 different opinions about everything, this thing succeeded in surviving anyhow. . . . One can wonder what made this possible. I think that it is primarily because we live in a world that for most people is unreal and a utopia. Each one of us has individually transcended the futile governmental paternity and has realized a life based on his or her own conditions. This is what unifies all of us, social outsiders and social losers. And from this attitude grows a mutual acceptance, a mutual solidarity and a common strength that obviously provokes and inspires.

But there were also other reasons for Christiania's continued growth. By 1973, as the international economic situation worsened, causing increased unemployment and cutbacks in social expenditures, Christiania showed that it could do relatively well with small means. Christianians worked independently, restoring buildings. They also began to deal directly with the heavy drug problem in the free city: they threw out all the heavy dope dealers and started voluntary treatment programs. Moreover, a variety of social misfits had found shelter in the workshops of the free city and were functioning productively.

By April 1976, Christiania had existed for five years, only six months legally and the rest under threat of evacuation. In spite of that threat, more and more people had moved in. Besides the original squatters, there came to the free city anyone who was dissatisfied or in conflict with society. In Christiania, such people found the freedom to practice whatever lifestyle they wanted.

Thus, the free city absorbed all kinds of people: Zen Buddhists, Taoists, Marxists, back-to-nature folks with goats and pigs, actors from the underground theater movement, anarchists, artists, poets, painters, musicians, filmmakers, craftspeople, academics, provincials, foreigners, drug addicts, dealers, criminals, runaways, healers, alcoholics, and yogis. For good or ill, the free city was open to everyone. And everyone came, as long as there was a room, a mattress, or a piece of grass on which to park a mobile shed or set a tent or wooden cabin.

By 1976, eight hundred people were living in Christiania: eight hundred individuals creating a self-sufficient, autonomous village; eight hundred souls formulating their own individual lives on their own premises. Amidst this almost inconceivable but colorful chaos, over the last twenty years, these people have created a politically, culturally, and socially powerful model of a pioneer city. Government bureaucrats call it a "social experiment"; Christianians call it "an experiment in how to make a society."

The Intended Evacuation

In spite of Christiania's successful growth, the Danish government decided that the area would have to be evacuated by April 1, 1976. The official reason was that heavy budget cuts had put an end to plans for construction of an opera and ballet school at the site; therefore, the Magistrate of Copenhagen planned to begin work on its housing project as soon as the area was cleared of its undesirable inhabitants.

But there was more to it than that. At this point, the leftist parties in the Danish government and the left wing of the Social Democratic party had lost interest in Christiania—especially since some right-wing politicians had begun using the settlement as an excuse for cutbacks in social programs. According to these demagogues, the people in Christiania were doing very well working "from hand to mouth," thus proving that it was unnecessary to give further aid to the most needy sectors of society. In this atmosphere, Christiania became a sacrificial lamb, a useless pawn on a political chessboard.

The Rainbow Army

In Christiania itself, proposed solutions to the evacuation dilemma were many and varied. Ideas ranged from complete compliance with the government's wishes to armed defense of the free city. Those who wanted to stay agreed on the need to fight for survival, but there was no agreement on the use of violence. How could a nonviolent army be made out of this motley group of individuals, some of whom were unable or unwilling to fight at all, while others were all too eager to start a shooting war against the system? How could the "fight" be organized and carried out?

In this time of desperation and chaos, some people despaired and left the free city, while others stayed on, endlessly discussing possible solutions to the dilemma. Then, from no one knows where, the answer came. And it came in the form of a rainbow, the only structure that could possibly unify all the inhabitants of the free city. Christianians decided to create an army under the flag of the rainbow, among whose broad spectrum of colors each person could find a suitable place. The call went out in *Ugespejlet*:

> By creating a Rainbow Army of nonviolent, hardworking people who all collaborate with each other, every individual in his or her own way, we can stand united, one for all and all for one, and overcome the threatening situation we are facing. Because we love each other, we can organize ourselves practically, in spite of all our differences.

As is normal for new ideas in Christiania, nobody really knew where the rainbow idea had come from. But as with rainbows themselves, the idea had appeared as if by magic after a violent storm, and its radiance and hope shone through for everyone. Eventually, that rainbow would stretch clear across Denmark and move people as far away as Holland, Sweden, Germany, France, and Italy to come and support the Christianian army.

The Rainbow Army had a double strategy and purpose: first, to create an internal structure in Christiania, making the free city as beautiful and smoothly functioning as possible; and second, to launch a multifaceted media campaign. The intention was to marshal strong public support for the free city, thus giving it some influence and power on the Danish political scene.

The recruitment and division of the army was easy. Each color of the rainbow was chosen to represent a special kind of work. Everyone could choose their own colors and work according to their personal inclinations and desires. In this way, everyone added his or her particular qualities and abilities to the army. In the end, the army reflected an attitude of outer readiness to fight, based on an inner balance— the kind of unity that arises when many different groups decide to cooperate in an equal and respectful way.

The regiments of the army were as follows. Red was for organization. These were the builders, the information disseminators and motivators who could initiate without taking control and lead without manipulating. Orange was for visual propaganda—for those who could spread knowledge through theater, music, postcards, paintings, films, and photos. Yellow was for child care and creativity—those who could build houses, create milieus and environments and nurse and care for people. Green was for supplies and storage; for bakeries, restaurants, shops, bars, and gardens; and for those who took care of the basic needs of life, cultivated the ground, collected supplies, and kept animals. Blue was for poets and dealers, the purveyors of dreams and cozy experiences—those who could help loosen the knots of the spirit and spread the highest knowledge and love. Purple was for the "chieftains, kings, and queens," the "servants of all," who chose to do the work of recycling and renovation, cleanup, and maintaining ecological balance. White was for physical and psychological healing and for the healers who practiced these arts. And black was for those who could keep order without resorting to violence or manipulation.

In the Rainbow Army, people indicated their inclinations and type of service by wearing a colored arm band. If a person decided to work in more than one area, he or she could wear all the colors that indicated those different services. Thus dressed and prepared, the Rainbow Army was ready for action.

The Battle of the Rainbow

Inside Christiania, the army prepared the battle grounds by cleaning up, planting flowers and trees, repairing and painting houses, and by finishing or building new houses. Houses that had previously been painted in bright colors received fresh coats of paint. Architecture became even more beautiful and inventive, and was spiced with crazier details and ideas. Mounds of garbage were carted away. Old bars and restaurants were restored, and new places were opened. Tremendous amounts of food and drink were stored. Workshops produced, refined, and sold their goods as never before.

Meanwhile, Christiania itself was inviting all of Denmark to come and see what the free city was all about. Thousands came—some for a couple of hours on a Sunday afternoon, some for a day or two, and others to stay and join in the efforts of the multicolored army. Some people came without any expectations, while others came filled with prejudices. Some came out of curiosity, and some came to show their support.

For weeks, a steady stream of visitors flowed in and out of Christiania. Scientists, teachers, laymen, and government types all saw the free city swarming with color and activity. They watched the Rainbow Army at work. They sat in restaurants and bars. They enjoyed the peace of the vehicle-free streets and the natural surroundings. They ate healthy food and listened to joyful music. And many of them walked away with a new attitude about Christiania.

Just as the Rainbow Army used many weapons in their battle for survival, their attack lines were also many and varied. One of the first things the warriors created was an organization called "Support Christiania," for the purpose of collecting money and supplies for the army. It started with headquarters in Copenhagen, but as the campaign grew, Support Christiania groups popped up in many other large Danish cities and even in places as far flung as London and Oslo.

Likewise, Christianian newspapers were distributed and sold all over the country, giving information about the free city, its lifestyles, and its goals, and calling on readers to join the Rainbow Army. "The free city is a symbol for the struggle of liberation inside the heart of you and me," read the call. "The free city is a sign of vitality within a society which is decaying and dying very fast. Christiania fights not for power, nor glory, nor for richness, but for love."

With bulletins, brochures, leaflets, postcards, and "Support Christiania" posters and stickers, the Rainbow Army invited everyone to visit the free city—especially for the final and decisive battle, slated for April 1.

The day of the final evacuation was slowly being transformed into a huge springtime peace festival. On that day, the Rainbow Army planned to receive the black-uniformed army of the city police with powerful and disarming weapons: a multitude of love and joy that would make all colors, including black, melt together in perfect harmony.

Again from the front page of *Ugespejlet* came the cry: "See you in Christiania. Spring and Peace Festival: from the 26th of March to the 11th of April. We will dress with the colors of the rainbow, according to our temperaments and the type of work we volunteered to do, and we will create the Rainbow Army, an army without generals and officers."

To add to the propaganda, some of the best musical bands in Denmark produced a popular LP entitled "The Christiania Record," which sold enormously well. In addition, the Christiania Action Theatre toured the whole country with a play, appropriately entitled *April Fool's Day*.

Activists also produced a profusion of radio and television programs. The most memorable and effective of the TV shows documented the visit to Christiania of the "Family Hansen," a middle-aged couple and their two children who had been invited to live in the free city for a week. In this way, the Danish TV audience could see for themselves what life in Christiania was really like.

Many Danes who had only heard negative things about the free city could now sit in their armchairs in front of their televisions and see how the Hansen family daily became more and more gentle in their criticisms and increasingly open to this fascinating new community. Like the Hansens themselves, most of Denmark finally had to admit that living in the free city seemed like living in a good, old-fashioned European village. Thus, the one-sided picture of Christiania that had been painted by the media (as a place filled with drug addicts and social cases) went by the wayside and was replaced with a truer picture of the free city as a place of low anxiety marked by togetherness, humor, and love.

Through the media, the rainbow consciousness rapidly spread throughout all of Denmark. During this time, Christianians even toured the country with slide shows and lectures, passing the word directly to schools, libraries, universities, youth clubs, factories, unions, and those who either could not or would not come to see for themselves. Christiania was rapidly becoming Denmark's main topic of conversation. Columns in Danish newspapers were filled with letters for and against Christiania.

The Rainbow Army was on the move—and growing. By now, support money was floating into Support Christiania headquarters. The number of members from these support groups was also growing. All the money received was immediately spent to produce new information and more propaganda.

The intensity of the campaign was enormous, as were the results. Hardly a person existed in Denmark who had no opinion about Christiania and what it represented. In less than six months, public opinion had changed from a vast majority against the free city to a clear majority for it.

A full month before "D-day," the Rainbow Army numbered in the thousands. Inside Christiania, the battleground was ready. The army had prepared the city to host thousands of soldiers. For the next three weeks, as well as for the Spring and Peace Festival itself, there were stands of food for everyone, theater and music every night, and daily discussions of all kinds at an open council held in a big circus tent.

The Decisive Battle

Those who entered Christiania on the morning of April 1, 1976, walked through an arch with a wide, brightly painted rainbow with a white dove of peace at its center. Above the rainbow, heavy spring clouds seemed ready to break loose, but they did not affect the crowd of thousands that had gathered to witness the decisive battle.

That day, the old military area and parade ground on which uniformed soldiers had exercised so stiffly for years had become a swirling ocean of color and activity. At the information booth, five women dressed in red were running around, directing the lines of guests coming through the gates. Old friends were meeting, and new friendships were being made. All the dialects of the Danish language mingled with the sounds of French, German, Italian, and English.

At a food stand, two green-clad youngsters were selling vegetarian pies. A tall Viking man dressed in purple was emptying litter boxes and showing people where to put their empty beer cans. Laughter and joyous screams were coming from a flock of people wearing orange arm ribbons—one of the local theater groups heading toward the circus tent. Dressed in blue, "dealers in visions" moved around in a happy daze, offering their hashish to anyone who wanted to buy.

Soon the area just inside the free city had become so crowded that it was hardly possible to move. An estimated twenty-five thousand people had congregated in Christiania—twenty-five thousand people eating, singing, drinking, and celebrating as a part of the most unusual army that had ever gathered anywhere: a Rainbow Army promoting peace and freedom for all.

It seemed impossible that anyone could destroy this immense ocean of colors. "When the bulldozers come, we just all lie down," someone said. "Yes, yes, we know," came the reply.

Everywhere, people were singing songs of defense, songs of joy and struggle. "They can't kill us, we are a part of themselves!" came the refrain. Even so, thousands of eyes kept glancing toward the entrance to the free city, waiting for the arrival of the police and the bulldozers.

But as the hours passed, the evacuation army did not appear, and rumors began circulating that the politicians and city planners had given up. For a long time, the Christianians dared not believe it was true, but finally it was confirmed: the free city would not be evacuated. The government had changed its plans. In a feeble attempt to save face, the bureaucrats now declared that the evacuation of Christiania would take place "without unnecessary delay," meaning at some undetermined time in the future.

The news spread through the crowd like a giant wave, first in whispers, then in unrestrained shouts of joy. When the shouting was over, there came an almost palpable silence, and the massive army began moving behind its rainbow banner, floating through the gates of the free city and into the streets of Copenhagen. Hundreds more joined in as the throngs marched toward the city's municipal building, where the colors of life finally spread out over the entire plaza. There, the Rainbow Army sang for victory and freedom, drowning out the sounds of traffic and the day's business.

Few politicians reacted visibly to the demonstration, so the army, having accomplished its goal, turned its back on the "building where laws are made" and headed back to Christiania. After returning, the thousands of peaceful demonstrators joined hands and completely encircled the free city—a dancing, singing circle of victorious Rainbow Warriors.

While the victory party was at its peak, the Christianians used their moment of power to undertake legal action against the government for not upholding the treaty of 1973 in which it had proclaimed the free city a social experiment. This was a shrewd move, for as long as legal action was pending, the city could not be evacuated.

In spite of its decisive victory, Christiania's tenure was still not secure. Since then, the free city has many times been forced to mobilize to avert other evacuation attempts and to fight again and again the massive internal problems of drugs and crime—problems that have grown heavier inside Christiania primarily because people from outside have tried to use the openness of the free city to secure a base for illegal activity.

Once again, the Christianians have successfully removed the heavy dope and drug dealers from outside, permitting only grass and hash to be sold inside the free city, and only by Christianians. They have also gotten rid of one of the most violent motorcycle gangs that had taken shelter there. In these and other ways, the Chrisianians have succeeded where outside society has often failed.

A Winter's Tale

By now, Christiania has survived for nearly two decades, despite governmental threats and immense internal problems. At the same time, the free city has provoked and continues to inspire the most impassioned discussions about new ways of living. It raises frequent debates about the rights of human beings to create their own lifestyles, even in opposition to established norms and rules. Christiania is a truly anarchistic, free society. It is also a profound enigma, the kind of society that both provokes questions and shatters fixed ideas.

Let me give you a personal example. In the early morning of January 2, 1987, in fifteen-degree-Celsius weather, I was sliding on icy paths in the vehicle-free city. I walked beside several buildings completely covered with snow, from which emanated the warm, homey smell of woodsmoke. Only a few hash dealers were out in the streets so early, and they seemed to be freezing as they showed their stashes to prospective buyers.

I stopped at the grocery and natural food store to buy some homemade, whole-wheat rolls, cheese, and chocolate milk. Instead of eating my provisions in the cozy warmth of the store, I left seeking solitude. I walked all the way to the channel that runs through the free city.

The channel, a couple hundred yards wide, was covered with ice. A few children were already ice skating, followed by a pack of Christianian dogs. Nobody else was around. I sat down in front of some mobile sheds facing the channel and contemplated the landscape on the other shore.

The place looked idyllic in winter. The garbage, the sometimes ill-attended gardens, the shagginess of some of the buildings—all were softened by snow. It looked like a new Alaska, a pioneer city in greens, blues, yellows, and reds.

While contemplating this natural wonder, my musing was suddenly interrupted by a hoarse voice from behind me. Someone was shouting, "Hey, you there, how are you? Did you have a good New Year's Eve?"

I was not in the mood that morning to start a conversation with some half-drunk foreigner or some "social case" in desperate need of contact; I simply wanted to be left alone. So I turned halfway toward the voice and answered in a classic, cool Danish way, "Thank you, I'm fine. Happy New Year to you, too." Then I proceeded to stare across the channel.

In spite of my rejecting tone, I heard the crunching sound of footsteps approaching. Then, just as I felt my annoyance turn to anger, I looked up to see a kind-looking man in his twenties standing before me with a snug, warm cat purring on his arm.

"You shouldn't sit here completely alone," he said as he handed me the cat. "Here—he will keep you warm." With these words and a smile, the man turned toward the warmth of his mobile shed again, leaving me with the cat.

With the cat in my arms, I began to contemplate the range of ideas and feelings I had just experienced—truly mirrors of the essence of Christiania. I thought of the unexpected beauty and peace to be found in the middle of a noisy, dirty city; of the individuality, integrity, and freedom I saw all about me—a double-faced freedom, cultivated, as it is, against the laws of society. I also thought about how this freedom should not be looked on from only one perspective; how on a personal level, freedom gives one the space for creativity and the possibility of realizing one's dreams, but how it can also bring a great deal of unrest, excess, and negatives of many kinds, including fear, anger, and prejudice.

Contemplation concluded, I stood up and returned the cat to his owner. Then I realized, for the first time in my life, that a cat can eat a dog, and that we should never have fixed ideas about anything.

The Faces of Christiania

Today, Christiania continues to have anything but fixed ideas, and its free thinking has led to many innovations. For example, the free city contains many large and small workshops. Among these are blacksmith shops that have produced cheap ecological ovens so that Christianians can heat their homes with recycled scrapwood instead of electricity. There are also unique bicycle shops that have given rise to the practical Christianian bicycle and bicycle trailer, the primary means of transportation in the nonmotorized free city. Other workshops produce everything from lumber and solar-powered machines to ceramics, candles, leather goods, shoes, and jewelry.

Christiania has a healing center that uses a plethora of alternative medicines and therapies. Somewhat incongruously, the free city also features "Pusher Street," the only place in Europe except Amsterdam where one can openly buy many brands of hashish.

Christiania has many fine restaurants and a very clean and beautiful bathhouse with a huge, integrated sauna. Here, one can take a bath with natural soaps and receive or give a free massage using the best of medicinal muds. There are several places to go dancing in

Christiania, places where famous bands and singers started their careers and where new groups make their debuts every year. These places, together with the theater hall, a variety of street theater groups, and Solvongnen, a very renowned Danish theater troupe, attract big audiences from all over Denmark.

Some people live and work full time in Christiania. Others live in the free city and work outside the community. Still others are either unable or choose not to work at all.

In Christiania, there are no laws and no official authority to tell anybody what to do. People do what they want to do or what needs to be done. There are no leaders to organize anyone's life, only those who start things and those who choose to help get things accomplished. There are no employees, except for people who decide to work, and these people do their work voluntarily.

There are eleven natural, organic areas inside Christiania and, therefore, eleven different, independent area councils. Nothing is agreed upon until everyone agrees to it; only consensus is valid. There are no rules for the economic infrastructure of the free city. Those who make profits in Christiania are encouraged to share them, but how much they share is always up to them. In the free city, nobody can force others to do what they are unwilling to do.

Christiania pays the Magistrate of Copenhagen for the use of electricity and water, and each inhabitant of the free city is encouraged to provide a small fee for those communal expenses. There is no central organization except for the Communal Council, where, again, nothing is agreed upon until everyone reaches consensus. The only responsibilities of the community are those it creates for itself. There are no limits to anyone's creativity or behavior except the limits established by each individual. Christiania is self-governed; likewise, each area, restaurant, bar, workshop, and person within it is self-governed.

Christiania freedom is double-edged, chosen and cultivated against the laws of society. Based on the conviction that people can do anything they want, this freedom invites both good and evil, like the faces of some ancient pagan gods. Look at such icons from one side and they show the face of beauty and goodness; from the other side ugliness and evil. Yet neither face can be taken away. If it were, the essence would no longer be God, but only a one-sided picture of reality.

People who try to grasp the solid essence or fundamental structure of the free city become hopelessly lost in flexibility and multiple antagonisms. Only when they forget about permanent structure do they begin to understand its true form. That is as it should be, for Christiania is like an amoeba—ever changing and flowing with the conditions around it but always moved by its own inner nature.

Postscript, October 1990

In the summer of 1986, the Danish parliament acknowledged the stubborn persistence of the Christianians by passing a law permitting the free city to exist on certain conditions: first, that all building and rebuilding in the area be stopped; second, that bars, restaurants, and workshops be legalized (with open accounts and payment of taxes); third, that a bioregional plan for the use of the area be drawn up.

For its part, the parliament agreed to give economic support for the urgently needed restoration of the original houses and for the health and social welfare of the area. A governmental group called the Christianian Secretarial Group, trusted by Christianians, was also appointed to negotiate plans and projects with the Christianians without altering their traditional means of making decisions.

Another remarkable law, passed by parliament in the summer of 1989, exempts Christiania from all existing laws about renting, owning, building, and rebuilding inside Christiania. This law leaves the inhabitants of the free city solely responsible to the Minister of Defense, who is in charge of the area.

This brings up a provocative question: Is it a victory for the Christianians to be set lawfully apart from the rest of society, with a government-approved chance for self-determination, or is it a major setback—a return to feudal times in which one's work and destiny were dependent on the will of one man?

According to the new federal law, it is important to maintain the "uniqueness" of Christiania. But this seems to be a contradiction in terms. How can uniqueness be maintained by legalization and normalization? Besides, in Christiania, there are as many opinions about the meaning of the word "normal" as there are inhabitants of the place.

At this point, the government has given economic help to restore some of the buildings. It has also given aid for various social projects such as crime prevention and an office for advice on social and legal questions. With the exception of expert help in restoration, all of these things are to be administered and carried out by Christianians.

On the other hand, the random building and rebuilding by Christianians has not really been stopped. Some restaurants, bars, and workshops have agreed to pay taxes and to have open accounts, while those that have not are regularly raided by the police.

The bioregional plan for the area, expected to pass in Parliament, has been drafted. According to this plan, the "town area" of Christiania is allowed to remain 90 percent as is, whereas the "countryside area" of Dyssen is planned as a recreational area for both Copenhageners and Christianians.

Whatever happens in the future—"normalization" or a new phase of the alternative society-within-a-society, Christiania, the free city, has already proved its success. It has taught that it is possible to live in love and respect instead of antagonism and competition; that it is possible to incorporate differences into a peaceful, workable unity. These teachings might very well serve not only as an inspiration to Denmark but to the entire world community.

Editor's note: Ria Bjerre is a Danish-born writer, dancer, actress, and untiring traveler. In the early seventies, she was part of the radical theater group Solvongnen in Christiania. Between 1973 and 1975, she toured Europe and Asia with the Hathi Babas performing group. Today, she lives part of the year in Denmark and the rest of the year in the community of Huehuecoyotl, Mexico.

This article was rewritten and edited by Brandt Morgan.

Pilgrimage to Huehuecoyotl
Jan Svante Vanbart and Alberto Ruz Buenfil

Among the new rainbow tribes born at the end of the sixties is Huehuecoyotl, "the Old, Old Coyote," a community located at the base of a mountain of the same name in Mexico. For years before we settled down, however, we were a highly nomadic tribe with many names. From 1968 to 1973, we were a guerrilla theater group known as "Chaos." From 1973 to 1977, we were called Hathi Baba's Transit Ashram Commune Unlimited. From 1978 to 1982, we were known

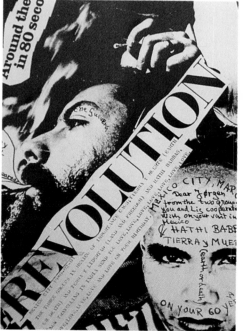

1. *Emblem of the Motherfuckers, New York, 1968.*

2. *Poster created by the Prophets of Chaos, 1970.*

3. *Abbie Hoffman and the Hogfarmer Wavy Gravy in a historical encounter, date unknown.*

4. *"The Hog Farm and Friends" book cover, California, 1979.*

5. *Woodstock collage, 1976.*

6. *Student march in Lund, Sweden, 1968; photographer Jan Svante Vanbart carrying banner at right of photo.*

7. *Postcard of Julian Beck and Judith Malina.*

8. *Danish cultural revolutionaries Jorgen Nash and Jens Jorgen Thorsen in a "happening" in Italy, 1969.*

9. *The group Chaos in Turkey, 1969.*

10. *Hathi Babas at a Tibetan camp, 1974.*

11. Ken Kesey with his bus, Further, on his Oregon farm, 1977.

12. Wavy Gravy telling stories to children at a Rainbow Gathering in Oregon, 1978.

13. Rainbow Gathering in Oregon, 1978.

14. "Patchs" bus at a barter fair in Okanogan Valley, Washington, 1978.

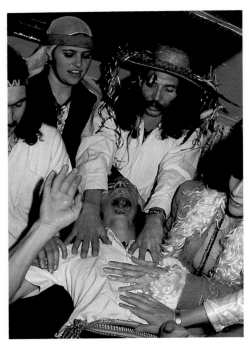

15. Marriage between the tribes, Round Mountain Ranch, California, 1979.

16. Kathleen Sartor and Tove Vils preparing for a performance, 1978.

17. *Fourth of July ceremony for world peace at Rainbow Gathering in Arizona, 1979.*

18. *Tribal council of Rainbow Warriors at Rainbow Gathering in Arizona, 1979.*

19. *Illuminated Elephants performing at the village of the Tarahumara Indians, 1980.*

20. *Peyote ritual with the Illuminated Elephants in Oaxtepec, Mexico, 1981.*

21. *Illuminated Elephants on top of the bus "Gitano 1," Atepec, Mexico, 1981.*

22. *Circle of Rainbow Warriors, Atepec, Mexico, 1981.*

23. Hopi kachina dance by children of the Illuminated Elephants, Atepec, Mexico, 1981.

24. Women from Huehuecoyotl, Morelos, Mexico, 1982.

25. A ceremony in Mexico City honoring the Aztec gods, 1983.

26. Children activists at an anti-nuke march in Mexico City, 1985.

27. Rainbow Gathering in Italy, 1985.

28. Puppets from the Bread and Puppet Theater museum, 1984.

29. Parvati with Pernille, 1986.

30. Greenpeace poster at Christiania, 1986.

31. The Arcoiris Community in Spain, 1986.

32. The Arcoiris Community in Spain, 1986.

33. Christiania, Denmark, 1987.

34. Christiania, Denmark, 1987.

35. Ceremony dedicated to Regina and the martyrs killed in 1968, Tlatelolco, Mexico, 1988.

36. Peter Berg and Judy Goldhaft (founders of the Diggers in the 1960s and of the Planet Drum Foundation) at a meeting with Spanish and Mexican ecologists, Vancouver, 1988.

37. *Alberto with Jose Salinas, captain of Aztec dancers in Palenque, Mexico, 1989.*

38. *Author with José Argüelles, Lloydine Argüelles, and Helen Lembaal at the pyramids at Palenque, Mexico, 1989.*

39. Celebration for world peace at the Mayan city of Etzdna, 1989.

40. Spring equinox ceremony in Chichén Itzá, Mexico, 1989.

41. *Ceremony for women inviting men into the circle, Uxmal, Mexico, 1979.*

42. Jim Berenholtz at the reopening of the Mayan ceremonial centers in Palenque, Mexico, 1989.

43. *Council of women elders at Kukulcan ceremony, Chichén Itzá, Mexico, 1989.*

44. *Fantuzzi with Rainbow children, 1989.*

45. Third festival of the Fifth World at the community house in Huehuecoyotl, Morelos, Mexico, 1989.

46. The group Puente de Wiricuta at the reopening of Mayan ceremonial centers, Palenque, Mexico, 1989.

47. Silent circle in preparation for uniting the sun and moon pyramids at the ceremonial center at Tikal, Guatemala, 1990.

48. Reopening of the ceremonial center at Tikal, Guatemala, 1990.

49. Maya-Quiché priestess Santa Isabel with a group of women at the ceremonial center at Copan, Honduras, spring equinox 1990.

50. Don Alejandro Perez Oxlaj, Mayan shaman of Totonicapan, 1990.

51. New Year's Eve meditation at the sacred sanctuary of Majagua, Manzanillo, Mexico, 1990.

52. Don Emilio, guardian of the temple of Cinteopa, near the village of Amatlan de Quetzalcoatl, Mexico, 1990.

53. Huehuecoyotl, in the mountains of Mexico, 1990.

54. Kathleen Sartor smoking sacred pipe in Huehuecoyotl, 1990.

55. Huehuecoyotl, Mexican god of music and dance, from the old codices of Mexico, 1982.

56. Conch-blowers under the sacred amate *tree at the conference of the guardians of the Earth at Huehuecoyotl, Morelos, Mexico, 1990.*

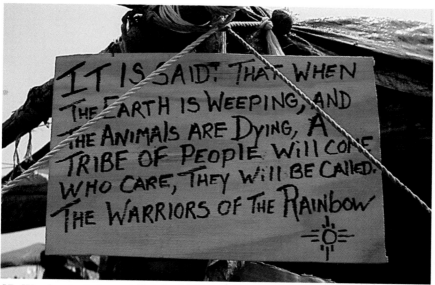

57. *Words of wisdom at Rainbow Gathering in Minnesota, 1990.*

58. *Peace pole ceremony at Rainbow Gathering in Minnesota, 1990.*

59. *The Gypsy tribe presenting their show at Rainbow Gathering in Minnesota, 1990.*

60. *(From left to right) Garrick Beck, Alberto Ruz Buenfil, and Chuck ("Montana") Mills (Garrick and Chuck are two of the founding brothers of the Rainbow Tribal Council), Minnesota, 1990.*

61. The "bicyclebus" at Rainbow Gathering in Minnesota, 1990.

62. The younger generation at the Rainbow Gathering in Minnesota, 1990.

63. Woodstock Nation banner at Rainbow Gathering in Minnesota, 1990.

64. Woodstock anniversary celebration, Woodstock, New York, 1990.

as the Illuminated Elephants. Since then, we have been, simply, the community of Huehuecoyotl.

Throughout these years, however, we have also been widely known as the Rainbow Messengers. Wherever our wanderings have taken us—literally all over the world—we have used theater, happenings, poetry, music, dance, and film to share what we feel are the most important values of the dawning "rainbow era."

"Chaos" was originally a radical performing group formed by six young people from Mexico City's National University and a couple of young radical American students. In June 1968, a few days after the death of Robert Kennedy, this small band of romantic revolutionaries decided to drop out of the academic world and join other thousands of youths in the creation of a new society.

We were a truly nomadic tribe of warriors. In 1968, we participated in the student rebellion in Mexico City, which was brutally smashed when hundreds of students were gunned down by the Mexican police in Plaza de Tlaltelolco during the Olympic Games. We also took part in various American underground activities, then moved to Europe to continue our radical wanderings.

Around the World in Eight Hundred Days

From 1969 to 1970, we were involved with a variety of European happenings: the last skirmishes of the French general strike movement; the founding of the German Commune Ein und Zwei in Berlin; the Provo and Kebauter squatters in Holland; and the libertarian groups that formed around the legendary Guiseppe Pinelli in Italy. We were also in Copenhagen during the first days after the occupation of the free city of Christiania and in London during the violent confrontation between the bands of Picadilly squatters and the British police. Finally, deciding to take a break, we stayed for a year at the Situationist Bauhaus of Drakabygget in southern Sweden.

From 1970 to 1971, together with the radical Scandinavian artists known as Drakabygget or the "Nest of Dragons," Chaos became known for its participation in wild happenings and rituals throughout the main cities of northern Europe. During this initial growth stage, the members of our young tribe blended with their Scandinavian counterparts. And with the first three children born from our group marriage, we took to new roads seeking adventure and change.

Between 1971 and 1973, we toured Africa and the Middle East. There, we came into close contact with many traditional tribes and ethnic groups. During our travels, we began to question many of our cultural and political ideas, and we gradually metamorphosed from a radical guerrilla theater band of the sixties into a young tribe of the New Age.

In 1973, our tribe now composed of people from at least seven different nationalities, we wandered even farther. Our road led through the Turkish mountains and over Khyber Pass in Afghanistan. After months of adventures, we reached India, where we stayed for an entire year. There, our babies were baptized in the sacred waters of the Ganges, and our name was changed to the "Hathi Babas," the Old, Wise Elephants.

Still traveling, we followed in the footsteps of the Beatles, the Dalai Lama, and the Sikhs. We learned about patience, humility, and the wisdom of yoga. Then, reaching the Bengali Ocean, we went on to the holy city of Puri, where we received an initiation in Kriya Yoga at the ashram of Paramahansa Yogananda. Finally, we crossed the ocean to Malaysia, Singapore, Java, Bali, and Australia.

In Australia, besides working to restock our "ark" and meeting with the Aborigines in their sanctity and misery, we encountered Fantuzzi's Butterfly Family doing their rainbow presentations in and around the city of Sydney. The "king of the rainbow gypsies" and his tribe were spreading their message everywhere—a magical blend of colors, a beautiful vision of the world metamorphosed with song, dance, and slides from all over the Earth.

Two years after our departure from the free city of Christiania, we landed on the Pacific Coast of Mexico. A few days later, we founded our first land base in San Jeronimo Lidice, on the outskirts of Mexico City. For the next year and a half we stayed there, baked bread, gave birth to our next couple of children, and did dozens of presentations in cultural centers, schools, streets, and parks. Slowly we became a theater group, and soon we began traveling in an old converted school bus—ten adults and five children.

The Dance of the Four Directions

In 1976, we headed north and reached Pescadero, just south of Santa Cruz in California. There, we had our first meeting with "The Rainbow Family." At first glance, we saw more than fifteen colorful buses just like ours, parked in the midst of smooth hills and green valleys. It felt good to be among so many brothers and sisters, gypsies of old times and new, "white Indians" and babies from all nations and races. We parked our green bus, raised the flag of the Hathi Babas, and joined in the celebration with our music and drums. We sang songs for Mother Earth and prayed to Grandfather Spirit Sun. And in the full-moon evening fire, our southern rhythms entered into the circle of the four directions.

In the winter of 1978, we found a temporary home base at Round Mountain Ranch north of the San Francisco Bay area. This community of radical therapists, feminists, and healers would be our social and spiritual center for the next two years. Round Mountain Ranch in California's Mendocino County was in the very heart of Ecotopia with its alternative communities, cooperatives, simple-living fairs, and self-sufficient settlements in the redwood and sequoia forests.

Those years were filled with happenings, rituals, plays, parties, and group healing sessions. We were taught the sweatlodge ritual by Melvin Chiloquim, a wise Indian from the Klamath River reservation in northern California. He came every full moon for over a year to Round Mountain. We became pipeholders and received a spiritual name, Kilokaga Nilaxi, "the small but powerful tribe looking for wisdom."

We by no means stayed at Round Mountain the whole time—there was too much to experience. Frequently, we all boarded our new fleet of colorful buses (named Kilokaga, Hikayana, Gitano 1, Prisma, and Jungle Queen) to travel in new directions and experience whatever fate had in store for us.

In July 1978, for example, we attended our first national Rainbow Gathering in the highlands of the state of Oregon. The Love Family had created a camp close to our idea of perfection. Baba Ram Dass was there, spooning out granola at sunrise every morning at the Hog Farm's encampment. Medicine Story, the old Indian poet, was also there, leading sweatlodge ceremonies by the river. On the Fourth of July, we danced the Dance of the Four Directions, then formed the

Great Meditation Circle: one hour of common silence to send out a united message of peace to the rest of the planet.

Young and old from many nations of the world came to the gathering. It was a truly international, intertribal, interracial, and interreligious convention. All colors were represented. Rainbows came and went with the forces of nature—the wind, rain, and sun all playing together. Then one day, all too soon, we bid farewell to our brothers and sisters: to Wavy Gravy, Fantuzzi, Garrick Beck, Sunny, Crazy Horse, Joaquin, and the others.

A couple of months later, after a season of picking apples and pears on the slopes of Mount Hood and the banks of the Columbia River, we pushed far into the cold, just below the Canadian border, where we experienced the Okanogan Valley and the annual Barter Fair of Washington State. Here was a place where money was unnecessary and where anything could be bartered: clothes, food, animals, herbs, medicines, bread, cookies, fresh apple juice, peyote buttons, Mendocino "sinsemilla" dope, dried fruits, garlic and potatoes—anything that could be used during the coming winter.

The Peace Pole Ceremony

While the other rainbow tribes were preparing for the dark, cold season ahead, we rainbow gypsies decided to move south again, back to our own sunny lands at Round Mountain Ranch in California. But we did not stay put for long. On July 5, 1979, we found ourselves at another Rainbow Gathering at the White Mountain Apache Reservation in the state of Arizona, preparing for a Peace Pole ceremony.

We, the Illuminated Elephants, as we were now called, had initiated this ceremony. We had spent several days carving, painting, and decorating the Peace Pole, then walked for several miles to plant it in the center of the gathering's circle of tipis. There, we shared our message, the Dance of the Flying Eagles. This event on July 5 became a new tradition, a ritual celebrated at every Rainbow Gathering thereafter.

By the time we met at the Peace Pole circle, we were close to five thousand strong—Rainbow Warriors with flags, music, instruments, garments, and symbols. Included in our number were the Hog Farmers with Wavy Gravy, the Hare Krishnas, Flower and Tree, the Dog Soldiers, Fantuzzi and the Butterfly Family, various indigenous tribes,

Japanese peace monks, and a black African prince named Cacoon and his family.

Each group had a song, dance, poem, or ritual for world peace. And when the pole, symbolizing the Great Tree of Life, was planted into Mother Earth, it was like a reenactment of the divine coupling— God thrusting his mighty penis into the warm womb of the Earth, making love with her and giving birth to all these tribes and families, songs and dances.

White Bear in the Land of the Hopi

Feeling strong, we next decided to go to the land of the Hopi, the People of Peace. The Hopi live within the Four Corners area, a place of mesas near the juncture of Arizona, New Mexico, Colorado, and Utah. We made our camp on a small plateau overlooking the sacred San Francisco Peaks, and from there we could see the lights of New Oraibi and the shadows of Old Oraibi, said to be the oldest permanently inhabited settlement in North America.

The Hopi, whose tribal symbol includes the colors of the four original races, have survived here in the middle of the Arizona desert for many centuries. Only their strong spirituality and cooperation with nature have sustained them in this extremely hostile world. Year after year, they have faithfully paid homage to all the sources of nature's life and energy through their ceremonial cycle and their kachina dances.

Simply waiting, we did not move from our camp for days. We wanted to see if we could make a real spiritual contact with this ancient tribe. One night, after about a week, a strong Hopi man came to our campfire. White Bear, the leader of the Sun Clan, had somehow learned of our arrival while he was purifying himself in the Grand Canyon for the upcoming kachina ceremonies. He had driven an entire day just to meet with us. Though he seemed to know everything about our group, he never revealed how he had learned it.

White Bear talked for hours. He told us about the creation and destruction of three former worlds and how the faithful Hopi had escaped all these catastrophes. He also told us about a certain kachina who in the near future would take off his mask in public, something that had never been done before. He also told us that he himself would soon be imprisoned and about the destruction of the fourth world.

The Third World War might be knocking at the door of humanity at any moment, he said, and the Hopi were again supposed to find the hidden entrance to the underworld. Unless the Federation of Planets intervened, this fourth world would be destroyed by wind and fire.

As this wise Hopi talked, we were all speechless. We just sat and kept the fire going. White Bear continued speaking about the coming of the fifth world, a world prophesied not only by the Hopi but by many other American Indian tribes. This was to be the world of the children and the gods. He told us how many tribes and individuals were already preparing themselves for a great purification. Only the pure of heart would survive, he said, and no other shelter but that heart would be available in the coming times of crisis. Then, he said, there would come a time when nine eagles would fly together in the sky and turn into a phoenix, which would initiate the rejuvenation of the planet.

When White Bear finally finished speaking, it was almost dawn. Finally, he stood up and said, "In case you are not the indicated people to receive this story, you will forget all I have told you by tomorrow morning. You won't be able to remember a word of it." And with these words, he said goodbye and disappeared into the night. More than ten years have passed since that night, and this is the first time I have dared to recall and put his message to paper.

White Bear's visit broke the ice for us with the Hopi. From that night on, we were invited to all the kachina ceremonies in the nearby villages. We lived in Hopiland for almost a month, experiencing some of the most important moments of our collective existence.

The Beginning

As the seventies came to a close, we began to feel we had finished our tasks in northern California. We ended our North American cycle with a new multimedia road show called *The Beginning*, based on a free adaptation of the *Tibetan Book of the Dead* and the life story of Isadora Duncan. This show, which we presented in towns throughout northern California and Oregon, was our way of bidding farewell to the seventies and welcoming the eighties.

The last of our California babies was born on an early morning of the winter solstice, under a rainbow, in the back of one of the buses. This, our seventh tribal baby, was named Paloma. Two months later, in the winter of 1980, we left Round Mountain Ranch and hit the road again, heading back to Mexico.

Pilgrimage to Palenque

The engines hummed smoothly as our line of rainbow-painted buses pushed slowly into the Sonora Desert, the home of the Yaqui Indians (mostly known through Carlos Castaneda's stories about the sorcerer Don Juan). We arrived just in time for a Yaqui ceremony. Their temple was filled with people chanting, singing, snoring, and praying, celebrating the Easter holiday, La Semana Santa. Some of the Yaqui were dressed in traditional clothes. Men, women, children, pigs, dogs, cats, and chickens all mixed in a colorful, noisy blend.

Next, we brought our songs, stories, dreams, and rainbow flag embroidered with the Hopi symbol to the land of the Tarahumaras in the state of Chihuahua, northern Mexico. We arrived while they were celebrating one of their cyclical corn ceremonies, and soon we were incorporated into their fiesta.

We performed our own ceremony for the Tarahumaras and their children in the schoolyard and in the village square. We included songs and dances from other groups we had met on our worldwide journey— the Tibetans, the Lapps, the Lakota, the Aborigines, the Inuit, and the new Greenpeace and Rainbow Tribal Council. We also left a Rainbow-Hopi flag there with the governor as a symbol of peace and goodwill. Silent faces the color of the earth watched our ceremony.

Our plan was to visit as many indigenous tribes as possible on our way to Chiapas in southern Mexico. We made it to San Andres Cohamiata, the land of the Huichols, just one month after Jerzy Grotowsky, the famous Polish theater director, had been thrown out of the village along with his entire troupe. We rode confidently into the village, but it was not easy to gain the acceptance of the suspicious Huichols. After almost a week of trials, we finally broke through their wall of mistrust, and with our drums, dances, and songs, we were appointed the official musicians, or *mariachis*, for the Huichol ceremony of Jikuri-Nerri.

From then on, we got an invitation every day to a different ranch, or *rancheria*, to play our music at various ceremonies and fiestas. Finally, we were invited to participate in the most important ceremony of all, held at the Huichol temple, or *caliguey*.

The *caliguey* was a dark and dusty place. Candle light threw shadows on the old mud walls. A small altar held flowers, corn, and burning copal, which produced a dense smoke, and pine branches covered the walls and part of the floor. In pairs, we joined in with the melodious song and danced with our shadows. Corn beer, or *tesguino*, was brought in and offered to the figures on the altar, then taken out and shared with all. Peyote-*jikuri* necklaces were hung around the altar.

Outside, the women made blue-corn tortillas, and as the night went on, Huichol men drunk with *tesguino* fell down on the ground, only to wake up later in the midst of the singing. The Wirikuta *"jikuri* hunters"* danced in a circle. Cane alcohol was brought out. Violins mixed with the now almost inaudible songs.

We drank the gravel-textured, bittersweet peyote mixture from a ceramic bowl, then earthly reality floated off. Time ran both ways. Wild-looking Huichols chased an agile deer that shone electric blue. They killed it again and again, and again and again it rose and fell. For an eternity, it seemed, the moon traveled from east to west. Only the tortillas and the *atole* drunk at sunrise brought us back to the here and now. Fallen heroes lay everywhere; only the women were busy. We took a long rest before it all started again in the afternoon. The celebration went on for more than a week.

Once again, a Rainbow flag stayed behind in the hands of the Huichol governors. On the last day of our stay, after almost a month in the Sierra, a shaman, or *marakame* priest, who had pulled down his pants to mock us the day of our arrival now agreed to baptize our little baby, Paloma. She received the spiritual name Curama. The circle had been completed. In fact, many of these Huichols from San Andres Cohamiata became our close friends and came to visit us years later at our new home in Huehuecoyotl.

More than a year after we left the Huichol Sierra, we found a camping base at an old Catholic church near Oaxtepec, in the state of Morelos. From this exotic, half-tropical place in the valley of eternal spring, we extended our tour throughout all of Mexico, working mainly with two cultural institutions, Bellas Artes and Fonapas. Then we went into southern Chiapas, into the jungle, into the old world of the Maya, the ancestors of the Lacandones.

We arrived in Chiapas in January 1981. There, in the jungle, we found a Lacandone hunter who reverently showed us the skull of a tiger he had killed only days before. There, we listened to the fine sound of oars breaking the water as we rode in a ten-meter dugout canoe across the surface of pearl-like Naha Lake. Around us, we could hear the screams of parrots and monkeys as we glided over water lilies on the surface of the "bottomless eye," suspended in time. And later, praying that spiders, reptiles, and deadly *nauyaca* snakes would kindly stay away, we took off our boots and slushed gaily through the muddy jungle path to the village of Naha.

There, we relaxed in the hut of Kayum, who played his guitar and taught us the songs of his people, the myths of creation, and the dreams that ruled their daily life. Many of these songs had been handed down to him by his father, Chan Kin, the last of the pure Mayan visionaries and men of knowledge. We have since used some of his songs in our own programs, bringing messages across invisible cultural borders.

At our last performance at the little plaza of Naha, we gave Kayum's elder brother Chan Kin, the chief of the village, another rainbow flag. And while the Lacandones remained in the dense jungle, we readied to move again toward our last important destination: the Temple of Inscriptions in Palenque, which we knew was awaiting us beyond the clouds of humid fog.

The Temple of Inscriptions

Finally we reached Palenque, the other end of the rainbow, ancient ritual ground of the once-splendid civilization of the Maya. With our Rainbow-Hopi flag, we ascended the steep steps of the Temple of Inscriptions and sat down at the top of the pyramid to meditate. All of Palenque was ours for the day, a special favor to Alberto Ruz Buenfil, whose archaeologist father, Alberto Ruz Lhuillier, had begun the famous excavation there in 1949.

Step by step, we descended into the humid heat of the pyramid— down into the royal chamber, the greatest Mayan discovery of the twentieth century. In the heart of the temple, we came upon the tomb of Lord Pacal.

It is possible that Pacal was a high priest, a nobleman, or an emperor. Some even say he was the incarnation of Quetzalcoatl, the mythical feathered serpent god. Swiss author Erik von Daniken sees

Pacal as a revered space traveler and his tomb as a stylized spaceship. Mexican-American author José Argüelles sees him as Pacal Votan, "Galactic Agent 13 66 56." Whoever he was, Pacal lay nailed into the great stone monoblock for more than a thousand years before his discovery in 1952. He is still there, stuck in the jaws of death, the reincarnational symbols of cross and corn growing from his heart.

In a final ceremony, we honored the "old men," the late Dr. Alberto Ruz Lhuillier and the one buried just below Lhuillier's greatest life's work—the discoverer and his discovery united in a strange karmic sleep.

Before we left Palenque, we again sang the songs of the Hopi, danced our interpretations of the kachina dances, and sang the chants and songs of the Sioux, the Tarahumaras, the Huichols, and the Lacandones. All of these mixed with our own songs of the rainbow as we gave thanks to the spirits that had guided us to our destination.

Huehuecoyotl: Home at Last

Now it was 1982, and our seven buses were parked in a mango-avocado grove outside the village of Yautepec in the Mexican state of Morelos. After more than two years of intensive traveling and performing, we were finally taking a rest. Now we found ourselves in the midst of a growth crisis. After many separations, ruptures, and a good deal of pain, our family needed a radical change in order to continue on together. We sent out some scouts to look for a new base—not just another temporary camping ground but a place we could truly call our home.

In the midst of this emotional commotion, some representatives of the Rainbow Tribal Council arrived unexpectedly from the north. The visit of our northern sisters and brothers gave us new light and energy. Also in the middle of this difficult transition, on March 6, 1982, another of our children was born. Her name was Parvati, which means "Blessing from the Sky, Wife of Krishna, the Perfect One." That same day, our four excited scouts returned to say that they had found a place for all of us to live.

The next day, we all went to the site, up in the Tepozteco Mountains in the state of Morelos—up past the huge caves where Emiliano Zapata and his men had hidden out during the Mexican Revolution. A steep, curving road took us through pine forests and old lava beds just below the Nahuatl village of Santo Domingo, Ocotitlan. A hidden path led up into thick forests inhabited only by goats and coyotes. Our new home was almost six thousand feet above sea level. This was the spot that the Great Spirit had picked for us—a five-acre piece of land hidden under Cerro del Mecac, the home of Ehecatl, the "Spirit of the Wind." Our new home already had a name. It was Huehuecoyotl, the land of the "Old, Old Coyote."

Under the generously extended branches of an *amate* tree, we found a perfect ritual space. There, in the sacred land of the Old, Old Coyote, the Aztec god of music and dance, we sang, danced, and planted our peace pole and our Hopi-Rainbow flag. After centuries of abandonment, this land was to be inhabited once more. The old Nahuatl-Zapata headquarters was to become a powerful place for our small tribe in search of wisdom.

Fifteen days later, Parvati was baptized under the *amate* tree. Her placenta was planted there, eventually giving birth to a cherry tree. The rainbow families from the north sang and played with us. Bells rang, conch shells sounded, aboriginal *didgeridoos* were heard for miles around, and ceremonial drums were beaten for a day and a night. The rainbow had found a new place to shine and grow. Leaping from the Earth, fed by white sunlight, and faceted by life-giving drops of water, it brought fire and water into spiritual union.

Parvati's Dream

Five years later, in 1987, our twelfth house was just being completed, and Huehuecoyotl had grown immensely. Our houses showed a great diversity in architectural style. They were made predominantly of adobe, combined with poles and boards made from fallen trees. Their shapes varied from round, ovular, and rectangular to hexagonal, octagonal, and pyramidal.

We divided our five-acre piece of land into personal and communal spaces. We captured water in a dam below a small seasonal waterfall that gushed from the pine forest above. This dam also became our first ceremonial site. There, we baptized our second Huehuecoyotl child, Carmen. And during the years, we have baptized all of our new young warriors: Ixchel, Tai, Laolin, Lianka, Emiliano, Ekihua, and Samanta.

On full-moon nights, we light the fire for a sweatlodge, the *temazcal*. We have set our lodge right in a place where men used to make charcoal before we came to Huehuecoyotl. Where once there was fire, there is now fire again—a cleansing fire. In the lodge, we sweat and sing and pray and smoke, circulating a pipe filled with kinnikinnick, sweet herbs, and tobacco to symbolize the fourth, or present, world. We have also added a fifth round of prayer to the traditional four to symbolize the fifth world—the world to come, the world of the gods and the children, a world that we have proclaimed to be here and now.

On the spring equinox of 1987, we held a festival to celebrate the fifth anniversary of Huehuecoyotl. This was a two-day celebration, with everything from kids' carnival and rock 'n' roll bands to Baharata Natyam Hindu dancers and an international restaurant. Altogether, there were more than seven hundred guests. Complete with firecrackers and magicians, it was a benefit celebration for the completion of the ceremonial house—a celebration of life . . . and of death.

Two months before the celebration, an electrical short-circuit had caused a fire that completely consumed one of our houses. Because of the asphyxiating smoke, we were able to get Parvati out only after it was too late to save her life. She had completed her mission here and had moved on to other realms. She, who was soon to be five years old and who had given us Huehuecoyotl on the day of her birth, had now departed. For the last time, we placed her under the *amate* where she had been baptized. From there, we carried her to the village of Santo Domingo, Ocotitlan, to her last resting place.

The procession, led by the children carrying the rainbow and Huehuecoyotl's flags, returned home in the afternoon. Sadness had turned to sweet melancholy. There is a saying that goes, "A village is not complete until you have buried your first son or daughter in the ground." Now, in the small graveyard of Ocotitlan, Parvati's fragile remains lie in a place where her spirit will play forever between pine trees, eucalyptus, and aloes. Life never ends: Parvati was and will ever be a happy being, and her memory will be with us always.

After nine days—when the spirit of a dead person rises, according to local shamans—we dreamed that Parvati was sitting in a well inside a cave. She looked upon us with curious eyes, without saying a word.

We felt that she was being cared for and that her spirit was now on its way. In this way, the Great Spirit calmed our restless minds.

The Legend of the Fourth Wise Man

On International Children's Day, we were asked to prepare a presentation for all the schools of Tepoztlan. We had three days to invent something, rehearse it, get the costumes ready, and add some music and songs to the show. The resulting play was called *The Legend of the Fourth Wise Man.*

We based our story on the biblical legend of the three wise men (Balthazar, Gaspar, and Melchior) and on the star that led them to the village of Bethlehem where Jesus was born. However, we wanted to construct a more appropriate legend for our own time, a legend for the New Age. If Balthazar had come from the south, he would have been an emissary of the black nations; Gaspar, who had come from the Far East, would have been an Oriental ambassador; and Melchior, who had come from the cold north, would have been the representative of the white family of humanity. To us, each of these men represented a different power: the first, magic; the second, wisdom; and the third, science and technology. But in this new era, the old myth was incomplete; we needed a fourth wise man. So we created a new myth.

Almost two thousand years ago, the star that guided the original three wise men to Bethlehem was most likely Halley's Comet. In 1987, according to our myth, Halley's Comet returned as a beautiful "star dancer" and cosmic healer who brought a red man with her. In our new legend, the red man introduced himself to the confused and somewhat angry original three as Tonatiuh de la Cruz, a representative of all the red nations of America, also called Tehuantizuyo or "Turtle Island."

After many adventures, misunderstandings, and even some serious arguments, the four wise men began a pilgrimage to the place where "Halley" had guided them, a place that would become the power center for the New Age. Finally, they arrived at a huge pyramid in the middle of the tropical forests of southern Mexico. Inside this pyramid lay the answer to the quest of the four wise men.

But one problem could not be solved: no one of them could open the pyramid. Despite Melchior's technical expertise, Balthazar's dance of power, and Gaspar's immense wisdom and concentration, nothing happened. Not even Tonatiuh's magical tricks were successful. The pyramid remained shining with promise and power, but closed.

Tonatiuh then proposed that the four try using their *combined* energies to discover the secret of the pyramid, so they all sat in one corner and concentrated. But all their efforts only shook the enormous generator; they needed help from the children. Only by uniting the love of innocent children with the combined wisdom of the four main cultures could they hope to reach the heart of all mysteries.

Thus, a huge circle of children joined hands around the pyramid, and the four wise men also joined in this circle. They closed their eyes and begin chanting a powerful, resonant "OM!" and slowly the pyramid lifted off the ground and departed into the universe, revealing at its core a Rainbow Child. This child had now been liberated from its mythical prison by an act of collective will, an act of love and wisdom. Only then could the fifth world begin, the world of the Rainbow Children who would bring happiness, light, and new life to our planet.

Today, the Rainbow Messengers of Huehuecoyotl continue traveling in the four directions, bringing with them messages from one culture to another, one people to another, one community to another through music, dance, poems, slide shows, rituals, and theater presentations. We try to set an example of how it is possible to weave a network of alternative solutions throughout the planet to begin the work of cleaning up the mess we have created through the centuries. And we share the optimistic certitude that it is possible to start building an ecotopian millennium: a world without nations, a world of light and love for generations of Rainbow Children yet to be born.

Editor's note: Jan Svante Vanbart is a writer-photographer, a pioneer in the Swedish alternative movement, and one of the founders of Huehuecoyotl. After attending the World Environmental Conference in Stockholm in 1972, he left Sweden and joined the nomadic Hathi Babas on a round-the-world pilgrimage and further adventures. He has written for Scandinavian newspapers and magazines and produced radio, television, and audiovisual shows in Europe and the United States documenting the history of the Rainbow Movement.

The Rainbow Communities in Spain
Alberto Ruz Buenfil

After the defeat of the Spanish Revolution of 1936-1939, General Francisco Franco took over power in Spain and held it until his death in 1975. His dictatorship provoked most Spanish intellectuals, artists, and libertarian politicians to leave their country. Most of the Spanish progressive thinkers either became political refugees or were exiled.

Spain lived through this long period sleeping beneath an apparent stability that was tightly maintained by repression, terrorism, and police control. This bred a cultural conservatism that for more than three decades kept the Spanish population away from the social changes that affected the rest of the world.

When Franco died in 1975, there was an explosion of change in Spain—especially among the youth, who were trying to regain the time that had been lost under fascism and to catch up with the rhythm of modern Europe. During these first years of rapid transformation, many new seeds of social change were planted and began to sprout all over Spain.

One of the hardiest of these early sprouts consisted of a group of people who gathered around a charismatic spiritual leader named Emilio Fiel. These people established a center for study and research near San Sebastian, a place they called Sadhana Tantra Ashram. There, they learned about yoga, naturalism, meditation, and the dynamics of group unity.

Soon after its founding, the center could no longer contain its original members. They needed more room to experiment and change. On September 20, 1978, the original seed exploded and gave birth to a new community.

The place chosen for the new community was an old monastery in the province of Navarra, twenty-seven kilometers from Pamplona. In Lizaso, "in the middle of a green valley between two rivers which feed it with mist and magic powers,"[5] as Fiel described it, was thus created the first Spanish tantric "Rainbow Community."

At the beginning, the original seed consisted of five individuals who restored the place. By the end of its first year, the ashram's population had grown to nearly thirty. These first residents began doing sweats, learning the rhythms of life, and discovering together the roots of peace and happiness. In their new center, they studied Eastern and Western techniques for personal growth such as pranayama, meditation, catharsis, and tantra, always seeking a balance between their internal growth and their collective process as a developing community.

By 1980, the community included more than eighty adults and ten children. Owing to the explosive climate of change in Spain, at least fifteen thousand visitors came through the community in a single year. Among them were students, apprentices, the curious, and the hangers-on. Lizaso quickly became too crowded, and Fiel and his friends began talking about creating a tantric Aquarian village that could accommodate as many as five hundred people.

At that point, Fiel was the unquestioned guru of the community, a talented conductor of an unusual orchestra. He was well schooled for the job. In 1968, he had been a representative of the Spanish student movement in France during the student revolt in Paris. He had also traveled extensively in the Far East, where he had been a disciple of great teachers such as Sri Aurobindo, Krishnamurti, and Bagwan Shree Rajneesh. Partly because of Fiel's charisma, Lizaso kept growing. It was, as Fiel called it, "a seed, the embryo of a new consciousness, of a new being that lives in Nature, free and harmoniously."[6]

In 1981, the new Rainbow Community seemed a true Noah's Ark. People were experimenting with all kinds of lifestyles: integral communitarian, tantric, and individual. The blending of styles developed in a space where each of its members could work and grow physically, emotionally, mentally, and spiritually. The community was turning into a real school of life.

In a country where a growing personal process had been forbidden for more than thirty years, thousands of young people had completely forgotten the meaning of the word "freedom." People had lost faith in traditional paths and schools, and they were in desperate need of new alternatives. The Rainbow Community offered many diverse types of workshops and classes for spiritual, emotional, and physical growth. It held weekend study camps, collective work sessions, and marathon courses. Sometimes more than two thousand people camped in the ashram's community areas in order to attend classes, and soon there was need for an even larger community center.

Accordingly, in 1981, the Initiate's School of the Rainbow Community was established in Arenys de Munt, near Barcelona. A dozen people left Lizaso to start working there, and by the following summer, the school began to welcome the most advanced seekers. Some of its intensive courses lasted more than five weeks.

In an interview published in *The Magician* magazine in the winter of 1980, Fiel explained some of the principles and techniques that were practiced at the Rainbow Community:

> More important than any technique is the desire of the individual to change and transform his life. The different techniques, such as catharsis, are only good to break apart the walls that prevent people from relating with the external world, to take apart the armors that impede us from being in contact with our inner feelings and thoughts. They are useful only to get away from "seriousness" and solemnity. Once you get through this stage, you enter into the inner exploration of trying to find new ways to confront life. Then you reach madness, and that is the time to become one with the whole, to reach total unification with the Universe.
>
> Tantra, in contrast with other teachings which are all rigid, disciplined and puritanical, is a teaching that avoids religious precepts, priests, churches and holy scriptures. Tantra is an inner integral search. Tantra is a synthesis of many other paths, because the sexual act is the direct path to cosmic fusion. It implies for each one to find their inherent dualism, their feminine and masculine principles.
>
> A community like the Rainbow is not meant for "special people" only, but for anyone, for people like you and me. People with problems, fears, joys and different abilities, people who are trying to transform their lives. If we are able to do it in small groups, then it means that we can do it as a whole, and that there is still hope for the world....
>
> We are reaching the point in which the world either destroys itself completely or develops a new consciousness, an awareness that is able to put an end to institutional religious, political, and geographical frontiers. What is most important to know is that in this new era, the Messiah is not going to be a special messenger coming from above. It is not going to be a Messiah that is external to ourselves. On the contrary, we are going to have to find our own inner Messiahs. We are *all* Buddhas....
>
> Besides this, the most important lesson for us humans is not to take things seriously, because seriousness encloses us inside frames and makes us believe that we are holding "the truth" and that our god is better than all others. We should never forget that life is only a *game!*[7]

On October 3–4, 1981, the members of Fiel's Rainbow Community hosted Spain's first Tribal Council of Rainbow Communities, which was attended by more than five hundred Spaniards. The main purpose of the council was to create new communities that could identify with the many colored paths of the rainbow. Those attending fell into two distinct categories: groups that were ready to live communally right away and groups that still needed to grow spiritually and emotionally before they could hope to become successful communities.

The symbol used to represent the council was a circle with three tipis, a ceremonial peace pipe, and an elder's power wand. These were placed beneath a buffalo's head representing Wakan Tanka, the Great Spirit of the North American Indians. Thus, for the first time on the "old continent," bands of "Spanish Indians" became inspired by the wisdom of the first inhabitants of Turtle Island. After two days of counseling, fifteen new communities were formed, with from six to as many as thirty members each.

Emilio Fiel was well aware of the rainbow's role as a bridge between past, present, and future. For the new Rainbow Warriors of the world, both those within the newly formed communities and outside them, he had the following message:

> In the middle of this world, which humans deplete without pity, destroying valleys and mountains with the deadly smokes coming from their cities, polluting the oceans with the vomit of their ignorance, we can still hear the outburst of the laughter of a Warrior. He is dancing his death dance, and he is sending his last call to all of us.
>
> His song is the chant of the Earth, and in his throat are all those beings and people who have walked the paths with a heart, one with Nature, telling us about their journeys: from the magic of all existing things to the infinite Nothingness.
>
> You all walk in a prodigious and marvelous world, a world which dearly loves you and offers the best fruits from its own body. The whole infinite sky kisses your chests every second, and the light of many suns and stars washes your blood. An indefinable mystery rests in each atom and fills all beings with benedictions. At each moment, the river of your life is transformed and all existence is renewed.
>
> Treat the world with gentleness and care. Do not deform it by putting unnecessary pressure on it. Every little thing is sacred. From the rock of the volcanos to the eagle in the mountains, all the living forms have to walk their own path, just like you. Watch them grow and die, dazzled by the Great Mystery.

You shall also die one day, and with you also will perish your beliefs, your morality, your schemes and your social goals. They will all disappear like this smoke in the air. Do not die in the boredom of habits and customs considered "honorable" which drag along others like a song repeating itself over and over in the midst of intoxication by alcohol. Do not ask nor expect anything. Do not trade life for anything. Trust yourself, trust life as it comes to you, trust your inner nature.

Dive into the silence of your soul and awaken the fire that sleeps there. Enjoy and love life without getting attached to anything. And whatever you do, do it fully. There is nothing else more important in this moment; each act of a Warrior is a sacred act. . . . Do not lower your head in the presence of anyone, and do not allow anyone to lower his or hers in your presence. A great Warrior is a simple person who is united to the Universe which protects him. Close your eyes and be honest with yourself, and the greatest humility will fill your hands.

Clean your mirror in the deepest solitude of your soul, and do not seek approval from any other world. Accept every person for who they are and do not interfere in their lives or try to impose your beliefs on them. Do not keep any creed, and unthrone reason and intelligence, as they should keep their proper place in your life.

Give your body its true place on Earth. Allow your feelings to guide your steps, and allow your actions to be fresh as dew in the early morning. Be just as life itself, unexpected. Break apart your weakness and do not consent to being dragged down by routine and monotony. Society rides like a blind, runaway horse, attracted by a cloud, a soap bubble; but the world will be perfect if you fight for understanding and seek for knowledge. Only then will eternity be with you and surround you. Fight all your life; the road has no end— and fight for the things that bring you joy, for the totality of being.

Conquer your weaknesses. Throw out the existing world and begin to learn from every little thing that you find in this new world you are discovering every day. Everything is alive. Observe carefully, especially those things that reason despises. Feel, allow your body to learn and know, because each sensation brings about the knowledge that you are seeking. Learn to focus your attention, to be more alert all the time. Attention is the sword of the Warrior, and it helps him destroy memories. Each day awake as if it were the last of your days and the beginning of a long journey. Walk toward the invisible world, following the paths that have a heart, and all your senses will open, as a flower filled with joy.

This is an endless road, and the only thing that really counts is walking; therefore, each step you take, each act you accomplish, do it

with impeccability, only for your pleasure, without expecting anything in return. Thus will you find in each act an indefinable secret,
and happiness will fill your whole being.

And when fog darkens your vision and freezing icebergs sting
your soul, remember my song. You will suffer when the known world
collapses, and you will be attached to it by chains that will hit your
wrinkled face when they break, as if they were waves of illusion fading
away without shape. And then, silently, you will hear a song, a sense-
less and absurd song. It will be the outburst of laughter of a Warrior
that, as unexpected as life itself, as love, as death, will call at the doors
of the Great Mystery.[8]

At the end of the first Tribal Council, the new communities departed
to begin their own adventures, and the decision to meet the following
year was taken by consensus. The idea was to have an "annual communities gathering" to share and trade experiences, creativity, and products. It was also decided that the groups would collectively produce
a book called *The Rainbow Communities*, summarizing their experiences.

The following winter, that of 1982–1983, instead of a book the
magazine *Arcoiris* ("The Rainbow") was born. Under the motto, "The
Union of Sky and Earth," issue "0" described the second Rainbow Tribal
Council in Spain. This event took place during the first few months
of 1983 at the school/community of Arenys de Munt.

Attending the council were representatives from all the new communities, as well as people who had become interested in the process
of community formation. Thus, the "rainbow awareness" quickly became a real social movement in Spain. Various communities were not
only meeting periodically to share information; they were also producing and trading articles such as organic food, crafts, publications,
cassettes, calendars, furniture, creams, and candles.

Also during 1983, another Spanish collective called Integral published a special issue of its periodical magazine, *Ecology, Health and
Natural Life*, in which Emilio Fiel was interviewed on the subject of
the evolution of the nuclear family into a holistic community:

> There will always be people who continue screaming that the only
> possible social organization for everyone is the nuclear family, in spite
> of all the terrible commotions which this traditional structure
> undergoes. These people have chosen to forget and ignore the exis-

tence of other social structures such as those among the northern Amerindians, many primitive societies, the first Essenian Christian communities and the alternative communities of all times.

If it is true that at a time in history the nuclear family helped humankind in its social organization, now for many decades this closed structure has turned into a cancerous sickness in the heart of humanity. It has become the origin of many mental perturbations and disturbances and the source of most illness among grownups, of their incapacity to love and the main reason for their distrust of other people.

To live inside a community means to live beyond possessiveness, to live in joy and freedom in a loving encounter. Children need to be in contact with many different people to increase their experiences about the world of grownups, and this can only be offered in a community where everything is possible, without authorities, power games or possessiveness.

In a commune, people can love each other at any moment, without struggling, without competition, sharing their bodies and souls at the same time. In communes, social obsession over sexuality disappears and all religions can blend into one spiritual experience: love beyond all differences. Communities can turn into a worldly paradise, here and now.

A commune is a place where freedom and love can turn into real experiences, where it is possible to make mistakes and also correct them, where one can confront the risks of learning. A community is a place where problems can be raised and solved, face to face, until our hearts are purged. In a community, each individual should be allowed to be exactly as they are, and nobody should try to change them or force them to be different. Each commune should create its own environment and structure, and change them according to its members' desires or needs, not copying other established forms. We should be able to doubt, to question ourselves until we get to the roots of our problems, and to develop our own discipline with an intense inner work.

It is very important that we learn to create our own environment in such a way that everything can acquire a sacred dimension. Places where we can develop our knowledge, express our emotions and allow our physical body to excel and relax, unifying the scientific, poetic and mystical spirit of each person. Our search for new meanings should grow in an environment without divisions or separations; in joy, laughter and play, not in hardship and asceticism.

The rainbow journey in search of the pot of gold requires from us the task of leaving behind the masks, games and deceits that society, the nuclear family, education, religion and other institutions have forced into our childhood. Only then will we be ready to acquire a new consciousness, a rainbow consciousness.[9]

In the winter of 1983–1984, issue 4 of *Arcoiris* was published with a report about the third Tribal Council of rainbow communities. To this gathering came representatives from communities all over Spain: Gredos, Hanta-Yo, Gulistan, Elorto, Kailashbati, Karma, Muntando, Shanti-Deva, Kala-Chakra, and many others. No one could doubt that the movement was growing by leaps and bounds. What had started out as a humble, grassroots urge to experiment with new forms of living had, in a few short years, blossomed into a flower whose fragrance was affecting an entire country.

The following year, 1984, the Rainbow Community made another important step in its evolution. Its members created a school of meditation in Alcover, Tarragona, where all the members of the different Spanish communities met to plan their future.

At that time, Alcover had the capacity to permanently lodge more than 150 members. At the same time, its school of meditation was able to hold dozens of students for an intense program of courses and workships. There were enough farming areas to produce most of the food needed for its members, as well as laboratories and workshops for crafts, carpentry, mechanics, textiles, and even an editorial workshop that subsequently produced a number of books. One of these was Fiel's *A Grain of Sand*, published in 1983, which emphasized more than ever the importance of individual action on behalf of the planet:

> Before the end of this millenium, if a large enough number of people are able to awaken their individual consciousnesses, humanity as a whole will be able to transform the chaotic situation the world is facing today. If that does not happen, we will face the worst planetary disaster in history.
>
> The moment has come in which each one of us should make a decision to make an evolutionary jump into the future. Our choice is either to submit to an old agonizing world or to participate in the creation of a new horizon of hope, which would allow us to enter into the mystery of an unnamed time to come and into the loving vibration of divinity.
>
> This transformation requires an inner discipline, accepted individually and voluntarily, exercised for many years, which will bring

us to the threshold of fulfillment and free us from the slavery of death. Through concentration, silent meditation, devotional ecstasies, conscious dreaming, the art of not-doing, the repetition of a mantra, purification of the subconscious mind or any other spiritual technique, we will be able to pierce through the most superficial layers of our personality. Only then will we be able to reach the depths of our inner being, and then new infinite spaces will open in front of us, taking us to marvelous worlds of emotion and feeling which lie far beyond the world of our reason.

Only by going through this process will we be able to transcend old dogmas and commandments and come into direct contact with a real spiritual experience, with the essence of life which dissolves personal, familiar, cultural, political and religious stinginess and pettiness.

These are times for action; we have wasted and exhausted enough words already. This is the last chance that humanity has for survival: the creation of a new humankind, carrying the love of Christ and the strength of Shakti, a force which will make destruction of this planet unnecessary and will act as a guide and witness to the transformation that will open the doors to the next evolutionary cycle.[10]

In the same book, Fiel talks about the meaning and importance of the rainbow in this coming planetary transformation:

The rainbow is the crossing point where whatever is human and divine meet. It is a great dynamo where the energies of everything and everyone blend and explode, creating new landscapes of joy and comprehension. . . .

The person who is able to balance harmoniously these seven energies reaches a state of natural ego or non-ego and the condition of illumination. The man or woman who reaches this state obtains a permanent center in his or her life, a permanent harmony which allows him or her to see the reality of life from a different perspective.[11]

And for those inclined to poke fun at the ideological principles of the Rainbow Community, calling their magazine *Anarchoiris*, Fiel gives this response:

Every day there are more and more citizens of the world who have replaced the mutilating idea of class, religion, nation or race, searching for the real function of their inner personal destiny within the totality of this known Universe on this planet. For these people it has now become obsolete to defend the Aryan or the black race, the proletarian class, those who speak Zulu, junkies, Christians, bisexuals or any other minority. And this is the main reason why there is such a proliferation of spiritual groups, group therapies, yoga centers, corporal expression courses and communities. All of these are different ways to affirm ourselves as *persons*, beyond the obscure forces of the masses and their stupid slogans.

We are tired of national anthems and hymns, statues, saviors of the world, revolutionaries, sexually obsessed characters disguised in black robes, raised arms and closed fists. This is the right moment for a personal awakening, for a change of our inner gravity, moving from the head center to the heart. This is the time for the birth of a new humanity which will unite for pleasure and not just for the sharing of suffering or grief.

And we are not talking about the creation of an Ecologist Army or a Libertarian, Communal system, but about the knowledge that we are one, in silence with the rest of our brothers and sisters on this planet, and that we are here to enjoy life in their company. Only then will we turn again into a nomadic tribal society, without territories or properties, and share a planetary, peaceful and loving culture.

We will become the dervishes of the New Age and the Warriors of the Aquarian Era. For a Warrior, the things which happen every day are not a benediction or a malediction but a challenge. A Warrior does not call the world unreal and is conscious of the powers that he or she can direct toward him or herself as well as to all the things that surround him or her. In this way, the world will turn into an infinite space for experimentation and liberation.[12]

In "The Light of the Zodiac," a program of activities for 1986 published by the Rainbow Community, the following workshops and courses were offered: catharsis, meditation, Sufi and Gnostic teachings, massage, t'ai chi, vipassana meditation, the art of living, reencounter with life and the sources of health, Kabbala, astrology, tarot, magic love and tantric union, sansara and dissolution of family archetypes, and an intensive rainbow meditation.

The community had turned into a veritable New Age "multiversity" for the awakening of planetary awareness. Besides these activities, community workshops produced garments made from natural fibers, pillows, anatomically shaped chairs, leather products, pottery, wax candles, mats, and an assortment of outer wear. The community was also satisfying most of the nutritional needs of its members, producing milk, yogurt, sprouts, vegetables, fruits, grains, cereals, eggs, bread, and many other wholesome foods.

In that same year, the community's editorial workshop published a new book by Emilio Fiel, entitled *Dharma Mandala: Toward a Global Vision*, in which Fiel summarized many of his ideas, experiences, and visions. With its own printing machines, the community now had a unique opportunity to publish its ideas as well as its years of real work and experience. Fiel and the members of the Rainbow Community were actually writing about putting their global vision to the test.

Dharma Mandala had a more ecological orientation, as evidenced by the following passage:

> When we awaken our human potentials, our creative forces, our lucid vision, serenity, emotions, and higher aspirations, we are contributing to a natural and harmonious improvement toward the relationships among humankind and toward the social and spiritual transformation of the Earth.
>
> In the world today, so many millions of people are opening to a meditative reality that we can truly speak about a planetary mutation in the perception of humankind. There are dozens of initiatic paths which are helping us to integrate the sacred into our daily lives and to have a better understanding of our true place in this Universe. . . .
>
> Today, there are thousands of people, young of mind and spirit, who have left behind the fear of insecurity and material egoism and are creating something new. . . . Most of society is against these people, but they side with the future and with the fantastic, radical and visionary changes to come. Today, only these people that we call the Rainbow Warriors are living in harmony both with physics and mysticism. They are the people of tomorrow and those who will survive the planet's crisis because they belong to a more human world. . . . [13]

In April 1987, the Rainbow Community in Alcover began to undergo a radical transformation. Its members defined it as a "qualitative leap." Once the rainbow had ascended, they said, it needed to return to Earth again, to transform the ladder of Jacob into a colored bridge. In order to complete this process, the Rainbow Community decided to fuse with a larger organization called Shambhala and to dedicate themselves to the fight for planetary healing.

In "The Path of the Heart and Fire," his first article published after this alliance took place, Fiel sent out a call to the followers of the rainbow path:

> The next months will represent a crucial step in the history of humanity. The American Indians from both north and south knew about this precise moment hundreds of years ago and even fixed the dates of the 16th and 17th of August as two days of great importance for the evolution of the whole planet.
>
> For the Amerindians of yesterday and tomorrow, the old Aztec Human-God figure of Quetzalcoatl, the Feathered Serpent, a deity which was the symbol for the creation of a new Sun, would be manifested in the form of 144,000 illuminated masters or Sun Dancers when the Earth would get stagnant and need it the most. And this moment would imply the beginning of a new humanity, a collective awakening of the whole of humankind.[14]

A few months later, at the time of Harmonic Convergence on August 16-17, 1987, Emilio Fiel decided that the time had come to end his role as spiritual leader of the Rainbow Community and that both he and the other members of the community should enter a new stage of their growth process. On those same two days, Fiel had several heart attacks, which he took as a clear sign that it was time to leave. Soon afterward, he departed from Alcover with a small group of his closest friends and his life's companion, Laksmi. They moved to the high Pyrenees, away from public life for a while, there to continue their work.

Meanwhile, the approximately eighty community members who decided to stay in Alcover adopted a new spiritual guide, this time a woman named Maha, who later took the name of Shakti. With this unusual decision, a series of drastic changes took place that verified the need for a qualitative leap within the community.

The Rainbow Community changed its name to Tierra Nueva, "New Earth," and in a public gathering its members declared their purpose of investigating and sharing new forms of human relationships through the transformation of consciousness and of working for the emergence of a new civilization.

In the fall of 1988, Emilio Fiel and Laksmi decided to travel to Mexico, expecting to find a new spiritual dimension in the deserts, mountains, and people of the "new continent." As a result of this journey, Fiel formulated the goals for his next adventure: to create a colored "bridge" between Mexico and Spain by the year 1992, the five hundredth anniversary of the arrival of Christopher Columbus to the lands named America.

In the high Sierra del Quemado, the sacred land of the Huichol Indians, Fiel and a group of Rainbow Warriors from Europe and Mexico named this new bridge "El Puente de Wirikuta." (*Wirikuta* is a Huichol word meaning "the place where the physical and spiritual worlds meet.") And since November 1988, Fiel's new group, as well as others recently formed, have been working simultaneously on both continents to awaken the Spanish people and the rest of Europe. Their ultimate purpose is to collaborate in the transformation of Europe by the ancient and new alternative cultures of America. In Fiel's words, the times are ripe for a spiritual awakening—for "Quetzalcoatl's recapture" of Europe.

I would like to conclude this chapter with a poem written by Fiel and dedicated to all the children of the Earth:

> With these musical notes and mysterious signs
> I hail to all Rainbow Children,
> And I share my happiness for partaking with them
> the multicolored sweetness of Gaia, our beautiful, battered Earth
>
> We welcome you among tantrikas and shamans
> beyond time, between nomadic dervishes and adventurers
> of the Tao, who with me wish you an exuberant life
> under the Sun and in the middle of the stars.
>
> I pray for my love to this gypsy woman who
> dances sweetly in the flames, and who will guide you
> through the Mysteries, protecting you always.
>
> Her eyes will not stop you in your struggle
> for purer air, for sharing the freedom of the sparrows
> and for the realization of your higher dreams
> in your fight against those petty beings who will
> fill your path with obstacles and waste.
>
> Our eyes look upon you as you play and inquire,
> sharing the warmth that you need to grow toward the sky
> and our hands weave boldly your uncertain future,
> until the moment in which you'll hold in your hands
> the steering wheel of your own lives.

Remember how difficult it will be to fly freely to the sky
and escape from the claws and tentacles of the mind,
trying to return to your lost home.

Be "nobody," transcending those opposites in struggle
and living as the rebellious children of humanity.

Forget about religions, borders, races, languages,
and realize fully the limitless human nature which
is revealed in that last and unique instant.

To all of you, Rainbow Children,
I dedicate with joy this song.

You are born in the middle of all colors
and every one of the people on this Earth
wishes you the greatest of possible fortunes.

And if one ominous day our beloved planet returns
violently to the original dust, do not forget
that we will meet again, in a world of light, out of this time.[15]

Chapter 5

Shining Specter of the Eighties

The Communist Manifesto of 1848 began with the words "A ghost is haunting the world, the ghost of communism." Today, the Berlin Wall has collapsed and state communism is all but dead. We have entered the New Age, and the manifesto for that age might begin, "A specter is healing the world, the shining specter of the rainbow."

The global healing we are experiencing is not the result of any particular group or social movement, it is the result of a new spirit; however, that spirit has become increasingly visible through the ecotopian rainbow movement that is rapidly spreading around the globe. From the beats and hippies of the sixties to the birth of Greenpeace and the American Rainbow Gatherings in the seventies and eighties, the rainbow spirit has begun to spread from the roots of the Tree of Life into the very roots and branches of society.

Today, the rainbow symbol shows up everywhere, from flags and windows to walls and bumper stickers. The rainbow is even used as an advertising tool to promote products that have little or nothing to do with its magical qualities. Still, its true spirit lives and grows, bathing the Earth and all creation in its healing light.

In this chapter, we will trace the expansion of the rainbow spirit through the eighties, both geographically and politically, observing how it spread and began to seep into the fabric of established society. Among its manifestations, we will explore the impact of the Rainbow Coalition created by the Reverend Jesse Jackson, the Arcoredes rainbow networks that have been working for social change in Mexico, the Rainbow Alliance that is causing rapid and positive change within the European Parliament, and the concept of "ecobanks" or "rainbow banks" that has taken root in Mexico and Europe.

These glimpses of history are only a few contemporary effects of the rainbow spirit on our global society during the eighties. Nevertheless, when considered together with the ongoing rainbow enterprises of the seventies and the sweeping political changes coming about on the world scene, they help to show more specifically how the rainbow is a harbinger of good news as we move into the last decade of the century and the beginning of a new millennium.

Jesse Jackson's Rainbow Coalition
Alberto Ruz Buenfil

Not all of the groups that adopted the rainbow as their symbol were inspired by a desire to bring about a global paradigm shift—at least not consciously. For example, the Rainbow Coalition, founded by the Reverend Jesse Jackson in 1984, was created primarily for political reasons. Even so, it had far-reaching consequences that have contributed greatly to the global shift in consciousness.

Jesse Louis Jackson was born in South Carolina in 1941. During the sixties, he moved to the black ghettoes of Chicago, where he became a Baptist preacher. Later, he joined the Civil Rights movement and became a close follower of black pacifist leaders such as Martin Luther King and Ralph Abernathy. In 1971, Jackson founded and became president of People United to Serve Humanity (PUSH), a new organization struggling to defend the civil rights of U.S. blacks.

Jackson first gained national attention when he openly challenged the credentials of the Illinois delegation at the 1972 Democratic National Convention, and in 1979, he was heavily criticized for supporting Palestine Liberation Organization (PLO) leader Yasser Arafat.

In 1983, Jackson played a key role in helping Chicago's Harold Washington become the first black mayor of a large U.S. city, a feat that earned him great popularity among black voters in the United States. As a result, Jackson decided to run for president in 1984.

From the beginning, he planned and conducted his campaign almost as a messianic crusade. Even Frank Watkins, Jackson's press secretary, expressed Jackson's mission as "more a prophetic than a political one." Jackson saw himself as contemporary David ready to confront Ronald Reagan, the biggest Goliath of the day, and he counted on as many as ten million black supporters.

Jackson knew he had little chance of being chosen as a presidential nominee by the relatively conservative Democratic Party. For this reason, he decided to create a more widespread political alliance, a coalition of organizations throughout the country with headquarters in Washington, D.C. This alliance was soon baptized the "Rainbow Coalition."

Headed by some twenty different state organizations, it was created as an independent force within the Democratic Party—a force that was intended to address not only the needs of black voters but the needs of *all* racial and economic minorities.

In the beginning, Jackson intended to use the Rainbow Coalition and the presidential campaign as a forum to make people more aware of the problems of U.S. minority groups. It was a perfect way to call the world's attention to the needs of people who otherwise would have no effective way of making themselves heard.

During the campaign, Jackson's popularity grew, in large part because of his personal charisma and the intensity of his colorful speeches. He also took advantage of his candidacy to make some bold and spectacular political moves, and in so doing he quickly learned how to use the enormous power of the media to his advantage.

Originally, there were eight Democratic candidates in the 1984 campaign. Only two of these besides Jackson survived the primaries: Walter Mondale and Gary Hart. Jackson's theatrical way of presenting himself, his rhetorical speeches, and his frequent use of biblical quotes generated more and more attention from voters both black and white, all over the country.

During the state conventions, the Rainbow Coalition widened its base, receiving support from groups of all denominations and colors. After only a few months of campaigning, Jackson became the champion of the poor, formulating a political platform that went "beyond races, religions, and geopolitical borders." He was also the first U.S. presidential candidate to openly declare his opposition to nuclear power plants and to the civil and military programs that depend on them.

His clear statements against the military budget, pesticides, and nuclear power gained him support from pacifists and environmentalists alike. Then in Texas, he won the support of Mexican-Americans. From there, he went south into Mexico, where he strongly condemned Ronald Reagan's interventionist policies in Central America and offered himself as an intermediary between the Central American people and the Department of State. He also attacked the Simpson-Mazzolli Bill, a proposed law to legalize the harassment and expulsion of Mexicans from southern agricultural states where they represented a majority of the work force.

In January 1984, Jackson traveled to the Middle East. There, during a meeting with Syrian president Hafez Assad, he secured the release of U.S. airman Robert Goodman, who had been shot down over Syrian-held territory in Lebanon the previous month. With this act, he drew international attention to himself and his campaign, and he took advantage of his position to make some pro-Arabic declarations and to assail Reagan's policies of terrorism in the Middle East.

Reagan had no alternative but to publicly thank Jackson for his "courageous personal mission of compassion," and Goodman was welcomed back as a national hero. With this deed, Jackson added new colors to his rainbow banner and new support to his growing campaign for the presidency.

However, not long afterward, Jackson made some serious political mistakes. Fearing for his personal safety, he asked Black Muslim leader Louis Farrakhan and some members of Farrakhan's paramilitary group, The Fruit of Islam, to serve as his bodyguards. Farrakhan abused his new position, viciously attacking the Jewish-American population and Judaism in general. He even publicly expressed his admiration for Adolf Hitler, thus provoking a strongly negative public reaction.

Then Jackson himself made an unforgivable mistake when he referred to the Jewish people as "Hymies" and to New York as "Hymietown." This anti-Semitic remark not only sparked a general attack from the conservative press, but also lost considerable credibility for Jackson's Rainbow Coalition. Because of it, many of Jackson's Jewish-American and southern Democratic allies left him.

Even after these major political blunders, however, Jackson was still able to win the support of black voters in Alabama, Florida, and Georgia, as well as in the ghettoes of the big northern cities. Their combined support made Jackson the most prominent black leader in the history of the United States. As his popularity grew, the Democratic Party began to worry about the role he might play at the Democratic National Convention in San Francisco, slated for July 1984.

In June, Jackson went to Cuba to meet with Fidel Castro. There, he obtained the release of forty-eight prisoners, including twenty-two U.S. citizens who had been accused of smuggling drugs and weapons. On the same trip, he journeyed to Panama and Nicaragua and met with Sandinista leader Daniel Ortega. In Nicaragua, he publicly condemned the presence of U.S. armed forces in Panama and Central America, as well as the support being given to the Salvadoran Contras by the U.S. State Department and the CIA.

At the conclusion of this journey, just before Jackson's plane landed again in the United States, a stewardess announced to all the passengers, "We have a rainbow on the left side of the aircraft." Many of those present took this as an omen, and a week later *Time* and *Newsweek* magazines were packed with photos of Jesse Jackson and the latest news of his unusual political crusade. Jackson now had strong and widespread support, not only from radical black voters and civil-rights organizations, but from Arabs, Hispanics, Chinese, and Japanese; pacifists and environmentalists; homosexuals and feminists; Central America supporters and white liberals. For the first time, the media had to take him seriously.

In June, Jackson announced that if he were chosen as the Democratic candidate for president, he would choose a woman as his running mate. His speeches and sermons became more and more messianic. His audiences cried, clapped, cheered, chanted, and screamed every time he took the microphone. Slogans such as "Win, Jesse, win," "It's time for a change," and "Rainbow! Rainbow!" became increasingly popular. By now, the Rainbow Coalition had become truly multicolored. Only 50 percent of its active members were black; the rest were a mix of people from all parts of the racial and social spectrum.

The 1984 Democratic Convention

Days before the Democratic National Convention in San Francisco, the Rainbow Coalition called for a "People's Convention" in Oakland, California. This convention featured workshops of many kinds: how to build local, regional, state, and national "Rainbow Alliances"; how to protect small farmers from agribusiness; how to fight the Simpson-Mazzolli Bill; how to stop U.S. intervention in Central America; and how to protect the civil rights of gays and prisoners. At this convention, dozens of unions and interdependent groups, as well as antimilitary and pacifist groups, were given full support by the Rainbow Coalition. Concurrently, pro-Jackson marches were held by the major labor union organizations on July 15 and 16, and a candlelight procession for gay rights drew people from every faith and walk of life.

During the first days of July, hundreds of groups and delegates converged on San Francisco. Walter Mondale had chosen Geraldine Ferraro as his running mate, Gary Hart had assumed the torch of the old Kennedy liberalism, and those who were unhappy with either of these options readied themselves to support Jesse Jackson in his crusade against the Reagan "Goliath."

As always, a plethora of groups used the convention as a forum for their goals, which included everything from nonnuclear policies to the legalization of marijuana. Among the personalities who spoke supporting Jackson were antinuclear activist Helen Caldicott, longtime pacifist leader Dave Dellinger, Native American leader Bill Wapehpah, South African poet Dennis Brutus, Chicano leader Velia Silva Garcia, and German Green Party member Uli Fischer.

On the first day of the convention, Jackson supporters held a huge peace march, and on July 17, they all waited for their leader's rousing convention speech. The Democratic Party feared that Jackson might break away and go independent, which to them would be a catastrophe. Without his support, neither Hart nor Mondale would have the majority of votes necessary to become the party's official candidate. In the streets outside the convention hall, thousands of people awaited Jackson's radical departure from the party.

When the dramatic moment arrived, however, Jackson checked his radical tendencies. Instead of breaking with the Democrats as his followers had hoped, he offered his support to the Mondale-Ferraro ticket and called on his followers to accept his decision: "The time has arrived, and now is the moment," he said. "The forces of our faith, hope, and dreams have triumphed, and we should stand up and rise all together."

Jackson acknowledged that neither he nor his party were perfect. But while he asked his Rainbow Coalition to support Mondale, he also emphasized that his concession was strategic. "God hasn't finished with me yet," he concluded, "and I ask my sympathizers to have a little more patience."

Disillusioned, thousands of Jackson followers decided to hold a "Counter-Republican Convention" and a "Caravan for Peace" during the Republican National Convention in Dallas in August. From San Francisco, hundreds of vehicles and thousands of Rainbow Coalition crusaders left for Texas, while other thousands headed in the same direction from the Rainbow Gathering for World Peace at California's Mount Shasta. Other hundreds of demonstrators, including representatives of Native American groups from all over the United States, left the "Peace Camp" that had gathered in the Four Corners area of New Mexico. All of these people had one major agenda for the summer of 1984: to change the world.

In Dallas, the Peace Caravan was met by the police, and hundreds were arrested or wounded. Then, in November, the Mondale-Ferraro ticket was crushed by the Reagan-Bush machine, leaving the U.S. and the world with the bleak prospect of another four years of conservative, authoritarian, militaristic leadership.

Toward a Rainbow Political Party

A year later, Jackson declared that even though it was painful to try to do good on Earth, this should not dissuade anyone from trying to realize "The Dream." Noting the time it takes for ideas to take root, he called on the Rainbow Coalition to reconvene as an umbrella organization for all minority groups. Jackson still recognized himself as a Democrat, but he saw the Rainbow Coalition as an organization independent of the Democratic Party.

In 1985, while continuing to count on the support of the Chicano, Arab-American, black, and feminist organizations, he planned a series of political actions, including a fundraising campaign, a protest of apartheid in South Africa, and a "National Convention of the Rainbow Coalition." In that year, Jackson traveled to Nicaragua, South Africa, Ethiopia, Somalia, and Sudan. The Rainbow Coalition established its central offices in Chicago, and up through 1987 Jackson continued to ask the dissidents of the Democratic Party for their support.

Preparing for the 1988 presidential election, Jackson's followers held a national convention in 1986, in order to establish Rainbow Coalition offices for district, state, and congressional races. Always seeking the support of ethnic, economic, and other minorities, the Rainbow Coalition restated its platform for 1988: more black delegates in the Democratic Party; more support for agriculture; cleanup of toxic wastes; and replacing nuclear power with alternative, renewable energy sources.

Jackson did not win the Democratic nomination for president in 1988; however, he was doubtless the most charismatic of the candidates, and he received widespread support from vast sectors of the U.S. population. His only real opponent in the Atlanta convention was Michael Dukakis, who finally was forced to adopt many of the ideas on Jackson's platform. In the end, Jackson did more to unite the Democrats in 1988 than any of the other candidates. In fact, it was partially because of Jackson's influence that the Republicans, even though they gained the presidency, lost their majority in the Senate and the House.

It is unlikely that the world will ever again hear from Dukakis and Gore as presidential candidates. By contrast, Jackson continues to grow as a political figure. He has also matured in his outlook and mode of expression. Just before the convention, in the July/August 1988 issue of *Mother Jones*, he reflected on the thrust of his campaign with the following words:

> Our agenda has been from the beginning peace, justice and jobs. Our ambition, to unite our constituency. Our deal, to capture the nation's imagination and find common ground for change.
>
> As I've campaigned this year, people have crossed ancient lines of race, religion and region to come together. They may be black or white or brown, but however different their numerators, the denominator is the same. They are victims of economic violence. They need a health care system, affordable housing, schools for their children. They grope for alternatives to war and threats of war, and to the growing isolation of the United States in the world community.

In spite of its two political "defeats," then, Jackson's Rainbow Coalition has won a far greater victory than most people imagine. In fact, it is the expression of a new and rapidly growing popular will. It is in the vanguard of a new spirit that is aligned not only with the rainbow actions of the seventies but with major world changes such as the Russian *perestroika* and *glasnost* directed by another charismatic leader, Mikhail Gorbachev. Regardless of whether the Rainbow Coalition evolves into a full-fledged political party, it is a powerful example of how the spirit of the rainbow is nurturing new growth and positive direction for the country and the world.

The Rainbow Networks in Mexico
Sandra Comneno

The words "net" and "web" have many meanings, but their basic concept is the same. They are strong, flexible structures composed of elements united in a common pattern or idea, and their strength is created by the interlocking pattern of the individual elements. In a net or web, everything is connected: one strand affects another, whether the web is one of good thoughts, a loosely knit group of individuals, or a worldwide communications web.

Such is the "rainbow network" in Mexico. This web of ecologically minded people began in February 1984, during a housing symposium held near the city of Toluca. At this symposium, a large number of Mexican alternative and environmental groups came together for the first time to discuss alternative sources of energy, appropriate technology, and related environmental concerns.

Of supreme importance to all of us at the symposium was the objective of resolving our differences and deciding what we could do together to help the planet. With these goals, the symposium became an opportunity for all of us "green" activists of Mexico to strengthen our common bonds and begin to form an effective network.

In the same month, the first meeting of the Net of Alternative Ecommunications (the REA) took place at the headquarters of Bioconservacion, a pioneering environmental association in Mexico City. We REA participants had high expectations. We spoke enthusiastically about the green movement in Mexico and about the possibility of starting an "organic products" market to benefit small farms and communities around Mexico City. We also spoke about creating an information network and a magazine to promote our visions and accomplishments.

Every month after that, the members of the newly formed REA network met in a different part of the country. At each meeting, we spent a whole day together, dedicating an hour or so to talking about the ecological situation in Mexico and then bartering our natural products in an atmosphere of friendship and tranquillity.

Each event was a bit like a party. Each month, we became more familiar with each other. We talked about social change, the quality of life, peaceful revolution, alternative medicine, and holistic education. From our beginnings in 1984 to June 1986, we had twenty-eight meetings and our membership steadily increased. The disparate strands of the green alternative movement were quickly knitting themselves into a stronger web.

In the fall of 1984, even before the end of our first year, the REA gave birth to an editorial cooperative called "Arcoredes," or "Net of Rainbows." We projected not just one, but dozens of "rainbow nets" that would stretch out all over the Earth, uniting all of us in the shining possibility of a better world. Arcoredes took the form of a quarterly magazine of the same name, produced by the REA and distributed throughout Mexico. Our idea was to create a true editorial cooperative in which all interested ecological groups could participate.

In the production of *Arcoredes, the Alternatives of Ecommunication* magazine, no one was forced to do anything; everything happened according to the will and energy of each individual. Another interesting aspect of the magazine was that any person or group could participate by buying one or two pages of space and doing whatever they wanted with it. In this way, *Arcoredes* became a huge collage of information that eloquently illustrated what the network was all about: an experiment in democratic, alternative communication.

Much to our surprise, within months *Arcoredes* was being read all over the world. It was sold not only all over Mexico but in the best alternative bookstores and newsstands of Europe, Japan, and South America. It was even presented at an ecological symposium in Nairobi, Kenya, and its distribution sparked a widespread exchange of ecological publications between numerous countries.

With the release of each issue of the magazine, the REA sponsored public events featuring music, slide shows, organic products, and discussions and presentations of all kinds. These events helped to promote the magazine.

However, in the fall of 1986, plagued by financial problems, *Arcoredes* was forced to discontinue publication. Temporarily, we found a voice in the cultural section of *El Dia*, one of Mexico's most widely read newspapers. *El Dia*'s editors offered us the "Spaces of Freedom" section in the Sunday edition of the paper. However, this was not the same. To feel constrained in our dream because of financial reasons was a defeat that left a bitter taste in our mouths.

Several of us continued to fill *El Dia*'s pages, taking turns writing articles each week for two more years. In this way, *Arcoredes* continued to exist until June 1988, when *El Dia* was taken over by the federal government. Subsequently, though, the editors of the paper's cultural supplement were all forced to resign and the "Spaces of Freedom" section disappeared, leaving a black hole in the alternative Mexican press that has yet to be filled.

The Sweatlodge of Our Dreams

Not to be dismayed, the REA network soon found another outlet for its idealism. Inspired by an audiovisual show created by REA members from three alternative communities, we put together a forty-minute show explaining through slides, music, and drama exactly what was happening to the planet and what could be done to reverse the trend. This multimedia presentation also explained how the network operated and how to get involved.

The show was entitled *Temazcal*, meaning "Sweatlodge," after the ceremonial cleansing lodge of the Native Americans. For the next two years, we presented it at schools, universities, cultural centers, public plazas, and state agencies throughout the country. In Mexico, *Temazcal* became known as the production that brought the "good green news" of the New Age. The show appealed to young and old alike and consistently raised people's environmental awareness.

As an offshoot of *Temazcal*, the REA network also formulated a series of minicourses featuring a number of practical things people could do to better the quality of their lives and tune into the rhythms of nature. These courses and workshops were followed by a series of conferences that took in-depth looks at many of the key causes of the world's ecological disasters. We also developed presentations for school children of all ages.

In these ways, *Temazcal* became part of a much more widely articulated project. In fact, even today, some of the original *Temazcal* performers, who now belong to a group called "Ecosolar," continue to develop this ambitious program, taking it not only to rural and indigenous communities of Mexico, but also to communities in Guatemala, El Salvador, and Nicaragua. Other REA and *Temazcal* members, such as myself, have taken on the ecological education of the children at our local primary school, Cetiliztli, where we have developed a pilot educational program for the state of Morelos.

Legacy of the 1985 Earthquake

After one of our *Temazcal* shows, someone asked me, "Where do you get all your energy?" After a long pause, I answered, "When two hands shake, there is always a subtle imprint left behind."

This is exactly what happened on the morning of September 19, 1985, when all of Mexico City began shaking uncontrollably in the throes of a massive earthquake. We held hands because we were scared; because, as far as we knew, it might be the last time we could hold hands; and because there was nothing else we could do. In the long run, though, the earthquake and all our cooperative hand holding brought us all closer together, made survival and rebuilding possible, and even changed the environmental direction of the country.

Two times that year, Mexico City was hit by devastating earthquakes, and those of us who survived were grateful to come out of the rubble unharmed. Not wanting to be alone or hoping to ease the pain, we REA members and friends held hands many times during those crises. At other times, we joined hands in an "Aum" of peace to restore our faith or to bring us a little tranquillity.

The earthquake was a time for testing the unity of the REA. Our work was constant, hard, and extensive on many fronts. Those hit by the quake were in dire need of basics: medical help, drinking water, food, shelter, and sleep. They also needed to know where to go, what to do about aftershocks, how to look for relatives and friends, how to stay sane, and in some cases how to go on living.

The REA organized itself in several ways. First, we formed the

"Green Brigades," a series of first-aid groups that offered both advice and practical solutions. Second, we improvised camps for the homeless, camps that included necessities such as dry outhouses, purified water storage, medicines, and relaxing music. We also established direct contact with people in an attempt to minimize emotional breakdown and panic.

The REA network was very effective. In fact, soon even the Mexican government officially recognized the importance of our work in easing Mexico City's pain. Two weeks after the first catastrophe, a meeting took place at the community of Huehuecoyotl for all the REA volunteers who had worked so hard. At sunset, seventy to eighty of us all held hands in a silent circle. The moon was rising in full splendor, and a slight tension filled the air. We were all preparing to go into the sweatlodge together.

Suddenly a rumor spread among us that the Mexican Minister of Ecology had come to thank us for our collective efforts and to find out more about our activities. No sooner had the rumor made its rounds than the minister appeared, dressed in high-heeled shoes, making her difficult way over the rocky road leading to Huehuecoyotl.

After the formal greetings were finished, I approached the minister and asked whether she wanted to join us in the sweatlodge. I explained that if she had not brought a towel, I would gladly lend her mine. She stared at me for a moment, then disappeared. A few days later, we discovered that a rumor had gotten around the city that some reckless fool had invited the minister to a forbidden ritual in the mountains of Tepoztlan, thus offending her sense of public decency. We were immediately marked as rash adventurers and "green terrorists."

For a Just Society in Harmony with Nature

Toward the end of November 1985, Mexico City hosted the First National Symposium on Ecology. After the September quakes, this event had suddenly taken on great national importance, and it quickly became a forum for debate about the ecological situation in Mexico.

For those of us in the REA, the symposium was the high point of two years of communal work, giving us direct access to a wide range of environmental thinkers and organizations. It also offered us an opportunity to evaluate the ecological progress of the nation.

Discussions at the symposium centered around the search for consensus on ecological issues, on prioritizing strategic actions, and on various proposals for a national environmental organization. Space was dedicated to exhibiting appropriate technologies and organic products and to ecological publications and slide shows.

The symposium helped us realize that in relatively few years our numbers had grown considerably and that we had come a long way with our own alternative, self-sufficient lifestyles. The gathering ended on Sunday, November 24, with an REA parade through the southern part of Mexico City. The march was for peace, disarmament, alternative energy, and an unpolluted world. It was also a call for cooperation and solidarity in our goal of healing the planet. The memory of the earthquake was still fresh in people's minds, and they were very open to our message. Though basically it was a march of protest, it came across as a celebration—a colorful return of hope parading through the gray, rubble-strewn streets of the city. It was an occasion to celebrate our unity, our common interest in taking the first steps toward a healthy future.

Decentralization

One of the main themes of the symposium had been decentralization—the need to ease the burden and danger by encouraging large populations of people to move away from the confines of Mexico City. After the terrifying experience of the earthquakes, many people had begun to realize how absurd it was to continue living inside the city with no prospect of getting out in the event of a disaster.

Consequently, several hundred families left Mexico City, and environmental groups began doing the same. On the one hand, the REA had even more interest in fighting for the rights of the urban people, since the government's abuse of power was growing more blatant by the month. On the other hand, there was also compelling evidence of a need to work in the countryside, to create new, functional alternatives to life in the city. Even within the REA, we felt these contradictions.

Gradually, a change began taking place. Small, decentralized networks were created, especially in the states of Morelos, Jalisco, Puebla, Chiapas, Veracruz, and Quintana Roo. Various groups throughout these states decided to start an exchange based on their regional needs.

Priority was given to local interests and to the support of country living over city living.

Our own experiences with Huehuecoyotl in the state of Morelos were stimulating and inspiring to many other newly formed communities, and several meetings were held in our region around the end of 1986. From these meetings, a small group was born, and together we planned a series of educational courses in the schools, a future "green university," and the exchange of alternative medicinal knowledge. Many of the most renowned healers and herbalists in Mexico accepted our invitation to share their wisdom with urban apprentices.

These and many other initiatives emerged from the idea of decentralization. The idea also led us to fruitful relationships with other bioregional networks, which helped greatly to focus our plans for the future.

Even so, the dispersion of people and energies that was primed by decentralization did not fit with our original vision of thinking and acting globally. As decentralization progressed and individual groups became increasingly absorbed by the needs of their own specific areas, the REA lost some of its strength and impact as a national network.

Only in 1990, almost four years later, did the local networks begin to reflect the kind of strength the REA had originally had as a national network. Today, in Morelos, Guadalajara, Veracruz, and Mexico City, the emerging eco-movement identifies more and more with the principles adopted by the bioregional congresses in the United States.

Deep Ecology in Mexico

In our hearts, many of us REA founders continued looking for an opportunity to initiate some new projects together. In mid-1987 we got our chance with the First Seminar and Conferences on Deep Ecology in Mexico. This seminar was held June 1–5 at the national School of Anthropology in Mexico City. It was organized by three of the groups that originally belonged to the REA: the Grupo de Estudios Ambientales, one of the Mexican collectives of the sixties that is trying to synthesize the principles of ecology with the traditions of indigenous cultures; Sobrevivencia, a similar group formed in Mexico City during the seventies; and the alternative community of Huehuecoyotl.

The seminar was a great opportunity for a much-needed debate among the green activists of Mexico. During that debate, we all learned the difference between ecology and "deep ecology." In non-scientific, social terms, the word "ecology" refers to all the methods, studies, alternative energy sources, and appropriate technologies that serve to bring our lives more in tune with nature (not to be confused with the "superficial ecology," the kind practiced by many governmental and private institutions to cover up their environmental crimes and mistakes). Deep ecology, on the other hand, is a philosophy that tries to deepen and complement an ecological lifestyle through a better understanding of the complexity and interrelationship of our global problems. It deals simultaneously with the theoretical, ethical, and moral aspects of ecology, and its ultimate purpose is to reestablish an equilibrium between humanity and nature. The deep ecology movement springs from diverse disciplines, including the natural sciences and the traditional popular and spiritual wisdom of ancient indigenous peoples. It promotes bioregionalism, unity in diversity, appropriate technology, better use of natural resources, and a respect for all life.

While organizing the event, we had many disagreements about the spiritual aspects of deep ecology. For some members of the environmental movement—especially those with a "leftist" understanding of the world—to speak of spirituality seemed out of place, almost heretical. However, we finally agreed that the time was right for a deeper approach.

In the end, we invited four speakers from the United States: Bill Deval, author of *Deep Ecology*; John Milton, president of the Threshold Foundation; David Haenke, one of the organizers of the First Bioregional Congress in the U.S.; and Peter Berg, president of Planet Drum Foundation. Their presentations gave us a clearer understanding of the reasons for our need to go deeper. By the end of the conference, we had spent two days in a closed room, letting go of all our doubts, fears, and inner needs. We came out with an increased desire to continue our work, not only in the external world but also in our own inner world. We understood better that nature is not just "out there," but also a part of ourselves.

After the seminar, some groups in the REA network continued to work independently, while others chose to join the government. Some formed a small "green party," while others formed a group called "The

One Hundred," a loose network of artists whose purpose is to help the national Ministry of Ecology in the "green" reconstruction of Mexico.

Over the years, the members of the REA network have grown together, each one harvesting his or her own needed fruits. A spirit of friendship, brotherhood, and community still prevails in our relationships, person to person and group to group. On August 16–17, 1987, for example, many of us celebrated Harmonic Convergence, an entering into the new Age of Aquarius prophesied by the esoteric legends of the Maya and North American Indians. This was a moment of great cosmic energy, and it helped to create a new phase of cleansing for our lives.

In 1988 in Tepoztlan, an hour away from Mexico City, a group of ecologists, artists, and parents (many of whom had participated in the REA network) began a project called Cetiliztli, a Nahuatl name meaning "staying together." Our main objective is to create an ecological center that will bring a number of long-term benefits to the entire community.

One of these is a new building for our ecological school for children, which has been functioning since 1982. This is the first holistic school in the state of Morelos and one of the very first Mexican models of environmental and spiritually oriented education.

Second, we intend to strengthen and expand a center for local indigenous women called Luna Nueva ("the new moon"), which has been working with the women of Santo Domingo, Ocotitlan, near Huehuecoyotl. We are also creating the first "green" university and an international library for the local community that will allow young people to get instruction in approriate technology, ecoshops, ecological planning, and related subjects.

In 1989, we received a piece of land in the valley of Atongo, and in August 1990 we began construction on the school. Included in this project will be a system to reclaim rainwater in cisterns, a patch of land for biological farming, a tank for pisciculture, and the new building for our elementary school.

Thus, we are seeking new alternatives of life for our children and ourselves, building the foundation for a freer and greener future—not only for us, but also as a model for future generations, here and in other places in the country and the world.

Now, the net has been cast, and the spider spins without ceasing. The once-small rainbow web has become huge, extending beyond all previous horizons. Now it is time to weave the threads more tightly and join them together. It is time to consolidate and explore the new geography and the new world that is growing within the web. For through the strands of that living, pulsating web flows the green blood that feeds the plants, the Earth, and all our relations.

Editor's note: During the seventies, Sandra Comneno was a radical activist in the Italian feminist movement. In 1980, she moved to Mexico, where she became one of the founders and main inspirations of the alternative community of Huehuecoyotl. She is one of the founders of the Arcoredes cooperative and has been continuously active in promoting the Mexican alternative movement. She is also a writer and a mother who is dedicated to helping her daughter, Ixchel, grow up as a free being.

The Rainbow Gatherings in Europe

Roots of the Gatherings
The European Rainbow Circle

In Europe, the Rainbow Gathering movement took root very gradually. It began in 1977 with a festival in which several thousand people shared in the first "Happening of the New Age." This festival, which was repeated in subsequent years, featured courses, songs, music, dance, theater, and workshops that focused on living simply with nature. After three years, however, the festivals were discontinued. Everyone had become too involved with projects of their own to make time for further celebrations.

Then two things helped to catalyze the gatherings. First, several people met one summer in a small village near Mount Truth, Switzerland, for what proved to be an inspiring summer experience in alternative community living. Second, some active members of the Swiss alternative press founded Friistarne Uni ("Free Star University"), which began to coordinate alternative living courses and activities.

This group's strongly provocative and liberal attitude met with official resistance. Intending to hold the free-minded movement in check, the Swiss government issued a number of restrictions, including the prohibition of mass gatherings. However, the first steps had already been taken, and in spite of continued governmental resistance, little could be done to stop the gathering movement.

Between 1980 and 1983, we met several times to live together in tipis, to organize small festivals, and to take various courses offered by the Free Star University. From these moments of togetherness, two of us were inspired to organize the first European Rainbow Gathering in Switzerland.

This was in early 1983, which left us very little time to prepare for the gathering by summer. Another drawback was our lack of experience. The two of us had attended Rainbow Gatherings in the United States, but aside from that, we had only our previous camping experience to rely on. The problems we faced were enormous. Ironically, though, our greatest problem proved not to be our lack of organizational experience, but getting permission from the Swiss government to gather peacefully in a public wilderness area.

We had chosen a lonely Swiss mountaintop not far from the Italian border. Because of the government's recalcitrance, we decided to move our site to Val di Campo on the Italian side of the mountain, where the Swiss authorities would be powerless and where, ten hours' walk from the nearest Italian village, the Italian police would not easily be able to reach us.

As the gathering convened, Swiss customs officials on the mountain border grew suspicious of the unusual movement of two hundred people (mostly Swiss and Germans) plus supply-laden horses and donkeys across the border, but before long we convinced them that we were doing nothing illegal. Finally, in the wilderness mountain surroundings of Val di Campo, we built our first community kitchen, tipi circle, latrines, information tent, sweatlodges, and, in a dry part of the riverbed, a stone temple called "Meditation Island."

For a first try, the gathering was small but successful. During the fifteen days we spent in natural solitude, we learned to work in council, listen to each other, and establish a primitive community from scratch. It was a good beginning.

Editor's note: The foregoing section was written collectively by Italian, French, and Swiss members of the European Rainbow Tribal Council.

The Gatherings Expand
Paolo Silkworm

About fifteen of us who convened for the first European Rainbow Gathering in 1983 met several times during the following year to deepen our spiritual bonds and develop ideas for the future. We also began to meet interested people from other European countries, and our problems intensified.

One problem was a multilingual council. Other problems included our lack of flexibility and a growing gap between the organizers of the gathering, the "Rainbow Hats," and its participants. Our main failing as organizers is that we neglected to get people to share the organizational load. In the end, the second gathering became an event enjoyed by many but planned and executed by very few. This was not as it should have been. As the American experience had already shown, the power of the gathering comes through everyone's participation.

For these reasons, in preparation for the 1985 gathering in Italy, we tried to get in touch with new people in every country on the continent and to get them involved early in the planning process. We also thought of shortening the event to prevent the loss of energy we had experienced during our previous two fifteen-day gatherings.

The site we chose for the 1985 gathering was near a tough mountain community called Acquacheta in the Tuscany Apennines in Italy. The only drawback of the area was the fact that it was on private property. Normally, we would have chosen a site on public land in order to add strength and legitimacy to our right of assembly. However, the land around Acquacheta had exceptional features, including thick woods and incredibly beautiful waterfalls. Thus, using some subtle diplomacy, we were granted use of the land, and in the process we learned much about how to negotiate and gain the trust of local people.

Because of our increased numbers and because of marked differences in language and national character, the 1985 gathering was somewhat chaotic. Even so, it included many joyful events and even some remarkable decisions, including an agreement between the Rainbow Council and the local authorities to jointly buy the land where the gathering had been held, in order to prevent the construction of a scenic road. However, from that summer on, the key word became "consolidation." We became acutely aware of the danger of expanding the size and scope of the gathering too fast; we still needed to stabilize.

For the site of the fourth gathering, we initially chose the Spanish Pyrenees Mountains in hopes of getting the French people involved, too. On the verge of the gathering, for logistical reasons, we moved the site to a mountain pass in French territory, and there we came to grips with the French police.

The police maintained that such an event would be unacceptable without proper authorization, yet at the same time they made it virtually impossible to obtain it. For two weeks, we tried to negotiate, without success. This put even more pressure on us as we struggled to establish a makeshift settlement to accommodate some two thousand people atop the windy pass. There, we also encountered a serious lack of water. This, coupled with ongoing police harassment, caused many of our number to give up and leave.

Finally, in a desperate move to avoid the police, the day after the gathering began we took shelter on top of a mountain seven hundred feet higher than the pass, a place so inaccessible that finally we were left alone.

From an objective perspective, the gathering could be considered a major failure—not only from a public relations standpoint but also because the lack of water and the bad weather combined to make it more a test of endurance than a collective celebration. On the second day, when the facilities were still not ready, a heavy, cold rain made the situation even worse.

Yet from another point of view, the gathering was a success in ways we could never have planned or foreseen. Finally the rain let up and the kitchen facilities were ready. Counting all the joyous welcome hugs, about fifteen hundred people came to the fourth gathering on the Col de Mantet, and the very toughness of the conditions there initiated our wished-for consolidation. Though we could not count on the evening tribal councils due to the bitter cold after sundown, spiritual activities were never lacking. Some tough aficionados even held all-night drumming sessions, finding warmth and comfort in their rhythms and in the blaze of the bonfires.

Gradually, both at the gathering and afterward, a new awareness dawned on us: we needed more frequent local meetings and better local coordination in order to make the next gathering a success. Our experience in the Pyrenees had also enhanced our wish to experience the rainbow vision more deeply. As if responding to this desire, the Spanish Comunidad del Arcoiris offered to host some of the organization meetings for 1987, and soon we chose Asturias, Spain as the site of our next gathering.

We made our festive camp in a sweet, grassy valley surrounded by rocky hills and mountains near the town of Asturias. The gathering was marked with bright flashes of creative enthusiasm, music and drums, night calls to dance in the middle of the tipi circle, and warm hearts and effusive hugs.

This gathering also inspired something else that was new to us. In spite of objections from the authorities, the local people themselves showed approval and benevolence. Even though it was an hour's walk to the camp from the nearest village, many village dwellers came to celebrate with us. In this way, we were even able to share the ancient legends of the place, a place where Celts had once held their own holy rituals and ceremonies.

The 1988 gathering was a real turning point. Our camp, scattered through a wide, flower-filled valley, again near Asturias in Spain, became the geographic glue that bonded many culturally diverse groups. Though the "neighborhoods" at the gathering encampment tended to organize themselves according to nationality, the continuous interchange of activity guaranteed a flow of energy and enthusiasm from one end of the camp to the other. We had finally succeeded in forming a polychromous area, a true linguistic and cultural rainbow, rich in Latin and Anglo-Saxon components.

Through correspondence, we had also created a living bridge across the ocean, a colored bridge that united the North American and European gatherings. This time, we had scheduled our European gathering for the week following the North American gathering. In this way, some people from both continents were able to participate in both. Moreover, never before at a European gathering had there been so much spontaneous cooperation in the construction and maintenance of facilities. Finally we were making good progress toward the creation of a multicultural village.

Editor's note: Paolo Silkworm first discovered the rainbow movement while wandering across the United States. After returning to his native Italy, he became one of the primary focalizers of the Rainbow Gatherings in Europe. Silkworm is also a cofounder of the Aquarius Community in Tuscany, Italy. He now lives with his family in northern Italy, getting ready for a wider and deeper community perspective.

The Making of Pasta Sciutta
Nina Schär

When I am asked what the Rainbow Gathering is all about, among the many important things I never fail to mention are the workshops. Personally, I have attended very few workshops due to my continuous involvement in organizing the gatherings. Even so, I have attended a few, and I remember well the beautiful human interaction that takes place within them.

One common workshop at the gatherings is cooking. During such a workshop, it would not be unusual to find three Italians, a Chilean, two Germans, a Spaniard, a Frenchman, and an American cooking lunch for three to five hundred people in a makeshift camp kitchen. The challenge is always to cook a good, nourishing meal with a few simple ingredients.

First, however, the would-be cooks have to agree on a common language. If this is not possible, they have to quickly learn to talk with their hands and use their common sense. For those who are not watching, the rest remains both a mystery and somewhat of a miracle.

As preparations progress, a rumor may begin to circulate: "We're eating on the plateau." Before long, another rumor makes the rounds: "It's raining; we're eating in the kitchen." Then: "Are you out of your mind? There isn't *room* enough in the kitchen!" Eventually, a burly German makes his way from the kitchen lugging a heavy pot of hot food and shouting, "Heiss, achtung, heiss!" And soon afterward, hungry people with bowls in hand are spooning the nutritious meal into their mouths. Perhaps the vegetables are a little raw, and perhaps the sleepy cook has even mistakenly put dog food in the stew instead of hamburger, but nobody cares.

One actual workshop I remember well was the cooking of fifty-five kilograms of *pasta sciutta*, a mix of numerous different pastas. Two Romans took responsibility for making the sauce. ("Don't worry," they assured us, "we are professionals.") A good many people took turns peeling and cutting vegetables and onions, then left, thinking everything else would take care of itself. The rest of us soon began sweating, having to continually keep turning the pasta over the hot fire.

By this time, most of the cooks were barefoot and half naked. Luckily, the huge pot of pasta had a faucet so that we could drain off the excess boiling liquid. But when we opened it, rigatoni noodles slithered out, one by one, along with the boiling water. A Swiss man, noticing our folly, came by and muttered something to the effect that we shouldn't be wasting so much precious water. At his urging, someone quickly brought a colander, which filled up within seconds and sprayed hot water everywhere.

Finally, we managed to shut the faucet, but the *pasta sciutta* lovers were badly shocked. One of these, an Italian named Franco, began yelling, "A rag, somebody gimme a rag! Come on, guys, let's take it away from the fire!" Five people rushed to lift the two-hundred-kilo pot with a pole through its handle. Shouts and curses erupted in several languages: "Scheisse, der Rauch! . . . Attention les pieds! . . . Moment mal! . . . Piano, porco diavolo, piano ragazzi!"

At this point, a stone shifted and the pot slid away from us all, leaning dangerously over the fire. Though the rope that held the pole got burned, eventually we managed to take the pot from the fire and the pasta from the water. Only a German photographer seemed to have enjoyed the whole process, eagerly snapping pictures of the whole hilarious mess.

At long last, our workshop was over and everyone was well fed. In spite of all the obstacles, our collective zeal and positive energy had seen it to a happy end. Now, having lost my mistrust for improvisation, I happily joined in the multilingual call to dinner: "Essen! . . . A comer! . . . Si mangia! . . . Time to eat, everyone!"

Editor's note: Nina Schär is a Swiss citizen who has been active in the Rainbow Gatherings in Europe. Today, she is working near the city of

Leon, building a "Peace Village" together with a group of young Rainbow Warriors from all over Europe.

The Gathering's Magic
The Sun Knights (Cavalieri del Sole)

We reached our first Rainbow Gathering in Italy after more than an hour of walking over Muraglione Pass, through woods, wading clear brooks, and breathing the perfumes dispersed in the mountain air.

After wading Acquacheta Creek, there in a large, grassy clearing between mountains, we were met with a most wonderful scene: Smoke was rising from the tops of tipis and campfires into a clear sunset sky. Several horses and cows were grazing freely, while children, dogs, men, and women played, tumbled, and haphazardly danced to the rhythm of the drums.

Around a big bonfire, many people—barefoot and shod, dressed and undressed—were dancing, following the slow setting of the sun. On the side of the clearing, on top of a grassy hill, peeped the roofs and ancient walls of an uninhabited village.

It would be impossible to describe all the sensations we felt at such a sight, to tell of the thoughts this scene brought to our minds. Suffice it to say, we had a strong feeling of being "home," of being reabsorbed in a dimension that, however new, felt familiar and warm.

The music moved us all deeply—the music of the air, the mountains, the happy, beating hearts, the hawks gliding high in the sky. But above all, what took hold of us was the magical beating of the drums. It was as if the sound had emerged from some great ancestral depth, as though the heart of the Earth itself were rising up toward heaven. Every day at sunset, the rhythm of the great drum grew stronger. Played by four people simultaneously, its music was joined by shouts, songs, bells, cymbals, and flutes. Flames reflected on the musicians' sweaty faces. Light shone on the sometimes frenzied, sometimes solemn movements of those who offered themselves to the secret forces of the night.

It was almost impossible to resist the call of the night. Some of us did not sleep for even one night, and quite often the dawn, shrouded in wet fog, found us still awake, heating our bread and coffee on the coals or singing our last songs.

One of these mornings, we happened to meet Sougi, the Zen monk. Sougi slept by night, but every morning before sunup he walked through the camp in his long gown, playing a thin, wooden flute, calling the faithful to their t'ai chi lessons. Five times a day, he could be seen reciting an ancient Vedic prayer and offering rice kernels to "Agni," the holy fire, which at other times was fueled with butter and cow excrement.

Music led us to glances, thoughts, and dreams we had never before imagined. Wisdom's holy wind inspired the Tribal Council, enlightening our minds and leading us Rainbow People to peaceful and harmonious solutions to our problems. Such was the gathering's magic.

Nobody knows why it is that the right things always seem to happen at the right time at such gatherings, yet they do. Often we found ourselves confused and amazed by the miracle of music played without knowing how, yet still the notes ran, stirring and heating our souls, riding clouds to the moon.

Back then, our musical technique was quite poor. But it didn't really matter because our sounds were necessary to express something we could not deny. So we used sound to find our long-forgotten connection to the life-restoring rhythms of nature. We used sound to open up again to the wind, grass, trees, and clouds that crowned the high mountains. And when at long last we felt grateful again for the rain, the cold, the hard stones, and the fire, it was because we were not afraid of life anymore and had once again found the blessed path that leads to inner contentment.

Editor's note: The Sun Knights (Cavalieri del Sole) and their spiritual leader, Gray Wolf, are part of a community located in the Bedizzole area of Italy. They produce musical cassettes that record the sounds, rhythms, and songs of the Rainbow artists.

The Rainbow Alliance in European Politics
Octavi Piulats

In less than a decade, a new "green" alliance has made rapid and powerful inroads into European politics. The alliance began in 1983, when a number of "green" political parties and alternative organizations met in Paris with the intent of creating a political platform of real opposition to the EEC, the conservative European Economic Community.

The action of these groups from many nations was motivated by the upcoming 1984 European parliamentary elections. For one thing, the groups wanted to form a "green confederacy" in order to consolidate their power. For another, they wanted to take advantage of the generous financial support that had been offered by the EEC to all European parties or alliances that took part in the 1984 elections. The EEC had declared that any party receiving a minimum of 5 percent of the votes in its own country and 1 percent of the collective vote in three countries had the right to a refund of all its campaign costs.

In April 1984, this group of European pacifist, ecologist, and other minority groups took on the collective name of "Rainbow Alliance." The constituent parties included Die Grünen of West Germany; Ecolo and Agalev of Belgium; Les Verts and Les Verts-Ecologie of France; the Ecological Party of Great Britain; the Comhontas Glas/Green Alliance of Ireland; the Greng Alternative of Luxembourg; the Grun Progressive Allianz of the Netherlands, the Groene Partij Nederland; and several small radical groups. At their convention, the groups agreed to the following platform: (1) to work for all of Europe according to a model different from that of the EEC—that is, to support a neutral, politically decentralized Europe, with full autonomy for each of its regions; (2) to strongly oppose the deployment of nuclear weapons, both in Eastern and Western Europe and to promote real disarmament and the dissolution of the two military power blocs, NATO and the Warsaw Pact; (3) to encourage and aid a consistent ecological policy, resisting the destruction of nature and the process of "asphalting" to which Europe was being subjected; (4) to fight discrimination against women, both in the workplace and in society at large; (5) to encourage a real aid policy for European workers on strike and to uphold the European "social state" model that was being eroded by the conservative governments; (6) to promote a new policy toward the Third World, reorganizing monetary and economic relationships with less favored countries and turning them into relationships based on fair exchange; (7) to uphold a model of Europe in which basic human rights are granted and exercised in full; and (8) to promote ecological agriculture and reduce the chemical pollution of consumer goods.

Growing Power in the European Parliament

The 1984 elections were not very satisfactory for the green and alternative parties. France's green parties went into the elections divided. Les Verts and Verts Party Ecologiste each won 3 percent of the national vote, neither reaching the 5 percent minimum that would allow a reimbursement of campaign costs and access to the European Parliament. Nor did the British or Irish green alliances gain parliament seats, each receiving only 0.5 percent of its country's total votes. Only Die Grünen, with 8.2 percent of the German vote, and the Agalev-Ecolo-Progressive Green Alliance of Belgium and the Netherlands gained access to the parliament.

This situation led the Rainbow Alliance to confer with other political groups, with the intention of forming a parliamentary group broad enough to unite their scattered forces. Thus, the Rainbow Alliance opened up to a greater diversity of regional and progressive political parties.

This move had a positive effect. Just a few years later, in May 1987, the Rainbow Alliance in the European Parliament numbered twenty deputies from ten political parties and six different countries. Since the parties were ideologically quite diverse in spite of their common green stance, they decided to subdivide into three different factions. Ecologist and alternative parties united in the so-called GRAEL faction, nationalist and regional parties formed the EVA, and Danish critics of the EEC formed the DKA. In 1987, the GRAEL faction had thirteen members in Parliament, the EVA had three members, and the DKA four.

Since 1987, the greens in Europe have gained a great deal of political power. Before 1987, France had almost no environmental movement at all. Two years later, Les Verts won almost 10 percent of the general vote. In April 1989, the Fifth Congress of the European Greens was held in Paris, with the enthusiastic presence of all the green organizations of the continent.

In June of that same year, at the European parliamentary elections, green parties in Belgium, Holland, Ireland, Italy, England, Greece, Luxembourg, and France made a strong showing. The British Green Party surprised everyone, winning 14 percent of the national vote and becoming the third most powerful political force in the country with almost two million followers. In similar fashion, the French Verts obtained 13 percent of the vote; the Italian Lista Verde and Arcobaleno (Rainbow Party) won 6.2 percent of the vote, twice the support it had won only two years before.

In the national elections of November 1989, the Swedish green party Miljopartiet increased the number of its votes by 500 percent, breaking through the 5 percent minimum-vote barrier and sending twenty deputies to their national parliament. In Spain, the various green organizations and parties, traditionally at odds with each other, finally came to an agreement and created a green confederation that also participated in the European elections.

Rainbow Structure and Activity

Theoretically, the most decisive branch in the Rainbow Alliance is the General Assembly. But since each of the alliance's three factions acts independently, the General Assembly does not often convene. Instead, the alliance's decisions are made by the "Rainbow Chair," a body that is composed of representatives from each of the three different factions. Four cochairs rotate every three months as representatives of the Rainbow Alliance in the parliament's agencies.

The Rainbow Alliance has vice presidents on several of the most influential of the commissions in the European Parliament: agriculture, environment, and internal regulations and affairs. In addition, it is represented on almost all the other parliamentary commissions with the exception of the Industry and Monetary Funds commissions.

On the commissions and in Parliament itself, the Rainbow Alliance invariably promotes positions that are contrary to the majority. Usually their reports and arguments are rejected by the plenary, but indirectly they exert a very strong influence, especially on the socialists and communists. Besides their parliamentary activity, GRAEL members often participate in extraparliamentary actions, such as demonstrations, political happenings, and organizing meetings on hot issues.

Philosophy and Objectives of Rainbow-GRAEL

As far as GRAEL is concerned, the EEC is characterized by the "mirage effect"—that is, to the EEC, appearances are more important than reality. Although the EEC claims to have the interests and welfare of all Europeans at heart, this is only true on minor issues related to culture and health; it is not true with respect to domestic and foreign policy in general.

The EEC's policy of capital accumulation and superindustrialization, generated through taxation of all Europeans, primarily serves multinational industries and bankers while threatening the health and environment of the taxpayers themselves. In contrast to the huge investments in such environmentally nefarious enterprises as cable TV, nuclear power plants, microelectronics, and more pollution-spouting automobiles, the government's small subsidies to farmers and merchants are mere bread crumbs. This aid, too, is an illusion. Farmers and merchants do not realize that in accepting these subsidies they are becoming more dependent on the multinational industries that dictate prices and methods of cultivation.

The average European is also being cheated through the EEC's foreign policy. EEC preaches peace, but it remains within the NATO Alliance, which because of its dependence on the U.S. can at any moment be turned into an instrument of aggression. Partly because of the Rainbow Alliance's opposition to the policies of the EEC, GRAEL in particular considers the European government's complaints about lack of solidarity mere crocodile tears. If there is a reluctance to give more power to the EEC, it is because European citizens do not fully believe that the European Parliament represents their true interests.

There has also been a great deal of debate over the issue of a future "United States of Europe." As far as GRAEL is concerned, Europe must avoid this kind of homogenization. GRAEL believes that because of its history and traditions, Europe must maintain its rich diversity, and that the proper choice is a federation of independent countries that will maintain respect for European diversity and autonomy.

What of the Future?

In summary, in the 1989 elections the Rainbow Alliance almost doubled the number of its European representatives—from twenty to thirty-eight deputies in three years. For the first time in history, the green votes in the European Parliament have become a decisive weight that can tip the scales that determine the outcome of the international political scene. Now there is even talk about creating the first "Green

International Party" to present a unified front in the continental elections.

For the first time in history, this party would include greens from both Western and Eastern Europe. This possibility has come about largely through the revolutionary Russian policies of glasnost and perestroika that have loosened the political structures of countries throughout Eastern Europe. Within Russia itself, these movements have also sparked the formation of numerous new environmental organizations, and today there is even talk of creating a green splinter group within the Russian Communist Party.

During the eighties, then, the Rainbow Alliance has grown almost astronomically, due to the rising sense of alarm over the destruction of the environment and the continued dehumanizing policies of the EEC. The nineties promise even greater change—change brought about by the need to respond to our environmental emergency and the fervent desire to create a harmonious means of living together in the world community of nations.

Editor's note: Octavi Piulats is a Spaniard by birth and a member of the editorial cooperative Integral in Barcelona. While studying philosophy in Germany, Piulats became a member of Die Grünen, the German Green Party. When he returned to Spain, he began to write about the international environmental situation. His writings include the most comprehensive Spanish report on the consequences of the Russian nuclear disaster at Chernobyl.

The Rainbow Banks
Alberto Ruz Buenfil

Economics has always been a predominant factor in human relationships, as well as in the relationship between humanity and the Earth. Until recently, most economic exchange has been based on purely "rational" criteria—productivity, development, and growth—without taking into consideration the natural relationship that keeps the ecosystem in balance. For some people, there seems to be an inherent contradiction between economics and ecology that will be resolved only when the two sciences are fused into one.

This should be both simple and natural. After all, both words come from the same Greek root, *oikos* or *eco*, which refers to everything that is related to the place where we live—not just our dwellings but also our bodies, our planet, and the place of the Earth in the solar system and the universe. As a step in that direction, we will see in this section how the rainbow consciousness has begun establishing the basis for a world economy—an economy based on a novel form of cooperativism called "ecobanks" or "rainbow banks."

The Popular Cases in Mexico

The Popular Cases are cooperative Mexican banking enterprises. Each Popular Case serves people of a specific locality. These are invariably people who are already bonded socially and culturally and who want to use their common capital to find solutions to their credit and savings needs. In a Popular Case, each member owns part of the company and can save, obtain low-interest loans, and participate in the company's direction.

The main purpose of a Popular Case is to hold the capital savings of its members. The capital, in turn, is used to protect the families of each member and to increase the resources of the cooperative. Through the solidarity it creates, it is also used to maintain a friendly community environment and to strengthen the bonds of trust between members of the community.

Above all else, Popular Cases are small-scale, personalized economic enterprises. They offer inexpensive credit and loans, and the beneficiaries of a deceased member receive double the amount of his or her savings. Popular Cases are the only financial institutions in Mexico that are established specifically to help each one of their members as well as the entire community.

Popular Cases were first established in Mexico in 1951. Even today, they represent one of the few examples in Latin America of self-governed economic power. One reason I mention this cooperative experience is because it is one of the oldest examples of an economic system by and for the people. Another is that the emblem of the Popular Cases is set on a multicolored background—a "rainbow flag" showing all the colors of the luminous spectrum.

The German Ecobanks

"Ecobanks," as they are called, are worker-owned, cooperative enterprises that provide for collective decisions about the use of money that is earned and invested. Ecobanks are developing quickly in such places as Scandinavia and West Germany, where there is a fast-growing movement toward cooperative enterprises. In an ecobank setup, members are both workers and owners in their own business as well as the decision makers on how their money is to be used. The result has been new forms of savings, credit, and loans.

One of the most well-known ecobanks in Germany is the Frankfurt Und Main, created in 1988. Its innovations and that of others in Germany are proving that there is a different way to operate financial institutions. One of these innovations is a system called KUVOG (*Kaufen und Verkaufen ohne Gold*), which means "to buy and sell without using gold." Another is using capital to promote enterprises such as permaculture, mass transportation, and other environmentally sound businesses.

In an article in the July 1989 issue of the Spanish magazine *Integral*, the founders of the Frankfurt Ecobank published a balance of operations after their first year of operation. After only one year, they reported sixteen thousand members and thirty thousand savings accounts. Since then, part of the bank's money has been used to increase its members' capital, and the rest is employed in various ecological and social-improvement projects.

According to the article, the success of the German ecobanks had already inspired the founding of a similar bank in Switzerland. Following its German model, the "Swiss Alternative Bank," as it is called, is not only promoting ecologically sound projects but is also trying to organize the first "Alternative Stock Exchange Centre" in Zurich for people who want to invest their money in environmentally sound ways.

The success of these initiatives suggests that the economic system of the future will be based on the principles established by the British economist E.F. Schumacher in his book *Small Is Beautiful*. In it, the author emphasizes the need to develop intermediate technologies, small industries of a size appropriate to small nations or bioregions. According to Schumacher, such small industries would declare the coming revolution to the rest of the world. The ecobanks are one such revolutionary industry.

The Rainbow Banks in Denmark

In 1985, a large circle of people from various popular social movements in Denmark decided to create the first Danish "Rainbow Bank." Their primary intent was to improve the quality of life, to help in the development of new alternative communities, and to increase the environmental consciousness of the bank's members and associates. Another of their goals was to let each member know exactly how his or her money was being used. The Rainbow Bank was created to invest solely in activities that support a sustainable, ecologically sound society—a small-scale society that is self-governed and that allows people to take control of their own destinies.

In 1986, the "Popular Movement for a Rainbow Bank" spread through all of Denmark, and in 1987, the bank began operations to finance (1) alternative forms of energy; (2) ecobiological agriculture; (3) new worker-owned enterprises; (4) construction and renovation of collective housing for people with few resources; (5) promotion of new progressive organizations both private and public; (6) investigation and research into cultural, social, and educational alternative projects; and (7) low-interest loans to members and associates. To become a member of a Rainbow Bank, one need only be a member of an organization, institution, or movement that identifies itself with social and personal transformation.

The loans from the Danish ecobank are of two different kinds: personal loans and loans for social projects. Personal loans have an interest rate that averages two percent lower than the lowest rate at most conventional banks, while project loans are given with even lower rates. One reason such low-interest loans are possible is that the members of the Rainbow Bank do not operate solely for profit but also for idealistic purposes. Another reason is that the Rainbow Bank's lack of luxurious offices and lavish publicity lowers its administrative costs, and those savings are passed on to its members.

The Rainbow Bank is administered by a council of nine representatives, each of whom is elected for one year. Six of these are members of the community and clients or associates; only three are professional staff who administrate, advise, and keep accounts. Half of the representatives are women, and all come from different bioregions of Denmark.

The Rainbow Bank has no branches or affiliates, but it supports the creation of new banks in places where groups of people are ready to start similarly independent institutions. As such, it is part of a larger network of independent ecobanks and alternative projects that have sprung up all over Denmark. The Rainbow Bank is also independent of all political organizations, and it includes people from the entire political spectrum. It is an inspiring example of how the rainbow concept can work in a very down-to-Earth, practical way.

One of the reasons the Popular Movement for a Rainbow Bank has met with such a positive response in Denmark is because of the widespread cooperative movement there. That movement is coordinated through an organization called KOKOO (Collective Coordination) based in Copenhagen. KOKOO is an alternative network that grew out of the communal movement of Christiania in the mid-1970s. Today, KOKOO includes more than ten thousand cooperatives, collectives, and communities from all over Europe, and KOKOO promotes the Popular Movement for a Rainbow Bank through periodic meetings and publications.

Through its cooperative movement and the Popular Movement for a Rainbow Bank, Denmark shows strong signs of a slowly emerging alternative society that promises to eventually overshadow and replace the old established system. To varying degrees, this is happening all over the world as the spirit of the rainbow ushers in a new ecotopian millennium.

Chapter 6

Toward the New Millennium

The Myth of the Eternal Return

We have seen that the rainbow is a universal archetype, present in all cultures and times. We have also seen that, in spite of their differences, many of the modern groups that identify with the rainbow have similar foundations and philosophies. In one way or another, all of them are trying to pave the way for a millennial change, for the dramatic and permanent shift from a world of exploitation to a world of ecological harmony and balance. These groups are the pioneers of a new society, the seeds of a new order.

Nevertheless, this kind of heroic pioneering is not really new. Such groups have often helped to rebalance humanity during times of upheaval. Their heroic behavior is also part of a mythical legacy that has been handed down to us since the dawn of our species. This legacy is called the "myth of the eternal return."

In his book *Myth and Reality*, anthropologist Mircea Eliade describes the myth of the eternal return as a living document registered in the body of time: as it was done yesterday, so it is being done today and will continue being done tomorrow.

The eternal return, then, is a mythical ritual that is symbolic of the periodic renovation of the world. But as with all myths, it is not just symbolic; it is also a collective action for change, and it is both our destiny and our privilege to take part in this great cosmic drama. While helping to renew the world, it is also quite natural for us to proclaim the coming of a New Age, for we are inspired by the memory of previous golden ages of the past.

Since 1958, when author Norman Cohn's book *The Pursuit of the*

Millennium first appeared, many scholars have searched for the roots of messianic and millennial movements, and most of them have arrived at similar conclusions. For example, the ancient legends say that the birth of a new era is always preceded by a great purification, a great cleansing or ritual death. Almost universally, mythical accounts of the end of the world describe apocalyptic events such as earthquakes, volcanic eruptions, fire, flood, and violent storms. These disasters symbolize the death and burial of the old world, from which springs the possibility of new life. They also symbolize a collective baptism through which humanity cleanses and regenerates itself. The end of such mythical disasters is often announced by the appearance of the rainbow, a sign from the cosmos that the purification has been completed.

In India, the Brahmins developed a doctrine about the end of the world based on the four ages of the Earth. The Buddhists and the Jainists share a similar myth about the eternal creation and destruction of the universe. This myth speaks of the horizon becoming inflamed; of multiple suns that will dry the seas and burn the lands; of a cosmic fire that will destroy the universe; and of flooding rains that will fall without ceasing. The myth also speaks of the cosmic serpent, the rainbow, that will herald a new beginning.

Similar myths of world destruction and transformation exist for almost every major culture and time. However, there is one major difference between the ancient myths and that of today: the potential means of destruction of the world are no longer purely natural. In 1945, humanity discovered a means of creating an artificial apocalypse through the power of atomic energy. Now, for the first time, we have in our hands a force that could stop the course of history and reduce our surroundings to rubble. Before, only the gods and nature possessed such power. It is partly for this reason that in our day the new "rainbow nations" have begun to form the embryo of a new humanity—a humanity whose purpose is to bypass the chasm of destruction and help to peacefully create a new ecotopian millennium.

The Legend of the Fifth Sun

This new humanity corresponds very closely to an ancient Aztecan and Mayan myth called Ollin Toniatiuh, or the Myth of the Fifth Sun.

According to the old codices, songs, and traditional stories, there were four suns before our present one. Each sun corresponded to one of the four primordial elements: water, earth, fire, and air; and with each cycle, there was a new Earth with a new flora and fauna and a new humanity. Each one of these four cycles ended in a cataclysm in which all of life was destroyed, in order to be reborn more perfectly evolved.

According to the ancient legends, in the year 13 of the Cane, the Fifth Sun was born in Teotihuacan with the sacrificial suicide of a man named Nanahuatzin, who became the god Quetzalcoatl (also known as the feathered serpent) as a reward for his heroic deed. With the Fifth Sun, also known as the Sun of Quetzalcoatl, the gods planted the seed of a new humanity on Earth—a better way of life that was to be ruled by the legendary Quetzalcoatl himself. At the moment of Quetzalcoatl's birth, the ancient wise men, who were also Toltec warriors, prophesied that the only way of enduring the cataclysms at the end of each millennial cycle was to have wisdom and a heart as firm as a rock.

The most familiar hieroglyph in the Aztec and Toltec temples of Mexico is a figure formed by four points and united by a common center. The number that corresponds to this center is five. This number, the bridge between heaven and Earth, symbolizes many things: the heart, the meeting place of opposites, the Fifth Sun, the heart of heaven, and Quetzalcoatl—all one and the same.

According to Mayan codices and stelae, the number five also symbolizes the planet Venus, which makes its periodic return in the evening sky each year. The Mayan wise men concluded that the Fifth Sun was the sun of the man-god Quetzalcoatl and that his heart was the planet Venus.

The myth of Quetzalcoatl indicates the beginning of the age of the "center." In the center of the Aztec calendar is the Fifth Sun, surrounded by the symbols of the other four ages that have preceded it. The Fifth Sun engenders life on Earth in all its richness, like the seed of a new cosmogony.

According to Laurette Sejourné, author of *America Precolumbiana*, Quetzalcoatl emphasized in his teaching the essential role that humanity plays in the maintenance of cosmic harmony, solely insured by constant spiritual regeneration.[1] In other words, the wind or power of the

Fifth Sun is the spiritual breath that gives rise to the eternal process of birth and growth. According to the ancient teachings of the Aztecs, the purpose of the Fifth Sun is to give human beings the knowledge of how to become "luminous beings"—to liberate ourselves from duality and resolve the contradictions between ourselves and nature.[2]

For the Aztecs themselves, the prophesied birth of the Fifth Sun coincided with the arrival of the Spaniards. Because of their prophecy, the Aztecs received the invaders as messengers of the gods. Subsequently, the ancient people of the New World suffered four hundred years of cruel domination. The newly arrived "messengers" in Mexico were nothing but vulgar conquerors in search of riches, and those who followed them to the north were more interested in land and manifest destiny than in ushering in a new age of spirit.

Nevertheless, during this difficult period in North American history, a new racial mix was created—a genetic and cultural blend of conqueror and conquered, master and slave. Eventually this mix expanded to include all the races of humanity, and from its spirit were born the new tribes of the rainbow era, the real messengers of the Fifth Sun and the builders of the fifth world.

Today, the centuries of strife between the Native Americans and whites are coming to an end. No longer are native peoples forced to continue in a state of unending war, hiding their spiritual roots. Instead, they are seeking a unification of all peoples, regardless of color, class, sex, or tribe. Instead of attacking the whites, they patiently seek to educate them in the ways of the pipe, sweatlodge, peyote, tobacco, and sun dance ceremonies. In this way, thousands of non-Indians have been introduced to Native American cosmogony and learned to respect and defend the "good red road."

Also, since the beatniks, hippies, and rainbow people opened the doors, many scientists, including ethnologists and anthropologists, have shed their traditional arrogance and cultural blinders and have become genuinely interested in learning about the indigenous cultures from the inside out. Likewise, environmentalists of all stripes, from greens and deep ecologists to bioregionalists and rainbow gatherers, have learned from the ancient teachings and are now using this knowledge in their common struggle to save the planet.

The fifth world, the world of the Fifth Sun, is no longer a prophecy of the "barbaric redskins"; it is fast becoming a spiritual-political reality for those all over the planet who recognize themselves as members of the same family: the family of Rainbow Warriors. Such warriors are not easily identified, since their visions and movements are many and varied. But collectively they are helping to bring about a massive shift in consciousness that is changing the way we see ourselves and all our relations.

The Aquarian Conspiracy

Another landmark in the present millennial movement was Marilyn Ferguson's book *The Aquarian Conspiracy: Personal and Social Transformation in the 1980s.* Ferguson's thesis is that there is a vast and informal global network of people and groups whose efforts are collectively bringing about a shift in human consciousness.

In researching her book, Ferguson made a deep and detailed investigation into the connections that link New Age groups all over the world. She sent thousands of questionnaires, interviewed hundreds of alternative groups and individuals involved in global change, and finally produced a book that is now considered a classic.

Beginning with Marshall McLuhan's concept of the "global village," Ferguson concluded that the Aquarian Conspiracy is an informal, spiritual alliance of all those people who have made a qualitative leap in their evolution.[3] These people, she says, possess an awareness of being planetary citizens; and through modern global communication, this consciousness is gradually spreading all over the planet.

According to Ferguson, the roots of this modern "revolt and creative protest" reach back to the European Gnostics and alchemists of the Middle Ages, as well as to American Transcendentalists such as Ralph Waldo Emerson and Henry David Thoreau.[4] In more modern times, the "conspirators" have been influenced by such divergent thinkers as Mohandas Gandhi, William James, Herman Hesse, Carl Jung, Marshall McLuhan, and Carlos Castaneda.

The conspirators start from the assumption that the present Christian, Piscean era is about to come to an end, and that with this change we are due for a new way of thinking characterized by a lack of certainty and an openness to new possibilities. This new way of thinking involves integrating our rational and intuitive capacities as well as our social roles, memories, dreams, and visions. According to Ferguson, the most important thing to an Aquarian Conspirator is to turn one's life into a message, to make it a process of experience and knowledge that does not necessarily lead to a definite goal. Instead, the goal becomes the road itself.

In considering this "new consciousness," it is also interesting to note Ferguson's analysis of the U.S. Revolution. According to her, the birth of the United States was inspired by "illuminated" people such as John Adams, Benjamin Franklin, George Washington, and Paul Revere, most of whom belonged to spiritual brotherhoods such as the Rosicrucians, the Masons, the Illuminati, and other metaphysical hermetic orders.

In its beginnings, the U.S. Revolution was a libertarian struggle, with civil disobedience as one of its most important democratic foundations. It received inspiration from both Eastern and Western philosophies. Its proponents conceived the world as organic, alive, and open. Reason and intuition were considered complementary rather than antagonistic to one another.

The Transcendentalists, who continued to express the spirit of the U.S. Revolution during the 1800s, anticipated many of the social movements of the twentieth century. They were both pacifists and abolitionists, and they created cooperative communities and artists' communes. Today, according to Ferguson, the U.S. Revolution has changed and expanded greatly. Since the 1950s, and especially since the 1960s, she says, a new revolution is being carried out in North America—a cultural revolution that could possibly start a world revolution, since many of the most advanced agents and the most radical transformers of social reality live right here in this part of the world.[5]

In California there is a school of "New Transcendentalists" based on the thinking of such men as Robinson Jeffers, John Muir, and Gary Snyder, which is working to synthesize science, art, and mysticism. Today, the New Transcendentalists and other tribes of Rainbow Warriors are helping to create a holistic way of seeing and relating to the world. As Ferguson says, Aquarian Conspirators are those who, after passing from the "outward activism" of the sixties to "living one's ideals" of the seventies, must now start changing the world to match the visions they have lived.[6] In this process, the tribe, the collective, and the network—all open, nonrigid social structures—become ideal vehicles for the next step in human evolution.

During the 1980s, the worldwide web of rainbow tribes began to weave itself into a loose meganetwork informally called SPINS, "Segments of Polycentric Integrated Networks," in which each segment or strand contributes to the whole but is also completely self-sufficient. This meganetwork now includes environmental networks to protect the Earth, psycho-spiritual networks to strengthen people internally, alternative education networks, holistic health networks, alternative economic networks, self-sufficiency networks, antinuclear networks, arts and crafts networks, and even computerized networks for the exchange of information on alternative services and products. All of these and other rainbow webs are jointly helping to materialize the ideals of the Aquarian Age.

The Aquarian Conspiracy is neither left nor right; it leans toward a radical center that is creating a new holistic future for the planet—a future in which it will be necessary to see reality with all three eyes: the left, the right, and the spiritual eye.

Ferguson's conclusion is that, for the first time in history, the dreams and visions of the "prophets of change" can now become reality through means that are already available to us. It is now possible, she says, to eliminate hunger, war, fear, and hostility through a collective shift in consciousness. We are all seeds and silent promises.

The City of Ram

One of the most coherent expressions of the Aquarian Revolution in our times is the Rainbow Community movement in Spain. Though I have already outlined the history of this movement in chapter 4, I would like here to touch on some of its plans for the coming millennium.

In his book *A Grain of Sand*, Rainbow Community founder Emilio Fiel introduces the heretical notion that Adam's tasting of the fruit of knowledge in the Garden of Eden was not only not a sin but the realization of his own divinity and the beginning of humanity's liberation. That is, with Adam's act of rebellion against the patriarchal order, humanity began to wake up and thus to win the real respect of God.

According to Fiel, this road toward human awakening and liberation leads to physical, mental, and emotional balance and goes through seven stages:

1. The search for security and avoidance of danger, the initial stage of the evolution of the human species;

2. Mastery of the external world, outward fighting for self-defense and domination;

3. Development of artistic capacities, language, thought, and the sacrifice of intuitive, right-brain functions to logical, left-brain functions;

4. Implantation of socio-sexual organization: family, education, social responsibility, fixed roles; sacrifice of the "eternal" for the political and religious needs of society;

5. Transcendence of spatial impressions and an ability to register sensations directly without mental interference;

6. Aesthetic flowering, letting go of the world of necessities, entering into the realm of the mystical;

7. Consciousness of death, letting go of the world of experience and the discovery of the interior God.[7]

According to this map, it is obvious that the major part of humanity is now in the fourth stage of its evolution, with small groups of people making their transition into the fifth stage or "fifth world." The sixth and seventh stages are still inconceivable to most of us at the moment, but they await us all.

In prose that evokes realities unimagined, Fiel expresses his own vision of these final stages of humanity:

> There is only one thing to do: redo or remake ourselves, reconstruct ourselves wholly, starting from the foundations of the great lie. To gather ourselves out of the nest of citizenship and madness so as to act without knowing the fever of frustrated desire. . . .
>
> Energy. The idea turns into woman, as Nietzsche would say. Logic turns into eros, truth into vertigo, and the person now free from his moral prison reflects in the deepest sense his passion for the unknown. Men and women become magical, being born in full, decrepit old age until their death, astounded and awed by youth in the maternal womb. . . . The being has now become the incarnation of superior

powers, and the days overflow with immense obedience, conditioning its breath to the torments of the spirit.

The poet, empty of symbols and flowers, slides between the stems of the clear forest, caressing the ancient stone with tenderness. Then he will cover the fires of dawn and plant the twilights of stars until he can rest in the spatial music of empty deserts. It is the last ballet without any story, white as snow, the mother city over a sacred rock that bestows knowledge, music, prayer, dance, and language.

This is the pilgrimage beyond colors, ecstatic silence. Smooth, white spaces that anticipate the signs. Now, the waves move quickly closer, savage and mysterious, searching for the treasures of those who possess a strong will. The men of wind and lightning.[8]

The Rainbow Community movement in Spain has had a coherent evolution through the years. The various Rainbow Communities are centers of alternative living, experiments in ecological survival, and cooperative centers of inner evolution and growth aimed at awakening the enormous, untapped human potential. Today, members of the Spanish Rainbow Communities are actually participating in mainstream municipal organizations. They do this in distinct ways, taking direct part in labor and management, in communal tasks, and in progressive ecological programs to benefit their particular bioregions.

They have also been working with a global perspective. In June 1986, for example, the Spanish Rainbow Communities and representatives of some twenty-five New Age organizations from five continents ratified the constitution of the newly formed World Congress Foundation (WCF), which has been trying to establish a popular assembly of nongovernmental associations in the United Nations. Among the WCF's planetary initiatives are a New World Congress for Peace and a televised festival for world unity, both of which took place in 1989, and a World Congress of Life slated for March 1991.

In 1987, the Spanish Rainbow Community movement also promoted the creation of a Federation for Planetary Integration in order to unite a large number of New Age associations all over the world. As part of its communication project with other networks, that same year the Rainbow Community published the first issue of its new magazine *Echoes of Shambhala*. In it was an editorial entitled "The Global Vision," which stated:

Humanity now confronts a challenge without precedent: either an elevation in consciousness is produced so that it can have access to a new evolutionary stage, or the human species will disappear from the surface of the Earth, at least as we know it. The challenge is to evolve so as to adapt to the new needs that make clear the danger of nuclear war, ecological disaster, violent conflict, economic crises, and scientific-technological exploitation. This can only be possible starting from a new world vision, a holistic, global vision . . . placing each phenomenon in relation to the global perspective that gives everything meaning.[9]

The Rainbow Community baptized 1987 the "Year of the Planetary Healing." That same year, Fiel began a pilgrimage to over twenty different cities in Spain. His objective was to help establish a living network of thousands of people who would lend their ideas and energies to help actualize world peace. Also through the Rainbow Community network, Fiel proposed the founding of the "City of Ram," a humane, spiritual society based on peace and cooperation rather than conflict and domination.

Today, the City of Ram is not just a vision; it is a well orchestrated reality centered in the community of Montral, Spain. Fiel's ideas and visions are also being actualized in other, more traditional Spanish cities, where his followers have chosen to continue their transformative work in the midst of mainstream society.

The New Age

In his book *Earth Ascending*, author José Argüelles proposes a new millennial interpretation of human history. According to Argüelles, history can be divided into seven stages that take it through its first great cycle. At the end of the first cycle comes the eighth stage. This is also the the first stage of the new cycle, much like the eighth note on the musical scale begins a new octave.

The seven stages, as follows, also correspond to the seven chakras and to the seven colors of the rainbow:

1. Red—the stage of nomadic, aboriginal humanity, the beginning of human evolution;

2. Orange—evolution of the aboriginal civilizations and the advent of agriculture;

3. Yellow—the birth of science and the arts, the Golden Age;

4. Green—growth, maturation, and an excess of confidence, the Imperial Age;

5. Blue—oriented to a spiritual idealism and religious mysticism characteristic of the Middle Ages;

6. Indigo—the Modern Age, with its emphasis on rationality, intellect, industry, and materialism, qualities leading to destruction of the life principle and Hiroshima, the end of history as we know it;

7. Violet—the post-atomic world, characterized by a new spirituality based on reintegration and synthesis. [10]

The eighth phase in this historical octave is associated with the color purple. It is both the end of one great human cycle and the beginning of a new one. According to Argüelles, it will be characterized by a planetary consciousness and in intuitive perception of the laws of nature.

In his historical scheme, Argüelles conceives the end of one period as the beginning of the next. Moreover, he believes that the energy of human evolution flows through the planet's seven chakras in much the same way that the vital energy flows through individual human beings. He likens this serpent-like energy flow to the kundalini force, which he believes is the human manifestation of the mythical "plumed serpent," Quetzalcoatl or Kukulcan.

Beyond the color purple, then, lies a planetary "rainbow," characterized both as a new era and as a celestial guardian who has always beckoned to humanity, goading it on toward greatness and the fulfillment of its true potential. As Argüelles puts it, this rainbow represents "a condition of complete planetary synthesis almost unthinkable today." [11]

In his search for the laws that rule the behavior of the universe, Argüelles has pointed out that there is a rather amazing relationship between the workings of humanity, the planet, and the universe. That is, all three systems share a common behavior—a behavior that obeys genetic programs stored not only in human DNA but also in the "psi field," a radioactive layer surrounding the Earth.

According to the discoveries of physicist Oliver Reiser, the energetic psi field does indeed operate much like DNA. [12] In effect, it serves as the collective memory of the planet. Moreover, this "earth cerebral cortex," as Argüelles calls it, has two hemispheres much like those of the human brain: an Occidental, "rational" hemisphere corresponding to the left brain and an Oriental, "intuitive" hemisphere that corresponds to the right brain.

Just like DNA, Argüelles says, the psi field serves to direct both the evolutionary process of the human species and that of the living planet. This implies that our genetic intelligence as a species as well as our collective memories are all part of the same planetary "mind."

After studying these relationships, Argüelles comes to the conclusion that of all the mythical models of humanity's evolution, none is better suited than that of the "plumed rainbow serpent," Quetzalcoatl or Kukulcan. For ages, both the serpent and the rainbow have represented knowledge, electrical energy, and the power of change and transformation. The plumed rainbow serpent is a psychogenetic model of the historical and evolutionary process itself. It represents a quest for a mythical hero who will be transformed into a temporal cosmic warrior: Quetzalcoatl, the archetypal Warrior of the Rainbow.

Paraphrasing Argüelles, with few variations the varied Mesoamerican histories of Quetzalcoatl fit into the following phases:

1. Quetzalcoatl appears as a cultural hero, bringing artistic and scientific knowledge. The man is also a great healer and spiritual leader, a messiah. This phase corresponds to the aboriginal prehistoric figure of the shaman as an embodiment of wisdom.

2. Quetzalcoatl founds an urban center, the city of Tollan. In this city, he becomes a civilizer and a great priest. The city itself is an example of the Golden Age, a sacred and pristine civilization.

3. Quetzalcoatl is tempted and defeated by the sorcerers of darkness, who deceive, degrade, and humiliate him. This moment represents the decay of the imperial system.

4. Quetzalcoatl awakens, regains consciousness of what has happened to him, but is unable to change the course of history. He decides to purify himself, calls on his people to abandon Tollan, and starts on a spiritual pilgrimage. He finally arrives at the "place of wisdom," and there he says his final farewell. This phase is the equivalent of the medieval and cosmopolitan stages of development.

5. Before leaving, Quetzalcoatl prophesies that he will return and that on that day Tollan will be redeemed. He then leaves in a raft made

of serpents, sailing toward the east, the place where the sun is born. For Argüelles, this phase represents the beginning of the global industrial era in which Quetzalcoatl is absent and in which the sense of the sacred has been lost. During this time, humanity lives in a state of collective amnesia, awaiting the return of Quetzalcoatl.

6. The return of Quetzalcoatl is manifested as the moment of reawakening of the sacred and the reestablishment of a new spiritual order. According to Argüelles, this will happen when humanity becomes unified, remembering its evolutionary process and beginning to act from the highest level of human consciousness.[13]

In *Earth Ascending*, there is a map that corresponds to this process, in which Quetzalcoatl is seen as a rainbow serpent whose head and tail meet in what corresponds to the beginning of posthistory, the moment the atomic bomb was detonated over Hiroshima in August 1945. This is sometimes referred to as the "year 0" of the post-Hiroshima era.

Posthistory, again according to Argüelles, is made up of two phases. The first he calls "radiosonic," indicating a synthesis of humanity with nature. The second, called "holonomical," is the road to planetary consciousness, the time of the Second Coming, the New World, the return of Quetzalcoatl.

For this global revolution to be realized, Argüelles notes, it is first necessary to create a global network of people who are consciously working for a "radiosonic" synthesis of humanity with nature. According to Argüelles, that network began profoundly influencing the global mind at the time of Harmonic Convergence in August 1987, when a critical mass of people joined to declare their determination to heal the planet. Following is the "Open Letter to 144,000 Rainbow Humans" that Argüelles and other New Age spokespeople sent to the four corners of the world announcing that event:

Beginning at dawn everywhere on the earth on Sunday, August 16, 1987, 144,000 humans are being called upon to create a complete field of trust by surrendering themselves to the planet and to the higher galactic intelligences which guide and monitor the planet.

At that time and continuing through Monday, August 17, the high galactic intelligences will be transmitting a collective planetary vision as well as messages of personal destiny to and through these people, the Rainbow Humans.

These dates, August 16-17, 1987, represent a window of galactic synchronization, the first to occur since humans began testing atomic weapons July 16, 1945. The testing and release of radiation into the atmosphere of the earth set up a signal which drew the immediate attention of the higher galactic intelligences, which humans refer to as UFOs or flying saucers ... All that the higher galactic intelligences have wished for humans to learn on a planetary scale is this: the only way to break the cycle of fear and destruction to which they have made themselves hostage is by creating a complete planetary field of trust. . . .

The optimum time for the creation of this complete planetary field of trust is August 16-17, 1987. The minimum number of humans required to create it and be with each other in conscious acknowledgment of their common act of surrender to the earth is 144,000. By their coming together, wherever they may be, beginning at dawn August 16, 1987, these 144,000 will establish a receptacle of galactic transmission. This will create a signal more powerful than the atomic signal at Los Alamos in 1945. In response, the higher galactic intelligences will stream communications in high-frequency beams to and through these 144,000 Rainbow Humans, catalyzing the mental field of the planet. The integrity maintained by these 144,000 humans over the two-day period will be felt by virtually every other human being on the planet in one way or another. Everyone will know and, depending on their own mental and spiritual development, will respond accordingly. . . .

Today, countless individuals, groups, and networks have identified with this millennial vision. No longer is Harmonic Convergence or the New Age movement a matter of theoretical fancy or philosophical theory; it is truly an international movement fueled by the ideas and energies of millions of people.

Ecotopia Here and Now

In the late seventies, Ernest Callenbach wrote a fictional book called *Ecotopia* that quickly became a cult classic of the environmental movement. In it, the inhabitants of northern California, Oregon, and Washington states had seceded from the union in 1980 and formed an independent nation called Ecotopia based on living in harmony with each other and the Earth. The book describes life in Ecotopia in 1999, as seen through the eyes of newspaper reporter William Weston, the first outsider to be allowed into the country since its secession.

In his private journals and communiques to the *Times Post*, Weston describes a land of natural foods, organic farming, recycled waste products, and nonpolluting forms of mass transportation. He describes a nonmilitary, nonindustrial economy based on cooperation rather than competition—an economy whose workers own and manage their own centers of production. He describes how the Ecotopians carefully manage their natural resources as well as their population. He writes about their ritual games, their sexuality, their seasonal ceremonies, and their political games. He also notes the absence of unemployment, the harmonious racial mix of people, the environmentally protective legislation, and the widespread use of clean, free, recyclable sources of energy such as the sun and the tides. In his research, Weston is surprised to discover that the Ecotopians' educational system is oriented toward creating an ecological, nonviolent consciousness and that the Ecotopians' health system is socialized, humane, and nonbureaucratic.

In the end, six weeks after his arrival, Ecotopia has so changed Weston's thinking that he decides to stay for the rest of his life. In a final note to his editor, he writes: "I have decided not to come back, Max. You'll understand why from the notebook. But thank you for sending me on this assignment, when neither you nor I knew where it might lead. It led me home."[14]

Ecotopia is fiction, yet in a sense it is not. All of yesterday's utopias form an integral part of today's reality. Our history is like a puzzle, with pieces of distinct visions, some ahead of their times, brought to us by the most sensitive beings of each epoch. Plato's *Republic*, Saint Augustine's *City of God*, Tommaso Campanella's *City of the Sun*, and Sir Thomas More's *Utopia* all helped to fashion social reality up to the sixteenth century. Similarly, English utopias such as Francis Bacon's *New Atlantis*, Hobbes' *Leviathan*, and James Harrington's *Oceania* served to set the ideological stage for the industrial society of the nineteenth and twentieth centuries.

In more recent times, the thinking of men such as Robert Owen, Charles Fourier, and Saint-Simon opened the road for communist and international utopians like Karl Marx, Friedrich Engels, and V.I. Lenin, whose thinking and action gave rise to the so-called "real socialist societies" of this century. Even in modern times, the science fiction utopias presented by authors and visionaries such as Jules Verne, H.G. Wells, Arthur Clarke, and Isaac Asimov have contributed to the creation of our modern, superindustrial society.

Now, at the end of the second millennium after Christ, the time has come for a new kind of utopia—a utopia that has its roots in the visions and libertarian philosophies of Bakunin, Kropotkin, Bookchin, and Illich. This new trend has been called "ecotopian," and its immediate antecedents can be found in the works of thinkers such as George Orwell, Aldous Huxley, B.F. Skinner, and Frank Herbert.

One of its most recent proponents is science-fiction writer Ursula LeGuin, whose main preoccupation is to present distinct models of ecotopian life. The heroes of LeGuin's novels are generally rebellious people who oppose the dominant social systems and who are struggling to create a new society on this or some other planet. Much like the Rainbow Warriors of today, they are generally anarchists or libertarian rebels, trapped between a highly industrialized capitalist society and a totalitarian socialist society.

In one of her least known novels, *The Eye of the Heron*, LeGuin relates the story of a colony in space called Victoria. Victoria is ruled by a system of feudal lords, but on the outskirts of the walled city live the "People of Peace," a social class dominated and brutalized by the Victorian nobles. The People of Peace are all political exiles, mostly pacifists and ecologists who have been deported from various countries of planet Earth and sent to Victoria to serve as free laborers and servants.

These people live by Gandhi's principles of nonviolent resistance and, when necessary, civil disobedience. Nevertheless, they all believe in the millennial promise that someday they will find a place where they can build their "Free Land." Meanwhile, they try to live a quiet life, committing themselves to the service of the feudal lords while not allowing themselves to be humiliated into conditioned obedience.

The head lord's daughter, Dona Luz, knows some of the People of Peace, and in spite of her education as a "lady," she has great sympathy for them. She is inspired not only by their endurance of injustice but also by their love of life, their simplicity, and their libertarian and democratic spirit.

When the confrontation between the lords and the people reaches its climax, Dona Luz joins the People of Peace and leaves with them to explore the wildest regions beyond the mountains. After many hardships, the exiles arrive at a place where they can begin to live again in harmony with the Earth. LeGuin's vision is remarkably similar to that of modern-day libertarians and Rainbow Warriors who are fighting for the creation of their own "Free Land"—a planet of peace and ecological harmony.

Aldous Huxley is another author who wrote novels with clear-cut ecotopian messages. Huxley traveled through many countries attempting to blend with the ways of some of the most primitive peoples. In the United States, for instance, he lived with the Hopi and Navajo and learned many of their rituals, ceremonies, tribal ways, and concepts about the world and its future. Huxley's ecological perspective is reflected in his novels *Brave New World* and, above all, *Island*, first published in 1961.

The latter book deals with a legendary island named Pala, situated in Southeast Asia. There, a small Buddhist community has been isolated for centuries. Its inhabitants are contemplative, passive people whose lives are ruled by simple ceremonies of communion. The youth of Pala have been educated in ecological principles and in the use of medicinal plants and a sacred hallucinogenic herb. For the most part, relations are harmonious between the people of Pala and their natural surroundings, and this harmony is complemented by appropriate soft technology accidentally brought to Pala with the arrival of a foreign physicist.

The plot of the story centers around the resistance of the islanders to the mercantile and commercial systems of the neighboring islands and to the intrusion of foreign companies that want to exploit their natural resources. It shows how the islanders use their innate knowledge and Buddhist approach to life in order to stop the "civilizing process" that has destroyed so much of the rest of the world. In so doing, the book offers a profound and important message to the modern world. That message is that the elementary knowledge of ecology leads directly to the elementary knowledge of Buddhism.

Other relatively recent works that have contributed greatly to the modern ecotopian movement include Peter Kropotkin's *Mutual Help* and Murray Bookchin's *Post-Scarcity Anarchism, Toward an Ecological*

Society, and *The Ecology of Freedom*. Bookchin's books in particular have inspired the ideas behind the modern deep ecology and social ecology movements.

Another profoundly influential ecotopian book is *Deep Ecology: Living as if Nature Mattered* by Bill Deval and George Sessions. Among other things, this book reevaluates the importance of native cultures. This reevaluation is not a romantic attempt to revive the ideal of the "noble savage"; on the contrary, the authors see it as the basis for a world philosophy that we can apply directly to modern society.

The deep ecologists of today do not propose to return to the Stone Age; they are merely looking to ancient cultures for inspiration and guidance. In fact, deep ecology forms the foundation of some of today's most radical environmental organizations. As the leaders of Greenpeace are fond of saying, ecology has shown us that humanity is not the center of life on the planet. All the Earth is a part of ourselves, and we must learn to respect her in the same way that we respect ourselves.

In *Deep Ecology* there is a chapter dedicated to the ecotopian philosophy and literature that expresses the visions and ideals of the movement. Like their utopian predecessors of all ages, most modern ecotopians know these ideals can never be fully achieved; still, they serve as as a compelling blueprint for a new future. In the authors' own words:

> The ecotopian visions serve to maintain a perspective between what our technocratic industrial societies should be and what they really are. They are helpful because they serve to develop an ecological consciousness in people and are part of an environmental program which offers possible alternatives . . . [15]

Today, as we have discussed in previous chapters, the evidence of a growing ecotopian society goes far beyond literature and philosophy. Even if all else escaped our notice, we would have to admit that its revolutionary spirit is expressed in the fall of the Berlin Wall and the political, ethnic, and cultural revolutions in Eastern Europe. Despite the ongoing global strife that is so prevalent in the news, these and other events are further indication that international power blocs, antagonism, and competition are all grinding to a halt.

Today, in the face of such events, our ancestors' prophetic visions of a world without borders appear less and less naive, and the possibility of the emergence of a "rainbow humanity," the ultimate utopian dream, now seems attainable within the next two decades.

I hope that the foregoing discussion has helped to show that the new ecotopian millennium is knocking on our door. In fact, we have been hearing its call for some time. In the sixties, the ecopacifist tribe of the Living Theatre sent a call to the people of this generation to construct their "Paradise Now!" In like manner, today the ecopacifist tribes of Rainbow Warriors are sending their own appeal to coming generations: "Ecotopia Here and Now!"

For All Our Relations

Today, as we approach the end of the millennium, the ancient legends are acquiring the characteristics of a new mythology. A collective messianic movement is being actualized by tribes of Rainbow Warriors all over the world. The legends are becoming more and more real, the myths are burning in people's hearts as never before. Day by day, the spiritual force of the rainbow is increasing in all corners of the planet.

Contrary to the tide of most great movements, the people who are contributing to this radical process of world change do not wait for the arrival of a savior, nor do they follow dictators or gurus in their urge to give substance to their myths. The Rainbow Warriors do not believe in an apocalyptic holocaust as a prerequisite to a new culture, nor do they believe in cultural transformation inspired by hatred or revenge. They know that the New Age will come about peacefully, and they know it will come about through their own collective efforts. This time the "messiah" is ourselves.

The ecotopian millennium will come about when science, art, ecology, and spirit unite with traditional wisdom to create a universal science of being. Only then will the brightest, clearest light shine upon the planet, giving its warmth to all the Earth's inhabitants.

Today, the four races of humanity have already walked through four separate worlds. Now, at this moment in the Earth's evolution, let us finally gather in a sacred circle, people of all races, sexes, ages, cultures, and beliefs. Let us sit together beneath a dome of branches and leather skins, in a universal sweatlodge where we can share our songs, prayers, visions, and our commitments in favor of life.

In the midst of this universal sweatlodge, let us purify ourselves of all the negativity we have accumulated through the centuries. When the ceremony is over, let us announce joyously to the four directions the birth of a fifth world. And when we open the door to the sun, let us behold the new dawn and salute it by pronouncing in unison the most profound and humble greeting of all time: *O'mta ku oyasin*— "Greetings to all our relations in the universe."

Rainbow Artists

During the last several decades, many artists have used their creativity to promote the values of the rainbow path. Some of these artists did not even realize why they were using the rainbow symbol; others, especially since the sixties, have been very aware of its implicit power. In this appendix, I would like to mention some of the artists I have come across who can be considered conscious Rainbow Warrior artists.

Arco Iris (The Rainbow)

Arco Iris is an international brotherhood of musicians who in 1969 joined together in a common commitment to love, peace, and art. The group's three principal members and composers are Danais Wynnycka, a Ukrainian by birth and the daughter of a spiritual teacher who was trained in Tibet by Buddhist monks; Ara Tokatlian, an Egyptian by birth and the group's musical leader; and Guillermo Bordarampe from Buenos Aires.

Already steeped in jazz, pop, and classical styles, in 1969 these people turned to the ancient traditions of South America. For years, they lived and studied with the Incas of Peru and Bolivia, becoming skilled practitioners of these people's unique instruments, melodies, and rhythms.

In its first eleven years of work, Arco Iris produced thirteen albums and numerous scores for films, documentaries, and TV commercials. Two of its albums, *Opera Sudamericana* and *Suite Agitor*, received Gold Record awards. In 1977, Arco Iris moved to the United States and began performing in clubs, universities, theaters, and correctional centers. Since then, the group has been living in a mountain ashram in California.

The members of Arco Iris see their work as a form of musical therapy. Their basic precepts are three: (1) to work toward a universal brotherhood, without distinction between race, sex, or social condition; (2) to study and respect all religions, arts, and sciences of the world; (3) and to investigate the latent psychic powers in humankind and in nature. The members of the group practice yoga, abstain from alcohol, tobacco, and other drugs, and continually purify their physical, emotional, and mental bodies.

In recent years, Arco Iris has toured the United States, South America, Europe, and Japan. Today, they continue sharing love, peace, and art with audiences of all ages and inclinations through a music that carries the ancient voices of the Andes. They do more than a hundred concerts a year, plus numerous workshops aimed at familiarizing children with the pre-Hispanic musical instruments of South America. Two of their most recent records are *Blue Pheasant* and *Peace Pipes*.

Dr. Now and the Rainbow Magic Circus

One hundred years ago, magicians were among the most sought-after stars in show business. During this "Golden Age of Magic," famous conjurors crisscrossed the world with spectacular mystery shows. They toured with a railroad car full of equipment and numerous assistants in order to present a magical extravaganza in a different city or town almost every night.

Today, the old-time magic show has returned in the form of Dr. Now and the Rainbow Magic Circus. Dr. Now was especially influenced by three famous performers: Robert Heller, an English magician of the nineteenth century; George Melies, a French magician of the 1890s; and Willard the Wizard, a magician, puppeteer, and escape artist of the 1930s.

The Rainbow Magic Circus can be defined as a mobile multimedia group that is interested in personal well-being and New Age environmental theater and music. Some of the Magic Circus's shows include *The Tantric Time Machine, Old Time Magic, Intergalactic Democratic Circus*, and *Planetary Mandala*, a symbolic multimedia healing ritual for global peace. This last presentation was a blend of sound, light, art, music, and dance based on mythological, mystical systems from all parts of the globe.

Using the ancient shamanic crafts of theater and magic, along with modern electronic projectors, synthesizers, and lasers, the group's performances are enhanced by Tibetan bells, bowls, and horns; ceremonial drums; and aboriginal instruments. These productions are offered out of deep respect and wisdom, as well as that fundamentally essential catalyst, humor.

Dr. Now describes the group's purpose as follows:

> As artists, we want to stimulate the human imagination to visualize a tranquil and harmonious future where peace is our next great adventure. We believe it is the true function of the artist to participate in the refocusing of human energy and human will toward the creation of global unity.
>
> It is the time to convert our destructive powers into cooperation, to "beat swords into plowshares," and to bring all of our tremendous resources, mental and physical, to bear on the challenge of manifesting peace, health, equality, and happiness on a global scale.[1]

Fantuzzi and the Rainbow Gypsies

The Rainbow Gypsies are an American group of jugglers, dancers, tightrope walkers, and musicians who traveled and performed in Europe during the sixties and in Asia, South America, and Australia during the seventies. They are led by a Puerto Rican named Fantuzzi.

Born in Spanish Harlem, Fantuzzi is a master conga drummer, an excellent dancer, and a gifted singer/composer. While in New York, he came across the Living Theatre tribe and became part of an extended tribe of off-Broadway experimental artists who lived in Greenwich Village in the early sixties. The first of Fantuzzi's albums was called *Warriors of the Rainbow*, the second *Peace on Earth*.

Fantuzzi and the Rainbow Gypsies first toured the world in 1971. In 1973, the group changed its name to the "Butterfly Rainbow Gypsies Family." In 1979, Fantuzzi received the "Song of the Year" award at the Los Angeles World Symposium for his song "Lost and Found." That same year, the Butterfly Family and the Illuminated Elephants, another traveling troupe, organized the first Rainbow Family Peace Pageant in Arizona. Ten years later, in 1989, Fantuzzi released a new album called *One Earth, One People*.

Fantuzzi has played with such performers as Bob Dylan, Stephen Stills, Billy Preston, Richie Havens, Baba Olatunji, and Joe Higgs. His song "Gemini Twin Star" became the title song for a major motion picture.

Today, Fantuzzi lives part time in Venice, California and part time in Santa Barbara, where he continues to share his enthusiasm and joy with people all over the planet. Speaking of his own music, he says, "I see it as being an instrument for the transformation that is happening today. It is an expression of joy which contributes to the process of the healing of the Earth."[2]

Warriors of the Rainbow
Fantuzzi

Warriors of the Rainbow
You don't have to fight,
Just let go of your ego,
Spread your wings and fly!
Spread your wings and fly!

Oh, Medicine River,
Oh, Ganges, make my soul clean,
Come on, give us our freedom
And some medicine dreams.

But I wish to be
A pure child
A pure child
Of divine energy!
Of divine energy!

Medicine people
Healing the people along,
All across the land,
If you are eager
To be one of the medicine men,
Jump outside your ego
And let the Great Spirit come in!
And let the Great Spirit come in!

Rainbow Warrior World Music and Arts Festival

It is our belief that human life is a gift through which the creative power can be known and expressed. This aspect of human existence is manifest in all cultures via their unique mythology, ceremonies, and arts. The purpose of the Rainbow Warrior Music and Arts Festivals is to honor and share these diverse expressions and to celebrate our common creative source.[3]

With this call, a group of concerned artists from Santa Fe, New Mexico began to organize and coordinate the first annual Rainbow Warrior Music and Arts Festival. The group was led by singer/songwriter Eliza Gilkyson, whose own music and poetry was deeply influenced by Pueblo Indian mythology.

The first event, held August 12, 1989 at the Paolo Soleri Amphitheater on the grounds of the Santa Fe Indian School, had two main purposes. One was celebration. The other was to create a fund that would support the spiritual and artistic traditions of indigenous peoples and offer grants to groups seeking to maintain biological diversity and ecological balance. It included an opening ceremony and traditional musicians, dancers, and storytellers from all over the world.

Some of the artists who performed at the festival included Harold Littlebird, a poet and singer from the pueblo of Santo Domingo; Foday Musa Suso, a West African oral historian and composer; the Cuicani ensemble with its Andean, Caribbean, and Nahuatl music; Mazatl Galindo with his pre-Columbian instruments from Mexico, South America, and Africa; Zuleikha, a dancer in the storytelling tradition of India and Afghanistan; Chilean political singer Consuelo Luz; and the Taos Pueblo and Hopi Second Mesa Dancers.

The second annual festival was held in August 1990. Gilkyson herself describes part of the festival's vision as follows: "In spite of the current world situation, we have every reason to hope, for within each of us is the potential for compassion, commitment, and heroic deeds. In our own small way, we are demonstrating this with the Rainbow Warrior Festival."[4] At the beginning of 1991, festival leaders were planning a tour throughout the world.

Song of the Rainbow Warrior
Eliza Gilkyson

Back in 1969, I took everything I owned
And blew out of California,
One more reckless rolling stone,
A child of the sixties
Headed for the great unknown.
But I was looking to find the Rainmaker
In the land he once called home.

When I rolled into Santa Fe,
I was running out of steam.
I took up with some people there
Who were living out their dream.
And gentle hands revealed my heart,
Laughter made me whole,
But the legends of Rainmaker
Blew a window to my soul.

And ooh, I was a Rainbow Warrior,
Crossing cloudy canyons
Of love and hope and change.
And ooh, another Rainbow Warrior
Dances for the maker of the rain.

The desert bleached my reason,
Possessions slipped away,
The sun beat down and burned the ground,
I planted every day.
But when I called out for the Rainmaker
And danced the ritual right,
The answers came on clouds of rain,
And thunder in the night.

And ooh, I was a Rainbow Warrior,
Crossing cloudy canyons

Of love and hope and change.
And ooh, another Rainbow Warrior
Dances for the maker of the rain.

Elu honkwa hliton iyane
Amitola tsina u-u-ne
Elu elu toma wahane
He-ya-hai-ya-he-ya-hai-yai elu
He-ya-hai-ya-he-ha-hai-yai elu.

*Translation of last stanza, a traditional Zuni
Native American song:*

Behold, see the rain drawing near.
Yonder see the far raven,
See the rainbow brightly decked and painted.
How beautiful the world!

Rainbow Songs, Chants, and Poems

Warriors of the Rainbow

Andres King Cobos, Huehuecoyotl, 1987
(Translated from the Spanish by John Oliver Simon)

From all the cardinal directions
They come embraced with future vision.
They are the green of life,
Transparency of twisted wind
In the roots of our great-grandparents.

They are the warriors, pacifist warriors
Who follow the ethic of quartz.

Each one twinkles like a star:
Red, orange, and yellow
Suns of magnetic pollen,
Tempered to the current
Of dazzling woods and plains.
Untiring walk in the smile
Or is sadness, never left behind
Of spellbound holy delicacy
Escaped from relativity of time,
History, that badly told tale.

They speak with the Lords of Night,
They love the song of crickets;
Everything has a language for their ears.
Each cloud is a cluster of stars . . .

Yes, they are the Warriors of the Rainbow
They play among suns,
Caressed by the hilly moons.

Blue as the wet, quiet fields
Or the azure stain of clouds,
Infinitely changing like the same sky
With its net of drunken foam,
Violet as humble flowers,
Peaceful and violent iridescence,
Purple like the bloody wine of joy.

Warriors of the Rainbow, guardians
Of Grandfather Fire, bringing the new
Fire from generation to generation,
Understanding the message as an enduring
Season cyclic for all that lives:
Stones and air have energetic soul.

Mute fire that devours hearts
Warriors of the Rainbow, simply
Conscious of white roses of August,
Plaintive orchids in the rain forest.

They do not deal in beauty, power, glory
Unmoved by usury and war.
Their daily struggle is love and seed
Construct new paths through miasmic
Human clamor of traffic and smoke,
Comfortable mirage of extinction.

Like multicolored transparent sunflowers,
Sparkling gems of arcane will.

Warriors of the Rainbow upon the earth,
Mathematical navigators of the wide sky
Listening to the earth's biorhythm;
Intuitively respecting the infinite
Creation of matter, image, and form;
    silence and voice,

The plot of life, ecosystems of nature,
Death with its plan of renewal.

Warriors of the Rainbow, roses,
Red purple initiation on the emerald blade,
Saturated passion that sings a living idea
Against the tricky time of bureaucratic clocks
And amputated rocking chairs eager for news;
Comfortable fatigue and corrupt machinery,
Manipulation, human garbage, cannon fodder;
A time of spectacular fashion,
Publicity and vanity in the coffin.

Warriors of the Rainbow daily struggling,
Helping, cooperating, indefatiguable,
Their effort and love for the work
Surprised and joyful in each new sun,
Returning to Paradise delighted by pollen
Between the clothesline and the cornfield,
Scattering the play of blue and green
Crowning the breasts of the maidens.

Innocent and generous dance of alliance!
Everything is here and now, we are ourselves
Because everything is holy, is holy . . .
The stones, the plants, the animals,
Men and children, divine women, the earth,
Space, the singing stream, the wind
Elemental fire; all being is holy

From the four directions reclaim their heritage
The Warriors of the Rainbow of time
Past and yet to come; shamans and wandering sadhus,
Roshis, Hopis, Huichol maracames, diggers, provos, Sufis,
Nomads, playful in the irreversible flowing situation,

Terrestrial and extraterrestrial beings of loving
    consciousness,
Geniuses and men of good will, all fighting
For communal peace ... devoted they will guard
The seed of the earth, to sprout creation
With a transparent flag and a multicolored song
Mysterious echo of volcanic origin
Penetrating sidereal genetic confines
Harmonizing numbers, languages and silence ...
Grave friction of comets and squeaking of death.

The sound of the battle of the rainbow
Is a peaceful song
    Rising among tonalities,
Singing from the igneous earth
    Yellow to the sky
Giving green to the flowery fields,
    Fathomless blue giving
Rain of white roses
    And violets
Oh, sweet illusion so rich and impalpable
Cause and effect in real loving unity
Arching our eyes to the luminous breath
Of the Bow in the sky in grace and harmony
Of the song of the Warrior of Peace.

The Temple of Clear Light
Emilio Fiel

Fly with me, beloved brothers and sisters of the Rainbow,
United in a dance which celebrates this sacred day.
Oh, oh, oh!

A shining look in the eyes, a smile in the lips,
Tenderness in the hands, let's dream for a moment
Of a nation without borders, without gods,
    without language
Without ambitions, without laws.

A marvelous people, filled with beauty and aliveness
Sharing the luminous fruits given to us by the sun.
And now, raise your eyes toward this celestial race
Which caresses the fields deep in silence.
Oh, oh, oh!

Walking through the vast paths of love,
Crossing the seven colored oceans,
You will reach the temple of clear light,
The heart of all the universes,
The origin of a God-created perfection.

I tell you that you can cross
All the dry deserts and the snows,
And reach the fruitful land of the rainbow,
The source of true freedom.
And there, where the city of dawn is hidden,
Our bodies filled with glory will play forever
In an eternal spring of hope and pleasure.

The Rainbow Pact
Pedro Vadhar

When everything begins with just a simple love,
When we all know how to look without fear,
When people gather for the sole purpose of sharing,
Someone will give happiness, someone will share peace.

Many of these will be the guides; among them will be
Those who, in the new day, will be witness to your path.
In this time of love, do not be afraid.

The seals are all broken, and clarity can finally be seen
In these times when it all seemed to be coming to an end.
We are not good, and we are not evil, we are not
      blue or red.
Here, we are all brothers and sisters, watching the
      mighty sun.

This is just a rainbow, a beautiful bridge
That can lead us toward the path of freedom.
In this time of love, do not be afraid.

And then darkness arrives, jumping among shadows,
Fulfilling its role, with no pain in its heart.
And someone who will give him or herself for all of us,
With no guns, only with love, closing thus the ring
And bringing forgiveness to everyone.

It is always the same story, which is part of the glory,
And which will finally bring the rains and bring peace.
In this time of love, do not be afraid.

The tribes are coming together for the last battle,
The Rainbow Gypsies, the Mayans from the South,
Our elders sharing their visions from the kingdoms of
      the Sun,
Our elders singing prayers that will reach all our hearts.

It is always the same story, which is part of the glory,
And will finally bring the rains and bring peace.
In this time of love, do not be afraid.

In the wind now are floating many messages for peace,
In the purest of silences that allow us to understand,
There are no thoughts, and reason is not speaking,
It is just a wonderful bridge reaching out to your heart.
In this time of love, do not be afraid.

*Note: This song was inspired by "No Guns," a woman from the
Rainbow Family who stood unarmed in front of a Jeep driven by an
aggressive man, trying to stop him from driving into the middle of a
silent circle of people who were praying for world peace. The driver
did not stop, running over No Guns and sending her to the hospital
for many months. Pedro Vadhar was present in that moment and felt
it as one of the most important of his life. He dedicates this song to
that woman and to that moment.*

Arcobaleno

The Community of the Cavalieri del Sole, Italy

We are walking along the paths of this world,
Looking for a road leading to the heart of the Earth.
Together we walk toward the mountains of love,
There where the fantastic dreams of life appear
In all their splendor.

It is the same vision which has guided us
Here where the dark veils of the world
Are transformed by beauty
Humanity does not know how much beauty there is
    in heaven
And we spend our precious lifetimes in darkness
Among the saddest of the clouds.

The world is sick, and we can hear the crying
Of animals, rivers, people,
There where darkness shows its threatening teeth.

Rainbow, oh Rainbow,
Guide us along the roads of the world.
Make us feel your deepest love.

We are walking along the paths of the earth,
Looking for cleaner roads that lead toward peace.
And together we sing as light butterflies,
Sharing with the people our colored flowery notes.

Your life may be short or very long, now you know it,
Your only hunger is to become one light with all colors.
Your life may be short or very long, now you know it,
Your only thirst is to share your certitude with all.

Otherwise, why would your steps have brought you all
    this long way home?

Don't you see it? Don't you feel it?
It is the rainbow that has called you.
There is no limit in the magic land of love,
There where beauty shines and vibrates
And where ignorance and pain disappear.

Rainbow, oh Rainbow,
Guide us along the roads of the world.
Rainbow, oh Rainbow,
Make us feel your deepest love.

Planetary Rainbow Anthem

Oh, say can you see
By the one light in all,
A New Age to embrace
At the call of all nations.
Where our children can play
In a world without war,
Where we stand hand in hand
In the grace of creation;
Where the rivers run clear,
Thru the forest pristine,
Where we learn how to live
In peace and harmony.
Oh, say do our hearts swell
With love and joy forever
On the planet of our birth,
Blessed with love on Earth.

Rainbow People

Rainbow Person,
Rainbow Person,
Go where you want to go,
Do what you want to do,
'Cause love is guiding you.
Rainbow Nation, discover yourself.
Rainbow Nation, discover yourself.

I Envision a World Called Rainbow

I envision a world called Rainbow,
Called Rainbow, called Rainbow.
We are the changing world called Rainbow.
We sing our prayers and
Praises across the land.
We send our visions across the land.
We are Rainbow.

Rainbow People, Come out Tonight

Rainbow people, won't you come out tonight,
Come out tonight, come out tonight?
Rainbow people, won't you come out tonight
And dance by the light of the moon?

Rainbow people, won't you come out today,
Come out today, come out today?
Rainbow people, won't you come out today,
And dance by the light of the sun?

I'd Rather Be Me than Watch TV

I'd rather be me than watch TV,
I think I'll go out and hug a tree:
I'd rather be me, I'd rather be free
And live life in simplicity.

I'll go out and find a stream.
There I'll listen and I'll dream,
Sit for a while with a flower,
Be in silence for an hour.

Peyote Song
(A Chant to the Four Directions)

Nih ho ney ney ney
Nih ho ney ney ney
Nih ho ney ney ney
Wih ho ney ney ney
Hey o wanna nih ho wey
Hey o wanna nih ho wey
Hey o wanna nih ho wey
Hey o wanna nih ho wey
Hey o wanna . . . yo wanna nih ho wey
Ney o nah, hey ney oh he.

Tongo
(From Kenya, Africa)

Tongo! Muchi frida kunda yo.
Tongo! Emeiliayah kunda yo.
Ooo ah lei . . . ooo ah lei
Mali pael mala wai
Mali pael mala wai
Tongo!
Tongo!
(Repeat)

Nam Yo Ho Rengen Kyo
(Buddhist Chant from Eastern India)

Chorus:
Nam yo ho rengen kyo
Nam yo ho rengen kyo
Nam yo ho rengen kyo
Nam yo ho rengen kyo
Nam yo ho rengen kyo
Nam yo ho rengen kyo!

Translation: "I devote myself to the mystic law,
the cause and effect of all things."

O Ko Ka Chita
(From the Lakota Sioux)

Chorus:
O ko ka chita
O-pa-tye-a-nyea-neh-ya
O ko ka chita
O-pa-tye-a-nyea-ya

Translation: "Oh, Mother Earth, we thank you for giving us life. Oh, Father Sun, in you we all are one!"

Hey Wichi Cha Yo
(We All Fly Like Eagles)
Lakota Sioux Chant Adapted by the Rainbow People

Hey wichi cha yo / Hey wichi cha yo
Hey ay yo / Hey ay yo
Hey wichi cha yo / Hey wichi cha yo
Hey ay yoo / Hey ay yoo

May we all fly like eagles
Flying so high,
Circling in the universe
On wings of pure light.

Hey wichi cha yo / Hey wichi cha yo
Hey ay yo / Hay ay yo
Hey wichi cha yo / Hey wichi cha yo
Hey ay yoo / Hey ay yoo

We are brothers and sisters,
Children of the light,
Here to make a better world
For everyone's delight.

May we all love each other,
Each other as one.
Love will heal our Mother Earth,
It's only just begun.

May we all grow together,
Together as one.
This is the New Age now,
The time has just begun.

Where we sit is holy,
Sacred is the ground.
The forests, mountains, rivers
Listen to the sound.

May we all be one family,
Open and true,
Clear with each other,
Nature, I and you.

May we all sing together,
Rejoicing in the sun;
We are all children of the Rainbow,
Of the New Age begun.

Directory of Rainbow Resources

Africa

Paul Denton, Box 10700, Bonteng Gaberones, Botswana, Africa.

Fob Fettig, Saft, Momambe, Swaziland, Africa.

Argentina

Mutantia, Miguel Grinberg, Cas. 260 Suc 12, Buenos Aires 1412, Argentina.

Australia

Les Beers, 10 Boondah Rd., Warriewood, New South Wales, 10012, Australia.

Maggie's Farm, P.O. Box 29, Bellingen 2454 Mid North Coast, Australia.

News From Home, Australian Association for Sustainable Communities, c/o Jura Book, 417 King St., Newtown, Sydney 2042, Australia.

Rainbow Archives, P.O. Box 390, Avalon 2107, Australia. Photos, records, posters, tapes, magazines, books, etc., of the rainbow movement in Australia.

Rainbow Region, Neighborhood Center, Cullam St. 2480, Nimbin, Australia.

Austria

Eva Schmid, Leonhart 4, SO63 Dellach/Maria Saal, Austria.

Dr. Roman Scweidlenka, Working Circle Hopi, Obersdorf 35 A-8983, Bad-Mitterndorf, Austria.

Michaela Zeller, Erlachgasse 18/14, 1100 Wien, Austria.

Belgium

Nora Bamsaghy, Champ de Mars 34 B, Bruxelles, Belgium.

Group Arc en Ciel (Alliance Verte Alternative Européene), Parlement Européen, 97-113, rue Belliardstr, B 1040 Bruxelles, Belgium.

Thomas Jean Pierre, 5 rue Opilarde, 6594 Beauwelz, Belgium.

Belize

Rainbow Tool, c/o Mom's Restaurant, Belize City, Belize.

Brazil
Colectivo Autogestao, C.P. 10512, Sao Paulo, Brazil.

Canada
Aarran Rainbow, P.O. Box 306, Stn. A, Vancouver, B.C. V6C-2M7, Canada.
Vince Cosimo, RR #1, Maynooth, ON KOL 2SO, Canada.
Journal de l'Arc-en-Ciel, 7833 St. Denis, Montreal, Quebec, Canada H2R 2E9.
Shawn Maxwell, 4858 King Edward Ave., Montreal, QU H4V 2J6, Canada.
Brian Sarwer, 152 Kamloops Ave., Ottawa, ON K1V-7C9, Canada.

Chile
Ecocomunidad, Brown Norte 675, Nunoa, Santiago de Chile, Chile.

Colombia
Comuna Autogestionaria, A. Aereo 66314, Medellin, Colombia.
Comunidad Cartago, A. Aereo 372, Cartago, Colombia.

Denmark
Helle Andersen, Autogena Christiania, 1407, Copenhagen K, Denmark.
Paul Antogena, Christiania 1407 Copenhagen K, Denmark.
KOKOO Kollective Koordination, Radhusstraede 13, 1466 K, Copenhagen, Denmark.
Mette Neerup, Tangmosevej 9, 8740 Braedstrup, Copenhagen, Denmark.
Regenbuebanken, Stig Jensen, Griffenfeldsgade 39 B 2. sal 3 dor, 2200, Copenhagen N, Denmark.

Ecuador
Johnny Lovewisdos, Casilla 237, Loja, Ecuador.

England
Julie Berger, 28 Clifton Road, Whitstable, Kent, CT5 1DQ, England.
Greenpeace International, Temple House, 25-26 High Street, Lewes, East Sussex BN2 7 LU, England
Philip Lee, Rainbow Info, 53 Claremont Road, Leamington SPA, Warwickshire CV31 3EH, England.
The Teachers, 18 Garth Road, Bangor, Wales, Great Britain.

Finland
Yirva Leea, Lehnpuu, 39100 Hameeskyro, Finland.

France
Pascal Emanuel Brighenti, Atelier Ariane, La Coume, Rennes Le Chateau F-11120, Couiza, France.

Community de l'Arche, La Boirie Noble, F 34260, Le Bousquet d'Orb, Herault, France.

Francois and Sarah Couplan, 5 rue Albert de Lapparen, F 75007, Paris, France. c/o Haut Ourgeas F-04330 Barreme, France.

Gerard Delesque and Kira, 1 Pl. Joffre, Drancy 93700, France.

Greenpeace International, 3 rue de la Bucherie 75005, Paris, France.

Germany

Connexions das Addressbuch Alternativ Projekt, Gisela Lotu, Verlag, Postfach 60, D-6334, Katzenelnbogen, West Germany.

Gabi Hombasch, St. Barbara, Eichbergerstrasse 26, 78 Freburg, West Germany.

Global Challenges Network, Lindwurmstrasse 88, 8000 Munchen, West Germany.

Ervin Spinge, Bernstroffstrasse 144 C, D 2000, Hamburg, West Germany.

UFA/Fabrik, Victoriastrasse 10-18, D. Berlin 42, West Germany.

Greece

Alternative Gallery, c/o Parrias, P.O. Box 20037 GR 11810, Athens, Greece.

Holland

Paul de Bruijn, De Marke G, Diepenveen, 7421GE, Holland.

International Communes Network, Rejksstrastweg 37, Nijmegen-Ubbergen 6574, Holland.

Ger Niessen, Waterlooseweg 8, Oudwaterloo, Beesel, Holland.

India

Chasram Das, Jai Sing Ghere, Vrindaban, Dis Mathura, U.P., India.

Shiva Dass, c/o Joe Banana, Anjura Beach, Bardez, Goa, India.

Israel

Robert Friedman, Shehal 73/15, Jerusalem, Israel.

Dam Gottesman, Kibbutz Shomrat, Enek Jezrael, Israel.

Chiam Tovia, 68 Raambam St., Paavana, Israel.

Italy

Arcobaleno Fiammegiante, C.P. 82, 80100, Italy.

Community Aquarius, Poggio alle Fonti, 53037 S. Gimignano (Si), Italy.

Community Cavalieri del Sole, Via Borghetto 16, 25081 Macesina, Bedizzole, (Bs), Italy.

Greenpeace International, Viale Menlio Gelsomini 28, 00153, Roma, Italy.

Magazine A, C.P. 17120, 20170, Milano, Italy.

Magazine AAM, Terra Nuova, C.P. 2, 50038, Scarperia (Fi), Italy.

Magazine Arcobaleno, Via S. Martino 59, Trento, Italy.

Mauricio di Gregorio, Via Enrico del Pozzo 10, 00146, Roma, Italy.

Paolo "Silkworm" Bigatti, Casa nel Bosco, 13080 Valduggia (Vc), Italy.

Rainbow Info, Rainier Neumann and Maurizio di Gregorio, Podere Pietro, Loc. Casamora, 52026 Pian di Sco (Ar), Italy.

Rainbow Peace Village, Cheggio, 28030 Viganella (No), Italy.

Romaniello Leonardo, Rainbow Circle, Via Buenos Aires 79, 10137 Torino, Italy.

Korea

Dr. Richard Burnesku, Chiropractic Clinic, Taegu University PO 21, Taegu 634, Korea.

Mexico

Alberto Ruz Buenfil, c/o Huehuecoyotl Community, A.P. 111, Tepoztlan, Morelos, Mexico.

Alfonso Gonzales, Juarez 65, Col. Santa Ursula Coapa, Mexico 22, D.F. Mexico.

Fabio and Laura Kuri, Bioregional Project in Morelos, A.P. 4-253, Cuernavaca, C.P. 62-431, Morelos, Mexico.

Cristina Mendoza, Sevilla 312, Portales, Mexico D.F., Mexico.

Arturo Pozo, Juarez 15-19, San Angel, Mexico City 01000, Mexico.

Rodolfo Rosas, Orizaba 13, Mexico D.F., Col Roma, Mexico.

New Zealand

Peter Gay, 16 Jarrow Pl., Christchurch 3, New Zealand.

Research Design, P.O. Box 110, Tokomaro Bay, East Capoe, New Zealand.

Tauhara Center, Mapara Road, Acacia Bay, Tampo, P.O. Box 125, Tampo, New Zealand.

Norway

Bernt Andersen, Berjmannsyej 17, N-1630 Fredrikstad, Norway.

Nina Bergittie Bentsen, Maarklosplass 10, 0479, Oslo 4, Norway.

Hans Jacob, Nigarden Brekke, 5743, Flam, Norway.

Kirsten Windus, Radar VN 47, 1152, Oslo 11, Norway.

Peru

Mel Saunders, Pyramid Research Center, c/o La Cabana, Casilla 42, Pucallpa, Peru.

Portugal

Marho Avramovic, Peace Fleet Coordinator, Monte Novo, Apto 107, 8900 Villareal de San Antonio, Portugal.

Ulrike and Family, Quinta da Ribeira, Vila Verde, 6270, Seia, Portugal.

Petra Waizman, Monte Verde, Santa Margarita de Serra, 7570 Grandola, Portugal.

Scotland

Findhorn Community, The Park, Forres, Scotland.

International Communes Network, Lauriston Hall, Castle Douglas, Kirkenbrideheshire, Scotland.

Soviet Union

Institute of Watertransport, Kunzmin Alexander Nikolaevich, Street Duinscaya, House 5/7, Leningrad 198033, USSR.

Yuri Popov, Moscow 111642, Novokosinkaya, DOM 18 KV 2, USSR.

Spain

Community Arcoiris (Tierra Nueva), Alcover, Tarragona, Spain.

Emilio Fiel, Jardin de Cristal, Rocabruna 17867 Comprodon, Girona, Spain.

Magazine Integral, Paseo Margall 371, 08032, Barcelona, Spain.

Planet Art, Marysol Gonzalez Sterling, Calle de las Fuentes 8, Madrid 28013, Spain.

Nina Schär, Rainbow Village Project, Lista de Correos, Bembire (Leon), Spain.

Susanna Soria, Diagonal 307-5, Barcelona 08013, Spain.

Javier Tavora, Finca los Molinos, Apartado 22, Cortec Ana 21230, Guelva, Spain.

Sweden

Comunidad, Box 15, 128 S-104 65, Stockholm, Sweden.

Modr Jord, Satarod PL, SV 2218, Linderd, Sweden.

Ingemar Karlsson, Urasa, Vackelsang, Smaland, Sweden.

Ting Meeting Info, Kai Vaara, Tapionkatn 30 AS 1, SF-33500 Tampere, Sweden.

Switzerland

Urs Fluery, Rainbow Circle, Box 111, CH 6600 Muralto, Switzerland.

Jean-Francois Henry, Dr. Kern 7, 2300 La Chaux de Fonds, Switzerland.

Worldwide Rainbow Info Network, Postfako 60 CH-8955 Oetwil, Switzerland.

United States

Arco Iris, c/o Danais and Ara Tokatlian, 2265 Westwood Blvd., Suite #321, Los Angeles, CA 90064.

Garrick Beck, c/o New York Rainbow, P.O. Box 1554, New York, NY 10009.

Fantuzzi, 2407 Wilshire Blvd., Los Angeles, CA 90064.

Hog Farm, 1600 Woosley Street, Berkeley, CA

Medicine Story: Mettanokit Spiritual Community, Another Place, Greenville, NH 03048.

Mystic Fire Video (films of the Living Theatre productions), 24 Horatio Street, New York, NY 10014, or 70 Greenwich Avenue #410, New York, NY 10011.

New York Rainbow, P.O. Box 1554, New York, NY 10009.

Palu, Rainbow Song, 518 Washington #5, Santa Cruz, CA 95060.

Peace Net, 3228 Sacramento Street, San Francisco, CA 94115.

Peace Project Media Mailing List, c/o Rainbow Hawk (Knapp) #84A0405, Drawer B, Stormville, NY 12582-0010.

Peace Village: Earth People's Park, Norton, VT 05907.

Peace Villages, c/o Barry "Plunker" Adams, Box 8574, Missoula, MT 59807.

Rainbow Family Net, 5885 Skyline Dr., Oakland, CA 94611.

Rainbow Farm, c/o Box 5577, Eugene, OR 97405.

Rainbow Gypsies, c/o Jiva, 828 Royal Street, Suite 523, New Orleans, LA, 70116.

Rainbow Magic Circus, Thaddeus Now, P.O. Box R, Ukiah, CA 95482.

The Rainbow Nation: An International Cooperative Community Guide, c/o Micheal John and the Rainbow Families, Box 154 Bodega, CA 94922.

Rainbow Peace Caravan, c/o Ray Barnes the Mothership Log, P.O. Box 981, Gatlinburg, TN 37738.

Rainbow Peace Projects Foundation, c/o Don Wirtshafter, 14 N. Court St., Athens, OH 45701.

Rainbow Peace Projects International Newsletter, c/o Diana Recycle for Peace, P.O. Box 1932, Walnut, CA 91788.

Rainbow Tribal Council Magazine, 515 E. Grant Rd., Suite 113, Tucson, AZ 85705.

Rainbow Warrior World Music and Arts Festival, P.O. Box 8627, Santa Fe, NM 87504.

Bill Weinberg, 40 Park Place, Brooklyn, NY 11217, USA.

Uruguay

Comunidad del Sur, Casilla 15229, Montevideo, Uruguay.

Comunidad G. de Freitas, Sarandi 935, Paysandu, Uruguay.

Notes

Chapter 1

1. Lama Anagarika Govinda, "Rainbow, Halo & Aura," in *The Rainbow Book*, F. Lanier Graham (New York: Random House, 1979), p. 219.

2. Ron Davidson, "The Sacred Art of Tibet," in *The Rainbow Book*, F. Lanier Graham (New York: Random House, 1979), p. 170.

3. Vincent Gaddis, *American Indian Myths and Mysteries* (New York: New American Library, 1977), p. 11. Quotation from A.M. Bolio's translation of the *Chilam Balam*.

4. Rutherford Platt, "What Is a Rainbow?" in *The Rainbow Book*, F. Lanier Graham (New York: Random House, 1979), p. 76.

Chapter 2

1. Vincent H. Gaddis, *American Indian Myths and Mysteries* (New York: New American Library, 1977), p. 197.

Chapter 3

1. Paul Goodman, "Human Nature and the Organized System," in *Growing Up Absurd* (New York: Random House, 1957), pp. 3-16.

2. Gary Snyder, *Earth House Hold* (New York: New Directions Books, 1957), pp. 92-93.

3. Ibid., pp. 113, 116.

4. Gene Anthony, *The Summer of Love* (Berkeley, CA: Celestial Arts, 1980), p. 148.

5. Gary Snyder, *Earth House Hold* (New York: New Directions Books, 1957), pp. 92-93.

6. Julian Beck, *The Life of the Theatre* (San Francisco: City Lights, 1972), meditation #11.

7. Ibid., #27.

8. Ibid., #24.

9. Ibid., #54.

10. Ibid., #45.

11. Ibid., #83.

12. Ibid., #37.

13. Ibid., #122.

14. Gene Anthony, *The Summer of Love* (Berkeley, CA: Celestial Arts, 1980), p. 122.

15. Wavy Gravy, *The Hog Farm and Friends* (New York and London: Links Books, 1974), p. 56.

16. Ibid., p. 68.

17. Ibid., p. 132.

18. Ibid., p. 143.

19. Ibid., p. 137.

20. Ibid., pp. 10-11.

21. Ben Morea and Ron Hahne, *Black Mask* 1, November, 1966.

22. Wavy Gravy, *The Hog Farm and Friends* (New York and London: Links Books, 1974), p. 108.

23. Seth Zuckerman, *Third North American Bioregional Congress Proceedings* (San Francisco, 1988), pp. 50-51. An interview with Peter Berg and Judy Goldhaft.

24. Abbie Hoffman, *Woodstock Nation* (New York: Vintage Books, 1969), p. 43.

25. Wavy Gravy, *The Hog Farm and Friends* (New York and London: Links Books, 1974), p. 77.

26. Ibid., pp. 79-80.

Chapter 4

1. Robert Hunter, *Warriors of the Rainbow* (New York: Holt, Rinehart & Winston, 1979).

2. David Robbie, *Eyes of Fire: The Last Voyage of the Rainbow Warrior* (Philadelphia: New Society Publishers, 1987), p. 92.

3. Alberto Ruz Buenfil, "Los Guerreros del Arcoiris," *El Gallo Illustrado*, 1985.

4. Michael Bowen and John May, *The Greenpeace Story* (London, 1989).

5. Emilio Fiel, "La Comunidad Tantrica del Arcoiris," *El Mago de la Nueva Era* 3, Winter 1980, p. 18.

6. Ibid.

7. Ibid., pp. 20-24.

8. Emilio Fiel, "Las Carcajadas del Guerrero," in *Despertar Interior y Cambio Colectivo* (Lizaso, Spain: Arcoiris, 1982), pp. 284-287. Trans. Alberto Ruz Buenfil.

9. Integral, "De la Familia a la Comunidad," *Vida en Comunidad*, no. 8, pp. 120-123.

10. Emilio Fiel, *Un Grano de Arena* (Lizaso, Spain: Arcoiris, 1983), p. 9. Trans. Alberto Ruz Buenfil.

11. Ibid., p. 11.

12. Emilio Fiel, "La Vision del Mundo del Guerrero" in *La Via del Corazon y del Fuego* (Lizaso, Spain: Arcoiris, 1987), pp. 22-25. Trans. Alberto Ruz Buenfil.

13. Emilio Fiel, "El despertar de la Consciencia Planetaria," *El Zodiaco de Luz*, Summer 1986, p. 6. Trans. Alberto Ruz Buenfil.

14. Emilio Fiel, "Un Espiritu, una Tierra, una Humanidad," in *La Via del Corazon y del Fuego* (Lizaso, Spain: Arcoiris/Shambhala, 1987), p. 5. Trans. Alberto Ruz Buenfil.

15. Emilio Fiel, poem from Arcoiris cassette, 1983. Trans. Alberto Ruz Buenfil.

Chapter 6

1. Laurette Sejourné, *America Precolombiana*, Vol. 21 (Milan: Feltrinelli, 1971), p. 85.

2. Ibid., p. 173. Trans. Alberto Ruz Buenfil.

3. Marilyn Ferguson, *The Aquarian Conspiracy: Personal and Social Transformation in the 1980s* (Los Angeles: J.P. Tarcher, 1980), pp. 55-56.

4. Ibid., pp. 46-47.

5. Ibid., pp. 205-210.

6. Ibid., p. 209.

7. Emilio Fiel, *Un Grano de Arena* (Lizaso, Spain: Arcoiris, 1983), pp. 229-231. Trans. Alberto Ruz Buenfil.

8. Ibid., pp. 220-21. Trans. Alberto Ruz Buenfil.

9. Emilio Fiel, "The Global Vision," *Echoes of Shambhala* 0, April, 1987. Trans. Alberto Ruz Buenfil.

10. José Argüelles, *Earth Ascending* (Santa Fe, NM: Bear & Company, 1988), p. 78.

11. Ibid., p. 78.

12. Ibid., pp. 15-17.

13. Ibid., p. 110.

14. Ernest Callenbach, *Ecotopia* (Berkeley, CA: Banyan Tree Books, 1975), p. 167.

15. Bill Deval and George Sessions, *Deep Ecology: Living as if Nature Mattered* (Salt Lake City: Peregrine Smith Books, 1985).

Appendix A

1. Rainbow Magic Circus brochure and press release.
2. "One Earth, One People" (Brochure promoting fall 1989 tour of Fantuzzi and the Flexible Band).
3. Rainbow Warrior Music and Arts Festival brochure, 1989.
4. Ibid.

Bibliography

Chapter 1

Bergua, Juan B. *Mitologia Universal*. Madrid: Editorial Ibericas, 1960.

Boyer, Carl B. *The Rainbow: From Myth to Mathematics*. Princeton, NJ: Princeton University Press, 1987.

Charles-Puech, Henri. *Las Religiones en los Pueblos sin Tradicion Escrita*. Vol. 11. Mexico City: Editorial Siglo XXI, 1982.

Eliade, Mircea. *Mito y Realidad*. Madrid: Guadarrama Editores, 1982.

Escobedo, J.C. *Enciclopedia de la mitologia*. Barcelona: De Vecchi S.A., 1972.

Graham, F. Lanier. *The Rainbow Book*. New York: Random House, 1979.

Humbert, J. *Mitologia griega y romana*. Mexico City: G. Gili, S.A., 1981.

Waldo, Bernasconi. *Cromoterapia: Per un rapporto equilibrato e terapeutico con i colori*. Milan: Ottaviano SRL, 1981.

Chapter 2

Berdella de la Espriella, Leopoldo. *Juan Sabalo*. Bogota: Carlos Valencia Editories, 1980.

Bergua, Juan B. *Mitologia Universal*. Madrid: Editorial Ibericas, 1960.

Blavatsky, H.P. *The Secret Doctrine*. Pasadena, CA: Theosophical University Press, 1974.

Caso, Alfonso. *El Pueblo del Sol*. Mexico City: Fondo de Cultura Economico, 1963.

Charles-Puech, Henri. *Las religiones en los pueblos sin tradicion escrita*. Vol. 11. Mexico City: Editorial Siglo XXI, 1982.

Column, Paedric. *Myths of the World*. New York: Grosset & Dunlap, 1930.

Courlander, Harold. *The Fourth World of the Hopis*. New York: Crown Publishers, 1972.

Ferguson, Marilyn. *The Aquarian Conspiracy: Personal and Social Transformation in the 1980s*. Los Angeles: J.P. Tarcher, 1980.

Gaddis, Vincent H. *American Indian Myths and Mysteries*. New York: New American Library, 1977.

Lhuillier, Alberto Ruz. *The Civilization of the Ancient Mayas*. Mexico City: Instituto Nacional de Antropologia e Historia, 1970.

Nuñes, Jose Corona. *Mitologia Tarasca*. Mexico City: Fondo de Cultura Economica, 1957.

Waters, Frank. *Book of the Hopi*. New York: Ballantine Books, 1969.

Willoya, William, and Vinson Brown. *Warriors of the Rainbow*. Happy Camp, CA: Naturegraph Publishers, Inc., 1962.

Chapter 3

Anthony, Gene. *The Summer of Love*. Berkeley, CA: Celestial Arts, 1980.

Beck, Julian. *The Life of the Theatre*. San Francisco: City Lights, 1972.

Berg, Peter. *The Digger Papers: Trip Without a Ticket and Other Texts*. Haight-Ashbury, CA: Free City Press, 1967.

Berti, Nico. "Spagna 36: Una rivoluzione contro il potere." *Magazine A*, 139 (August-September, 1986).

Bookchin, Murray. *Post-Scarcity Anarchism*. New York: Ramparts Press, 1971.

Brand, Stewart. *The Whole Earth Catalog*. New York, Random House, 1971.

Brand, Stewart, and Art Kleiner. *News That Stayed News (1974-1984: Ten Years of the Coevolution Quarterly)*. San Francisco: North Point Press, 1986.

Burroughs, William. *El Lunch Desnudo*. Barcelona, Spain: Club Brughera, 1980.

Creagh, Ronald. *Laboratori d'utopia*. Milan: Antistato, 1985.

Goodman, Paul. *Growing Up Absurd*. New York: Random House, 1957.

Gravy, Wavy. *The Hog Farm and Friends*. New York and London: Links Books, 1974.

Hoffman, Abbie. *Woodstock Nation*. New York: Vintage Books, 1969.

_____ . *Revolution for the Hell of It*. New York: Dial Press, 1968.

Kerouac, Jack. *Angeles de desolacion*. Barcelona: Biblioteca Universal Caralt, 1980.

_____ . *Los Vagabundos del Dharma*. Barcelona: Club Brughera, 1982.

_____ . *On the Road*. New York: Viking Press, 1957.

Kesey, Ken. *Garage Sale*. New York: Viking Press, 1973.

Miralles, Alberto. *Nuevos rumbos del teatro*. Barcelona: Salvat Editores, 1974.

Perry, Charles. *The Haight-Ashbury: A History*. New York: Random House, 1984.

Rubin, Jerry. *Do It!* New York: Simon & Schuster, 1970.

————. *We Are Everywhere.* New York: Harper & Row, 1979.

Snyder, Gary. *Earth House Hold.* New York: New Directions Books, 1957.

Wolfe, Tom. *The Electric Kool Aid Acid Test.* New York: Farrar-Strauss & Giroux, 1968.

Yuhmayo, Albert R. *No Mad Living, Gypsies and Scapegoats.* Mendocino, CA: Pomo Tierra Press, 1977.

Chapter 4

Adams, Barry P. *Where Have All the Flower Children Gone?* Missoula, MT: Michael Spradlin Crater, 1988.

Aesenda, Marco. "Greenpeace: Multinazionale dell' ecologia" *Magazine Airone* 55 (1985).

Australian Association for Sustainable Communities. "News from Home." *Review* 3, no. 2 (March 1986)

Beck, Garrick. *Basic Rainbow.* New York: Rainbow Council, 1986.

Blum, Jacques. *Fristaden Christiania.* Copenhagen: Nationalmuseet, 1976.

Buenfil, Alberto Ruz. "Los Guerreros del arcoiris de la Greenpeace Internacional." *El Gallo Ilustrado* magazine in *El Dia*, 1985.

Buenfil, Alberto Ruz, and Sandra Comneno. "Rainbow Nation." *Magazine Frigidaire*, 56-57 (1985).

Catpoh. *Christiania: 1,000 persones — 300 chiens une commune libre.* Paris: Editions Alternative et Paralleles, 1978.

Christianitter. *Christiania et Samfund i Storbyen.* Copenhagen: Nationalmuseet, 1976.

Comunidad Arcoiris. *Despertar interior y cambio colectivo.* Lizaso, Spain: Comunidad Arcoiris, 1982.

————. *El Zodiaco de la Luz.* Alcover, Spain: Comunidad Arcoiris, 1986.

Esman, Eva. *Der er en regnbue over Christiania.* Copenhagen, 1976.

Fiel, Emilio. *Dharma Mandala: Haca una vision global.* Alcover, Spain: Communidad Arcoiris, 1986.

————. *Un grano de arena.* Lizaso, Spain: Comunidad Arcoiris, 1983.

Garlington, Phil. "The Return of the Flower Children." *California* (October 1984).

Howe, Steve Douglas. *Anotherland: A Film Script.* Larkspur, CA: Anotherland Productions, 1977.

Hunter, Robert. *Warriors of the Rainbow.* New York: Holt, Rinehart & Winston, 1986.

Kapleau, Philip. *The Wheel of Life and Death*. New York: Doubleday, 1989.

Klovedall, Ebbe, and Reich Gylendal. "Til forsvar for masselinsen og de rettetro." *Ugespejlet* (1976).

Lovetand, Per. "Christiania som integrenet funktion i Kobenhavn Arkitekten." *Arkitekten* (1974).

Maggie's Farm Media Center, Australia. *Alternative Network Magazine* 34 (1986).

McGee, Terry. *Nimbin Centenary: 1882-1982*. Nimbin, Australia: Aquarius Foundation RSL, 1983.

McTaggert, David, and Robert Hunter. Greenpeace III: *Journey into the Bomb*. London: Collins, 1978.

Mollerup, Peter, and Keld Lovetand. *Fristadens Christiania's udvikling*. Copenhagen: Christiania's Publications, 1976.

Morgan, Robin, and Brian Whitaker. *Rainbow Warrior: The French Attempt to Sink Greenpeace*. London: Arrow Books, 1986.

Nimbin Community Press. *Nimbin News Magazine* 9, no. 6 (1986-1987).

Peace Dream Productions. *First Annual Rainbow Warrior Music & Arts Festival*. Santa Fe, NM, 1989.

Plum, Neils Munk. *Hvad med Christiania?* Copenhagen: Eget Forlag, 1975.

Rasmussen, Steen Eiler. *Omkring Christiania*. Copenhagen: Gyldendals Traneboger, 1976.

Reddersen, Jacob. *Fremtidsbyen eller slumghettoer: om Christiania & remisevenget i velkaerdsstaten*. Copenhagen: Ruc Publications, 1985.

Robbie, David. *Eyes of Fire: The Last Voyage of the Rainbow Warrior*. Philadephia: New Society Publishers, 1987.

Sjorslev, Inger. *Christiania: A Freetown*. Copenhagen: Nationalmuseet, 1977.

Terania Native Forest Action Group. *The Message of Terania*. New South Wales, Australia: Terania Media, 1979.

"Vida en Comunidad." *Integral* (1983). Number 8 in a collection of "Monographies."

Weinberg, Bill. "Rainbow Lore: An Interview with Garrick Beck." *Downtown* (October-November, 1989).

_____ . "Rainbow Warriors and the Ecotopian Millennium: An Interview with Alberto Ruz." *Downtown* (September 1990)

Wilkinson, Pete. "Greenpeace: The Rainbow Warriors." *AAM Terra Nuova* 26 (1986).

Chapter 5

AAM Terra Nuova. "Atti del campo su bioregionalismo e ritorno alla terra: a manifesto." *AAM Terra Nuova* (1989).

Aha. "Interes Bulletin zum Projekte A." *Aha* (March 1987).

Aivanhov, O.M. *La Nuova Terra*. Milan: Prosveta, 1987.

Alter, Jonathan. "Jesse Jackson: The Power Broker." *Newsweek* (March 21, 1988).

Arcana. *Ma l'amor mio non muore*. Rome: Arcana Editrice, 1971.

————. *Vivere Insieme*. Rome: Arcana Editrice, 1974.

Arcoredes: Alternativas de E-Comunicacion nos. 1-4 (1984-1985).

Bailey, A.A. and Maestro Tibetano D.K. *Trattato dei sette raggi*. Rome: Edizioni Nuova Era, 1987.

Buenfil, Alberto Ruz, ed. *Lo Verde Sobre la Piel: Notas sobre Ecologia Profunda*. Mexico City: Huehuecoyotl and Escuela Nacional de Antropologia e Historia, 1987.

Confederacion Mexicana de Cajas Populares. *Estatuto de las Cajas Populares*. Mexico City: CMCP Editories, 1986.

Damanhur. *Le Nuove Comunita*. Baldissero Canavese, Italy: Edizioni Horus, 1983.

Deval, Bill, and George Sessions. *Deep Ecology: Living as if Nature Mattered*. Salt Lake City: Peregrine Smith Books, 1985.

Francescato, D. and G. *Famiglie aperte, le comuni*. Milan: Feltrinelli, 1967.

Green, Mark, and James Ledbetter. "The Conventions: 20 Solutions." *Mother Jones* (July-August, 1988).

Hawk, Rainbow (Paul Knapp). "Rainbow Peace Projects." Paper written at Attica Correctional Facility, New York, 1987.

Hollstein, Walter. *Underground*. Milan: Ed Sansoni, 1971.

Jackson, Jesse. "What We've Won." *Mother Jones* (July-August 1988).

Jensen, Stig. "Regnbue Okonomi." *KOKOO* 3 (August 1989).

KOKOO. *Bulletin of Information of the Cooperative Coordination Center in Denmark*. Copenhagen, 1986.

Muwakkil, Salim. "Jackson's Challenge." *The Progressive* (July 1987).

Peace Village Council. *A Presentation of the Peace Village Plan*. Drain, OR: Rainbow Tribal Council, 1980.

Piulats, Octavi. "La Coalicion Arcoiris." *Integral* 9, no. 90 (1987).

Pivano, F. *C'era una volta un Beat*. Rome: Arcana Editrice, 1976.

Rainbow Tribal Council. "Peace Village." Brochure. Drain, OR: Rainbow Publications, 1979.

"Regnbue Banken: den Alternative Bank." Brochure. Folkebevaegelsen for Regnbue Banken. Odense, Denmark, 1986.

Rivier, F.M. Kalachakra: *The Tantric Initiation of the Dalai Lama.* Rome: Edizioni Mediterranee, 1985.

Stampa Alternativa. *Commune Agricola.* Rome: Savelli, 1978.

Tasini, Jonathan. "Lining up New York's Blue Collar Vote." *Village Voice* (March 29, 1988).

Wills, Gary. "Making History with Silo Sam." *Time* (March 21, 1988).

Wilkins, Roger. "Ending the Power Shortage." *Mother Jones* (July-August 1988).

Chapter 6

Argüelles, José. *Earth Ascending.* Santa Fe, NM: Bear & Co., 1988.

———— . *The Feminine, Spacious as the Sky.* Boulder, CO: Shambhala Publications, 1977.

———— . *The Mayan Factor: Path Beyond Technology.* Santa Fe, NM: Bear & Co., 1987.

———— . *Surfers of Zuvuya.* Santa Fe, NM: Bear & Co., 1989.

Barabas, Alicia M. *Utopias Indias: Movimientos Socioreligiosos en Mexico.* Mexico City: Editorial Grijalbo, 1989.

Bookchin, Murray. *The Ecology of Freedom.* Palo Alto, CA: Cheshire Books, 1982.

———— . *Post-Scarcity Anarchism.* New York: Ramparts Press, 1971.

———— . *Toward an Ecological Society.* Montreal: Black Rose Books, 1980.

Cabo de Villa, Jose. *Feria de Utopias.* Madrid: Biblioteca de Autores Cristianos, 1974.

Callenbach, Ernest. *Ecotopia.* Berkeley, CA: Banyan Tree Books, 1975.

———— . *Ecotopia Emerging.* Berkeley, CA: Banyan Tree Books, 1981.

Cohn, Norman. *The Pursuit of the Millennium.* Barcelona: Barral, 1972.

Creagh, Ronald, and Alberto Ruz Buenfil. *Laboratori d'Utopia.* Milan: Antistato, 1985.

Deval, Bill, and George Sessions. *Deep Ecology: Living as if Nature Mattered.* Salt Lake City: Peregrine Smith Books, 1985.

"Ecofilosofias." *Integral* 3 (1984).

Eliade, Mircea. *Tratado de la Historia de las Religiones.* Mexico City: Biblioteca ERA, 1972.

Fiel, Emilio. "El Espiritu de la Ciudad de Ram." *Arcoiris* 5 (1985).

Gabayet, Jacques, ed. *Hacia el Nuevo Milenio.* Vols. 1 and 2. Mexico City: Villicana y Casa Abierta al Tiempo, 1986.

Herbert, Frank. *The Dune Series*. New York: Berkeley Books, 1977.

Huxley, Aldous. *Brave New World*. New York: Harper & Row, 1932.

Lawrence, D.H. *El Arcoiris*. Madrid: Brughera Libro Amigo, 1980.

———— . *Il Serpente Piumato*. Milan: Monadori, 1981.

LeGuin, Ursula. *The Dispossessed*. New York: Harper & Row, 1974.

———— . *The Eye of the Heron*. New York: Harper & Row, 1984.

———— . *La Mano Sinistra delle Tenebre*. Bologne, Italy: Libra Editrice, 1971.

Orwell, George. *1984*. Madrid: Destino, 1952.

———— . *Rebelion en la Granja*. Mexico City: Editorial Antorcha, 1983.

Pereira de Quiroz, Maria Isaura. *Historia y Etnologia de los Movimientos Mesianicos*. Mexico City: Siglo XXI, 1969.

Plum, Werner. *Utopias Inglesas*. Bogota: Ediciones Internacionales, 1978.

Portilla, Miguel Leon. *Los Antiguos Mexicanos a traves de Sus Cronicas y Cantares*. Mexico City: Fondo de Cultura Economica, 1983.

Sejourné, Laurette. *America Precolombiana*. Vol. 21. Milan: Feltrinelli, 1971.

———— . *Pensamiento y Religion del Mexico Antiguo*. Mexico City: Fondo de Cultura Economica, 1984.

Skinner, B.F. *Walden Two*. New York: MacMillan Publishing Co., 1984.

Snyder, Gary. *Earth House Hold*. New York: New Directions Books, 1957.

Wilhelm, Richard, and Cary F. Baynes, trans. *The I Ching or Book of Changes*. New York: Bollingen Foundation, 1950.

About the Author

Alberto Ruz Buenfil, an international activist and performer, was born in Mexico City on September 11, 1945. A world traveler since his early childhood, he is the son of Dr. Alberto Ruz Lhuillier, the noted French-Cuban-Mexican archaeologist who discovered the Royal Tomb of Palenque and who helped to reconstruct some of the major Mayan ceremonial centers in southern Mexico.

During the sixties, Ruz Buenfil taught French and studied economics, political science, philosophy, and psychology at the University of Mexico City, and took part in the Mexican political student movement. He was deeply influenced by the U.S. "beat" literature of the fifties and the antiwar and Third World movements of the sixties, as well as by his journeys to revolutionary Cuba.

In 1968, Ruz Buenfil traveled to the United States, where he helped to organize the Berkeley Commune in California and the Poor People's Campaign in Washington, D.C. There he met many leaders of various minority and student organizations.

During the first half of the seventies, Ruz Buenfil lived and traveled in Europe, the Middle East, and the Far East with the guerrilla theater group Chaos (later called the Hathi Babas). In Europe, the group came into close contact with most of the avant-garde organizations of Europe: the German communes in Berlin; the Dutch Provo and Kebauter movements in Amsterdam; the early squatter bands in Copenhagen and London; and the French radical situationists. During this time, Ruz Buenfil also experienced the lifeways of many peoples who live close to the Earth—including the nomadic Kurds of the Turkish deserts, the Berbers of the Sahara, the Moroccan "Blue Men," the Bedouins of Palestine, and the Canary Islanders.

In India, Tibet, and Malaysia, Ruz Buenfil and the Hathi Babas added the Eastern arts, philosophy, and religion to their repertoire of experience, then returned to Mexico in 1975. There, the group, now composed of fifteen members (including five children), lived by producing and selling whole-grain bread and crafts, and through street theater performances.

Ruz Buenfil and his tribe, now called the Illuminated Elephants, moved back to California in mid-1976 and began a spiritual-social odyssey, taking part in Rainbow Gatherings, simple-living workshops, fairs, and festivals all along the West Coast. Traveling in a seven-bus caravan, they presented street shows in California, Oregon, Washington, and Arizona before deciding to find a permanent home in Mexico.

Ruz Buenfil is the father of three children and a cofounder of the community of Huehuecoyotl in the Mexican state of Morelos. Since 1982, Huehuecoyotl has become a major attraction for artists, environmentalists, spiritual teachers, and travelers, and a center for events, parties, and workshops. There Ruz Buenfil has spent most of his time producing articles, books, films, and honey. His articles on ecology and alternative living have appeared in publications all over the world, particularly in Europe, the United States, and Central and South America.

Ruz Buenfil's travels have brought him into contact not only with many of the leaders of today's environmental and alternative living movements, but with a wide variety of native peoples all over the world.

In 1989, his new group, El Puente de Wirikuta, helped to organize a series of ceremonies to celebrate the reopening of the Mayan initiatic centers in Mexico. At the five-hundredth anniversary of Christopher Columbus's arrival in the New World, Ruz Buenfil and El Puente de Wirikuta are committed to creating a spiritual "bridge" between the Americas and the rest of the world.

BOOKS OF RELATED INTEREST
BY BEAR & COMPANY

THE GREAT TURNING
Personal Peace, Global Victory
by Craig Schindler & Gary Lapid

THE MAYAN FACTOR
Path Beyond Technology
by José Argüelles

PROFILES IN WISDOM
Native Elders Speak about the Earth
by Steven S.H. McFadden

THE RETURN OF PAHANA
A Hopi Myth
by Robert Boissière

RETURN OF THE THUNDERBEINGS
A New Paradigm of Ancient Shamanism
by Iron Thunderhorse & Donn Le Vie, Jr.

SACRED PLACES
How the Living Earth Seeks Our Friendship
by James Swan

SECRETS OF MAYAN SCIENCE/RELIGION
by Hunbatz Men

Contact your local bookseller or write:
BEAR & COMPANY
P.O. Drawer 2860
Santa Fe, NM 87504